Lecture Notes in Business Information Processing 441

Series Editors

Wil van der Aalst ⓘ
RWTH Aachen University, Aachen, Germany

John Mylopoulos ⓘ
University of Trento, Trento, Italy

Sudha Ram ⓘ
University of Arizona, Tucson, AZ, USA

Michael Rosemann ⓘ
Queensland University of Technology, Brisbane, QLD, Australia

Clemens Szyperski
Microsoft Research, Redmond, WA, USA

More information about this series at https://link.springer.com/bookseries/7911

David Aveiro · Henderik A. Proper ·
Sérgio Guerreiro · Marne de Vries (Eds.)

Advances in
Enterprise Engineering XV

11th Enterprise Engineering Working Conference, EEWC 2021
Virtual Event, November 12, 2021
and December 16–17, 2021
Revised Selected Papers

 Springer

Editors
David Aveiro ⓘD
University of Madeira
Funchal, Portugal

Sérgio Guerreiro ⓘD
University of Lisbon
Lisbon, Portugal

Henderik A. Proper ⓘD
Luxembourg Institute of Science
and Technology
Esch-sur-Alzette, Luxembourg

Marne de Vries
University of Pretoria
Pretoria, South Africa

ISSN 1865-1348   ISSN 1865-1356 (electronic)
Lecture Notes in Business Information Processing
ISBN 978-3-031-11519-6   ISBN 978-3-031-11520-2 (eBook)
https://doi.org/10.1007/978-3-031-11520-2

This Springer imprint is published by the registered company Springer Nature Switzerland AG
The registered company address is: Gewerbestrasse 11, 6330 Cham, Switzerland

Preface

This book contains the revised papers of the 11th Enterprise Engineering Working Conference, EEWC 2021, held online on November 12 and during December 16–17, 2021. It was organized, by the CIAO! Enterprise Engineering Network (CEEN), a community of academics and practitioners who strive to contribute to the development of the discipline of enterprise engineering (EE), and to apply it in practice. The aim is to develop a holistic and general systems theory-based understanding of how to (re)design and run enterprises effectively. The ambition is to develop a consistent and coherent set of theories, models, and associated methods that enable enterprises to reflect, in a systematic way, on how to realize improvements, and assist them, in practice, in achieving their aspirations.

In doing so, sound empirical and scientific foundations should underlie all efforts and all organizational aspects that are relevant should be considered, while combining already existing knowledge from the scientific fields of information systems, software engineering, and management, as well as philosophy, semiotics, and sociology, among others. In other words, the (re)design of an enterprise and the subsequent implementation of changes should be the consequence of rationalized decisions that take into account the nature and reality of the enterprise and its environment, and respect relevant empirical and scientific principles.

Enterprises are considered as systems whose reality has a dual nature by being simultaneously, on the one hand, centrally and purposefully (re)designed, and, on the other hand, emergent in a distributed way, given the fact that its main agents, the humans that are the "pearls" of the organization, act with free will in a creative and responsible (or sometimes not) way. We acknowledge that, in practice, the development of enterprises is not always a purely rational/evidence-based process. As such, we believe the field of EE aims to provide evidence-based insights into the design and evolution of enterprises and the consequences of different choices irrespective of the way decisions are made.

The origin of the scientific foundations of our present body of knowledge is the CIAO! (Communication, Information, Action, Organization) Paradigm as expressed in our Enterprise Engineering Manifesto and the paper "The Discipline of Enterprise Engineering". In this paradigm, organization is considered to emerge in human communication, through the intermediate roles of information and action. Based on the CIAO! Paradigm, several theories have been developed, and are still being proposed. They are published as technical reports.

CEEN welcomes proposals of improvements to our current body of knowledge, as well as the inclusion of compliant and alternative views, always keeping in mind the need to maintain global systemic coherence, consistency, and scientific rigor of the entire EE body of knowledge as a prerequisite for the consolidation of this new engineering discipline. Yearly events like the Enterprise Engineering Working Conference and associated Doctoral Consortium are organized to promote the presentation of EE research and application in practice, as well as discussions on the contents and current state of our body of theories and methods.

Since 2005, CEEN has organized the CIAO! Workshop and, since 2008, its proceedings have been published as Advances in Enterprise Engineering in the Springer LNBIP series. From 2011 onwards, this workshop was replaced by the Enterprise Engineering Working Conference (EEWC). The 2021 edition of the EEWC was a special one as it marked the merger of CEEN, the EE-Network.eu, and the Enterprise Engineering Institute in an integrated network, concerned with the development of theory-based and practice-proven methods, techniques, and tools for enterprise engineering.

This volume contains the proceedings of EEWC 2021, which received 16 submissions. Each submission was reviewed (double-blind) by three members of the Program Committee (PC) which recommended if the paper was good enough for presentation at the conference or not. After the conference presentations, authors were given the opportunity to improve their papers according to the reviewers feedback and discussions at the conference and submit a new version of the paper, together with a changes report. Papers were then subject to a second review round by PC chairs, with input, as needed, from the PC members who originally reviewed the paper. After the second review round, final decisions were taken regarding paper acceptance for the proceedings, resulting in the five full papers and three short papers in this volume. In pursuit of the spirit of a working conference, it is now the norm of EEWC to publish post-proceedings, where the papers that were presented are made available to conference participants, and are revised and extended by the authors taking in account the discussions that happened at the conference, the feedback of the reviewers, and new developments that might have taken place in the research during/after the conference. This year's online format included two keynotes, of which two respective invited papers resulted and are included in this proceedings.

EEWC aims to address the challenges that modern and complex enterprises are facing in a rapidly changing world. The participants of the working conference share a belief that dealing with these challenges requires rigorous and scientific solutions, focusing on the design and engineering of enterprises. The goal of EEWC is to stimulate interaction between the different stakeholders, scientists, and practitioners, interested in making enterprise engineering a reality.

We thank all the participants, authors, and reviewers for their contributions to EEWC 2021 and hope that you find these proceedings useful to your explorations on current enterprise engineering challenges.

April 2022

David Aveiro
Henderik Proper
Sérgio Guerreiro
Marne de Vries

Organization

EEWC 2021 was the eleventh working conference in this successful series. These events are aimed at addressing the challenges that modern and complex enterprises are facing in a rapidly changing world. The participants in these events share the belief that dealing with these challenges requires rigorous and scientific solutions, focusing on the design and engineering of enterprises.

This conviction has led to the effort of annually organizing an international working conference on the topic of enterprise engineering, in order to bring together all stakeholders interested in making enterprise engineering a reality. This means that not only scientists are invited but also practitioners. Moreover, it also means that the conference is aimed at active participation, discussion, and exchange of ideas in order to stimulate future cooperation among the participants. This makes EEWC a working conference contributing to the further development of enterprise engineering as a mature discipline.

The organization of EEWC 2021 and the peer review of the contributions to the conference were accomplished by an outstanding international team of experts in the fields of enterprise engineering. The following is the organizational structure of EEWC 2021.

Program Chairs

David Aveiro	University of Madeira, ARDITI and NOVA-LINCS, Portugal
Henderik A. Proper	Luxembourg Institute of Science and Technology, Luxembourg
Sérgio Guerreiro	INESC-ID, IST, Portugal
Marne De Vries	University of Pretoria, South Africa

Program Committee

Carlos Páscoa	Instituto Superior de Educação e Ciências, Portugal
Christian Huemer	Vienna University of Technology, Austria
Eduard Babkin	Higher School of Economics - Nizhny Novgorod, Russia
Florian Matthes	Technical University of Munich, Germany
Geert Poels	Ghent University, Belgium
Gil Regev	Ecole Polytechnique Fédérale de Lausanne, Switzerland
Graham Mcleod	Inspired.org, South Africa

Hans Mulder	University of Antwerp, Belgium
Jaap Gordijn	Vrije Universiteit Amsterdam, The Netherlands
Jan Verelst	University of Antwerp, Belgium
Jens Gulden	Utrecht University, Netherlands
José Tribolet	Instituto Superior Tecnico, Universidade de Lisboa, Portugal
Julio Cesar Nardi	Federal Institute of Espírito Santo, Brazil
Junichi Iijima	Tokyo University of Science, Japan
Marcela Vegetti	Universidad Tecnológica Nacional, Argentina
Marcello Bax	Federal University of Minas Gerais, Brazil
Maria-Eugenia Iacob	University of Twente, The Netherlands
Martin Op 't Land	Capgemini, The Netherlands
Mauricio Almeida	Federal University of Minas Gerais, Brazil
Miguel Mira Da Silva	Instituto Superior Tecnico, Universidade de Lisboa, Portugal
Monika Kaczmarek	University of Duisburg-Essen, Germany
Niek Pluijmert	INQA Quality Consultants BV, The Netherlands
Peter Loos	Saarland University, Germany
Petr Kremen	Czech Technical University in Prague, Czech Republic
Robert Lagerström	KTH Royal Institute of Technology, Sweden
Robert Pergl	Czech Technical University in Prague, Czech Republic
Robert Winter	University of St. Gallen, Switzerland
Rony Flatscher	Wirtschaftsuniversität Wien, Austria
Stefan Strecker	University of Hagen, Germany
Stephan Aier	University of St. Gallen, Switzerland
Stijn Hoppenbrouwers	HAN University of Applied Sciences, The Netherlands
Tatiana Poletaeva	Higher School of Economics - Nizhny Novgorod, Russia
Tiago Prince Sales	Free University of Bozen-Bolzano, Italy

Contents

Invited Papers from Keynote Presentations

Conceptual Modeling and Artificial Intelligence: Challenges
and Opportunities for Enterprise Engineering 3
  Dominik Bork

Toward AI-Native Enterprise 10
  Vinay Kulkarni

Presented Papers

Modeling Payments and Linked Obligation Settlements 21
  Glenda Amaral, Tiago Prince Sales, and Giancarlo Guizzardi

Towards an Ontology Network in Finance and Economics 42
  Glenda Amaral, Tiago Prince Sales, and Giancarlo Guizzardi

Flexible Enterprise Optimization with Constraint Programming 58
  Sytze P. E. Andringa and Neil Yorke-Smith

Adapting and Evaluating the Story-Card-Method 74
  Marné De Vries

Business Driven Microservice Design: An Enterprise Ontology Based
Approach to API Specifications 95
  Marien R. Krouwel and Martin Op 't Land

Evaluation of the Perceived Quality and Functionality of Fact Model
Diagrams in DEMO 114
  Dulce Pacheco, David Aveiro, Bernardo Gouveia, and Duarte Pinto

Towards the X-Theory: An Evaluation of the Perceived Quality
and Functionality of DEMO's Process Model 129
  Dulce Pacheco, David Aveiro, Duarte Pinto, and Bernardo Gouveia

Use of EA Models in Organizational AI Solution Development 149
  Kurt Sandkuhl and Jack Daniel Rittelmeyer

Author Index 167

Invited Papers from Keynote Presentations

Conceptual Modeling and Artificial Intelligence: Challenges and Opportunities for Enterprise Engineering

Dominik Bork$^{(\boxtimes)}$

Business Informatics Group, TU Wien, Vienna, Austria
`dominik.bork@tuwien.ac.at`

Abstract. Conceptual modeling applies abstraction to reduce the complexity of a system under study to produce a human interpretable, formalized representation (i.e., a conceptual model). Such models enable understanding and communication among humans and processing by machines. Artificial Intelligence (AI) algorithms are also applied to complex realities (regularly represented by vast amounts of data) to identify patterns or classify entities in the data automatically. However, AI differs from conceptual modeling because the results are often neither comprehensible nor explainable nor reproducible. AI systems often act as a black box; not even their developers can explain their behavior. The uptake of AI is recognizable across all disciplines and domains, both in academia and industry. The enterprise engineering field is no exception to this trend. In this paper, which is based on a keynote delivered at EEWC 2021, we present selected recent contributions at the intersection of conceptual modeling and AI, thereby shedding light on challenges and opportunities for enterprise engineering.

Keywords: Conceptual modeling · Model-driven software engineering · Artificial intelligence · Machine learning

1 Introduction

Artificial Intelligence (AI) applications are conquering more and more domains in recent years with the increasing availability of vast amounts of data. The now dominant paradigm of data-driven AI employs big data to build intelligent applications and support fact-based decision-making. The focus of data-driven AI is on learning (domain) models and keeping those models up-to-date by using statistical methods and machine learning (ML) over big data – in contrast to the manual modeling approach prevalent in traditional, knowledge-based AI. While data-driven AI has led to significant breakthroughs, it also comes with several

© Springer Nature Switzerland AG 2022
D. Aveiro et al. (Eds.): EEWC 2021, LNBIP 441, pp. 3–9, 2022.
https://doi.org/10.1007/978-3-031-11520-2_1

disadvantages. First, models generated by AI often cannot be inspected and comprehended by a human being, thus lacking explainability and establishing challenges toward the utilization of such approaches in enterprises [5]. Furthermore, integrating pre-existing domain knowledge into learned models – before or after learning – is complex.

In contrast to AI, conceptual modeling (CM) is human-driven. Humans are in charge of applying abstraction and creating a simplified representation of a system under study for a specific purpose. Consequently, conceptual models are comprehensible and foster understanding of existing and the design of new systems. Models enable visual analysis, easy comprehension, and formalized representation using a commonly agreed-upon modeling language. However, some of these positive attributes are mitigated when models get very large (scalability) or the complexity of the system under study is still too high.

Only recently, the first workshops focusing on the intersection of CM and AI emerged [3,14]. CMAI research aims at combining the specific strengths of the CM and AI while mitigating some of the mutual weaknesses. Table 1 shows a comparison of conceptual modeling and artificial intelligence along the dimensions *Nature*, *Outcome*, and *Prerequisites*.

Table 1. Compatibility of conceptual modeling and AI

Dimension	Conceptual modeling	Artificial intelligence
Nature	Explicit knowledge representation	Able to learn implicit knowledge
	Human-centered	Machine-centered
	Limited data	Vast amounts of data
	Low to medium complexity	Huge complexity
Prerequisites	Domain knowledge	Vast amounts of data
	High method expertise	Low to medium method expertise
Outcome	Human comprehension	Limited/no human comprehension
	Transparent	Limited/No Transparency
Effort	Medium to high	Low (except data cleansing)

2   Conceptual Modeling and AI Research Framework

In the following, we introduce a research framework for positioning and presenting conceptual modeling and artificial intelligence research based on [1]. The framework, visualized in Fig. 1 positions the two research fields of conceptual modeling and artificial intelligence orthogonal to one another, thereby shaping four concrete CMAI research categories. These CMAI categories are based on the contribution of the respective research disciplines. Works like [2] apply genetic

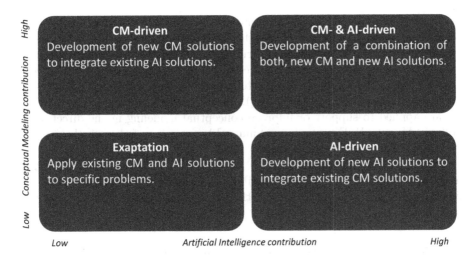

Fig. 1. Conceptual modeling and artificial intelligence research framework

algorithms and heuristic search to automatically partition overarching data models into smaller, more understandable modules. Even fewer works attempt to show possibilities of improving AI-based systems by using CM [11]. As such, the CMAI research framework not only serves the purpose of classifying existing works it also sheds light on, thus far, underrepresented CMAI research areas.

Exaptation CMAI. Following the definition of exaptation research in Design Science Research given by Gregor and Hever [8], we define exaptation research in conceptual modeling and artificial intelligence as one that combines existing solutions from both fields to target a specific problem.

CM-driven CMAI. In this category of CMAI research, all papers aim to develop new conceptual modeling solutions to be combined with existing AI solutions to target a specific problem. Such research primarily contributes to the conceptual modeling research community.

AI-driven CMAI. In this category, all papers aim to develop new AI solutions to be combined with existing conceptual modeling solutions to target a specific problem. Such research primarily contributes to the artificial intelligence research community.

CM- & AI-driven CMAI. In this category, all CMAI research aims to make contributions to both scientific fields, i.e., research that improves existing or develops new AI and CM solutions to target a specific problem.

3   Challenges and Opportunities for Enterprise Engineering

In the following, a selection of recent CMAI research outputs is briefly presented to showcase both challenges and opportunities emerging for the Enterprise Engineering community. The choice is based on a literature survey and past and ongoing research of the author himself.

Conceptual modeling and AI are mutually compatible disciplines and therefore present mutual benefits to each other. We present the selected literature in the two directions of how CM can contribute to AI and how AI can contribute to CM in the context of Enterprise Engineering. The unique characteristics of conceptual modeling are used and applied to improve AI techniques and applications in the direction of CM2AI (CM → AI). The other way around, AI characteristics are applied to support or improve conceptual modeling in the direction of AI2CM (AI → CM). Eventually, real mutual benefits manifest in single research outcomes are characterized by (CM ↔ AI).

Table 2 shows the characteristics of selected CMAI research outcomes mapped to the CMAI research contribution framework (Fig. 1), the research direction (CM2AI, AI2CM, or both), the modeling language, and the AI technique used.

Table 2. Mapping CMAI selected works to CMAI research framework

Work	Direction	CM language	AI technique	CMAI type
[15]	CM → AI	Archimate	General AI	Exaptation
[12]	AI → CM	EER	Machine Learning	Exaptation
[9]	CM → AI	GSL	Machine Learning	CM-Driven
[7]	CM → AI	iStar	Multi-Agent Systems	CM-Driven
[4]	AI → CM	UML or DSML	NLP	AI-Driven
[6]	AI → CM	UMLDSL	Machine Learning	AI-Driven
[2]	CM ↔ AI	ER	Genetic Algorithms	CM-&AI-Driven
[10]	CM ↔ AI	UML	Genetic Algorithms	CM-&AI-Driven

3.1 Opportunities of Conceptual Modeling for AI

Artificial Intelligence increases business intelligence and automates various tasks or services. However, enterprise systems do not quickly adapt or understand AI methods due to AI's high complexity and black box characteristic. Conceptual modeling provides a visual representation of systems and domain- and purpose-specific abstraction. Conceptual modeling can make AI more accessible to non-experts in AI by supporting transparency, an accessible way of tuning and configuring AI parameters, and AI performance. By supporting the easy incorporation of AI methods, conceptual modeling can increase business opportunities.

In EEWC'21, Sandkuhl and Rittelmeyer observe that different AI applications require additional prerequisites in an organizational IT landscape, some of which can be extracted from an EA model [15]. The authors propose a method component adding to enterprise architecture management, which describes how the organizational context of AI can be determined as support for AI requirements analysis and feasibility studies. The modeling language used in this work is ArchiMate, and the method is applied to support general AI requirements. This work applies existing CM concepts to support AI. Therefore, we mapped this work as Exaptation in our framework.

Conceptual modeling is combined with ML for the explainability of ML models, providing human-understandable accounts of why a machine learning model produces specific outputs. To improve explainability, Lukyanenko et al. [12] propose *superimposition*, an approach that maps the features that are important to a machine learning model's decision outcomes to a conceptual model of an application domain. Machine learning algorithms are applied to Extended Entity-Relationship (EER) models. The research direction is from AI towards CM as AI methods are applied to conceptual models. The contribution is mapped to Exaptation as the work uses existing CM and AI methods to realize the explainability of AI.

The behavior of ML components, e.g., neural networks, is inductively derived from training data and thus uncertain and imperfect. Quality assessment heavily depends on and is restricted by a test data set or what has been tried among many possibilities. To this end, Ishikawa [9] proposes an MLQ framework for assessing the quality of ML components and ML-based systems. This work uses Goal Structuring Notation (GSN) as the modeling language for designing the proposed MLQ framework. In this work, new conceptual modeling concepts are used to develop a solution for AI. Therefore, this work follows the CM $\rightarrow$ AI direction and is mapped to the CM-Driven contribution type in our framework.

Multi-Agent Systems (MAS) involve various agents that interact with each other to achieve their goals. The modeling of MAS with different rational agents is a non-trivial task due to the specificity of their domain concepts, also at the requirements level. To this end, Goncalves et al. [7] present an approach to model MAS with rational agents at the requirements level using iStar. This work uses existing conceptual modeling concepts to support Multi-Agent Systems in AI; therefore, we position this work in the CM $\rightarrow$ AI direction and as a CM-Driven contribution type in our framework.

3.2 Opportunities of AI for Conceptual Modeling

Modelers face a high cognitive load to understand a multitude of complex abstractions and their relationships. Conceptual models contain a plethora of structural and semantic information. Machine learning-based AI methods can use conceptual model repositories to learn patterns within conceptual models to assist conceptual modelers with context- and domain-aware assistance in conceptual modeling tools. Current intelligent modeling assistants (IMAs) lack adaptability and flexibility for tool builders and do not facilitate understanding the differences and commonalities of IMAs for modelers. To this end, Mussbacher et al. [13] present a conceptual reference framework (RF-IMA) and its properties to identify the foundations for intelligent modeling assistance.

Various works have focused on model and metamodel completion and evolution. An NLP-based assistant is proposed by Burgueno et al. [4] to support auto-complete suggestions for the partial model under construction based on the automatic analysis of the textual information available for the project (contextual knowledge) and its related business domain (general knowledge). In this work, existing NLP techniques support existing conceptual modeling tools with UML or other domain-specific languages. Therefore, we position this work's contribution as AI-Driven in our framework.

A graph neural network (GNN) based recommender system is proposed by Di Rocco et al. [6] to assist modelers in performing the specification of metamodels and models. This work is also AI-Driven as Machine Learning based solutions are developed and used to support conceptual model specification. The modeling language used in this work is UMLDSL.

Modularization helps the comprehensibility and maintainability of models by breaking down a monolith into a modular structure. A genetic algorithm-based modularization approach is presented by Bork et al. [2] to modularize ER models using the meta-heuristics search approach. The evaluation results prove the approach's effectiveness and efficiency and outperform humans. A metamodel-model co-evolution approach is presented by Kessentini et al. [10] that refines an initial model instantiated from the previous metamodel version to make it as conforming as possible to the new metamodel version. This work uses genetic algorithms on UML models to support conceptual model evolution. These two works develop new concepts for both CM & AI. Therefore, we classify these works as CM&AI-Driven in our framework.

4   Concluding Remarks

This paper reflects a keynote speech delivered at the 11th Enterprise Engineering Working Conference (EEWC) 2021. The focus was to shed light on the current research stream that combines Conceptual Modeling with Artificial Intelligence (CMAI). This paper proposes a framework to characterize CMAI research contributions and reports on selected recent CMAI research.

The paper shows that CMAI research can contribute to the diverse needs and challenges of enterprise engineering. The selected works span from the use of AI to support: i) method engineers in designing new modeling languages, ii) modelers in creating models, and iii) model users in coping with the complexity of large models by providing modularizations. We further show how conceptual models can enable non-AI experts to develop and analyze AI systems.

This paper aims to provide pointers to exemplary works that have the potential to steer discussions that eventually lead to new research contributions from the enterprise engineering community.

Acknowledgements. The author wants to thank the organization committee of EEWC 2021 and the EEWC steering committee for the invitation to deliver a keynote. Moreover, the author wants to thank Syed Juned Ali for supporting the preparation of the keynote and this paper.

References

1. Bork, D.: Conceptual modeling and artificial intelligence: mutual benefits from complementary worlds. arXiv preprint arXiv:2110.08637 (2021)
2. Bork, D., Garmendia, A., Wimmer, M.: Towards a multi-objective modularization approach for entity-relationship models. In: ER Forum/Posters/Demos, pp. 45–58 (2020)
3. Burgueño, L., Burdusel, A., Gérard, S., Wimmer, M.: Preface to MDE intelligence 2019: 1st workshop on artificial intelligence and model-driven engineering. In: 22nd ACM/IEEE International Conference on Model Driven Engineering Languages and Systems Companion, MODELS Companion 2019, pp. 168–169. IEEE (2019)
4. Burgueño, L., Clarisó, R., Gérard, S., Li, S., Cabot, J.: An NLP-based architecture for the autocompletion of partial domain models. In: La Rosa, M., Sadiq, S., Teniente, E. (eds.) CAiSE 2021. LNCS, vol. 12751, pp. 91–106. Springer, Cham (2021). https://doi.org/10.1007/978-3-030-79382-1_6
5. Buxmann, P.: Interview with Karl-Heinz Streibich on "Artificial Intelligence". Bus. Inf. Syst. Eng. **63**(1), 69–70 (2021)
6. Di Rocco, J., Di Sipio, C., Di Ruscio, D., Nguyen, P.T.: A GNN-based recommender system to assist the specification of metamodels and models. In: 2021 ACM/IEEE 24th International Conference on Model Driven Engineering Languages and Systems (MODELS), pp. 70–81. IEEE (2021)
7. Gonçalves, E., Araujo, J., Castro, J.: iStar4RationalAgents: modeling requirements of multi-agent systems with rational agents. In: Laender, A.H.F., Pernici, B., Lim, E.-P., de Oliveira, J.P.M. (eds.) ER 2019. LNCS, vol. 11788, pp. 558–566. Springer, Cham (2019). https://doi.org/10.1007/978-3-030-33223-5_46
8. Gregor, S., Hevner, A.R.: Positioning and presenting design science research for maximum impact. MIS Q. **37**(2), 337–355 (2013)
9. Ishikawa, F.: Concepts in quality assessment for machine learning - from test data to arguments. In: Trujillo, J.C., et al. (eds.) ER 2018. LNCS, vol. 11157, pp. 536–544. Springer, Cham (2018). https://doi.org/10.1007/978-3-030-00847-5_39
10. Kessentini, W., Sahraoui, H., Wimmer, M.: Automated metamodel/model co-evolution: a search-based approach. Inf. Softw. Technol. **106**, 49–67 (2019)
11. Lukyanenko, R., Castellanos, A., Parsons, J., Tremblay, M.C., Storey, V.C.: Using conceptual modeling to support machine learning. In: Cappiello, C., Ruiz, M. (eds.) International Conference on Advanced Information Systems Engineering, pp. 170–181. Springer, Cham (2019). https://doi.org/10.1007/978-3-030-21297-1_15
12. Lukyanenko, R., Castellanos, A., Storey, V.C., Castillo, A., Tremblay, M.C., Parsons, J.: Superimposition: augmenting machine learning outputs with conceptual models for explainable AI. In: Grossmann, G., Ram, S. (eds.) International Conference on Conceptual Modeling, pp. 26–34. Springer, Cham (2020). https://doi.org/10.1007/978-3-030-65847-2_3
13. Mussbacher, G., et al.: Opportunities in intelligent modeling assistance. Softw. Syst. Model. **19**(5), 1045–1053 (2020). https://doi.org/10.1007/s10270-020-00814-5
14. Reimer, U., Bork, D., Fettke, P., Tropmann-Frick, M.: Preface of the first workshop models in AI. In: Companion Proceedings of Modellierung 2020 Short, Workshop and Tools & Demo Papers, pp. 128–129. CEUR Workshop Proceedings (2020)
15. Sandkuhl, K., Rittelmeyer, J.D.: Use of EA models in organizational AI solution development. In: 2021 11th Enterprise Engineering Working Conference (EEWC 2021) (2021)

Toward AI-Native Enterprise

Vinay Kulkarni[✉]

Tata Consultancy Services Research, 54B, Industrial Estate, Hadapsar, Pune 411021, India
vinay.vkulkarni@tcs.com

Abstract. Enterprises are fast evolving into hyperconnected ecosystems that need to continue meeting the stated goals in a dynamic environment that changes along multiple dimensions. Ability to respond to these changes in an ever-shrinking window of opportunity is a critical need that has remained unfulfilled. With enterprises increasingly reliant on software systems, these need to be amenable to quick adaptation in order to effect these decisions. We propose an approach aimed at meeting these needs in a holistic, automated, and human-in-loop manner. The proposed approach builds further upon proven ideas from Modelling & simulation, Artificial Intelligence, and Control Theory, and is validated in part on real-world industry-scale problems.

Keywords: Adaptive enterprise · Digital twin · Reinforcement learning

1 Motivation

Enterprises of future will be hyperconnected complex ecosystems (or system of systems) operating in dynamic uncertain environments. They will need to continue delivering the stated goals in the face of unforeseen changes along multiple dimensions such as events opening up new opportunities or constraining the existing ones, competitor actions, regulatory regime, law of the land, and technology advance/obsolescence. The goals too could keep changing over time. Customers will demand highly personalized service and user experience which would keep changing over time. These dynamics will play out equally significantly across the three planes of enterprise: **Intent** plane that deals with defining goals and strategies for achieving them, **Process** plane that deals with operationalization of the strategy in terms of business processes, roles & responsibilities, and workforce assignment, and **Systems** plane that deals with providing mechanical advantage through automation of the process plane to the extent possible. Thus, a change may originate in one plane and ripple through to the other planes. Given the increased rate of change, the time window available for bringing the three planes back in sync will continue to shrink. This will put several hitherto unseen demands on enterprises namely regulatory compliance at optimal cost with minimal exposure to risk, responsive decision-making in the face of uncertainty, and swift adaptation to support continuous transformation without compromising on certainty.

D. Aveiro et al. (Eds.): EEWC 2021, LNBIP 441, pp. 10–17, 2022.
https://doi.org/10.1007/978-3-031-11520-2_2

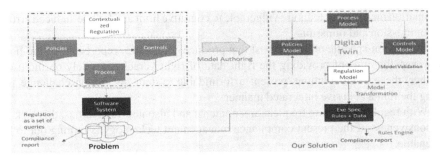

Fig. 1. Regulatory compliance

We argue that current practice is found wanting to meet these critical needs. We propose a solution that aims to meet these needs in a more satisfactory manner and illustrate its efficacy on a real-world industry scale use case. We then propose an architecture that integrates the various components into a whole. We conclude by describing preparedness to support this architecture and list future research needed.

2 Regulatory Compliance

2.1 The Problem

Enterprises today face unprecedented regulation. With over 50000 regulatory alerts a year, the regulatory landscape is complex and constantly changing. Enforcement by regulators is strict, and stiff penalties apart, non-compliance leads to loss of reputation and brand value. US companies alone have paid close to $320 billion in fines since 2008. Studies show up to 70% of management time being spent on compliance related issues. Regulatory compliance therefore figures among the top five CEO-level concerns in enterprises worldwide[1].

Regulators issue guidelines to guard against specific risks in enterprises conducting their business. Enterprise needs to respond by putting in place internal policies to enforce regulatory guidelines and implement policies through appropriate controls to mitigate risks. The regulations need to be interpreted correctly into policies and controls in enterprise context. The enterprise information scattered into structured, semi-structured and unstructured information sources needs to be examined to check if these obligations hold. If not, the non-conformant data element needs to be flagged in the light of the appropriate obligation. Figure 1 depicts a schematic of regulatory compliance problem. Moreover, non-compliance risk needs to be computed.

2.2 Current Practice

Current practice uses document-centric compliance management tools such as GRC frameworks[2] that put heavy analysis and synthesis burden on human experts. Lack of

---

[1] https://www.leanmethods.com/resources/articles/top-ten-problems-faced-business/.

[2] https://www.ibm.com/cloud/learn/grc.

automation means these tools are vulnerable to cognitive limit and fatigue-induced errors of commission and omission.

Regulation-specific offerings exist that produce compliance reports out-of-the-box. However, the onus of providing the right data of right veracity is solely on the user. Further, these point-solutions present a formidable system integration challenge for using them in a cohesive integrated manner.

With regulators issuing frequent amendments and also new regulations, this lack of responsiveness of the present compliance management technology is turning out to be untenable.

Regulatory compliance has attracted research community as well where the focus has been on rigor and automation using formal techniques to check compliance [1, 2]. These have seen poor adoption in industry due to the difficulty of manually coming up with formal specifications of regulation rules from the regulation document in natural language text. Also, research approaches do not address the entire compliance management process.

2.3 Our Solution

We take a holistic approach to address the issues outlined above by changing current document-centric focus of compliance practice to a model-driven approach as shown in Fig. 1.

We provide assistance for model authoring from source text documents using natural-language processing and machine-learning extraction techniques, and a near-natural language interface [3]. Legal and domain experts together author models of the regulation, policies, controls, and business processes from their respective source documents to create a compliance-specific digital twin of the enterprise which is amenable to automated analysis and transformation.

We provide technology support for domain experts to validate these models for consistency and correctness thus enabling early detection of errors. The validated models are automatically transformed into an executable form with clear identification of the necessary & sufficient data for compliance checking [4]. We provide technology to pull this data from wherever it exists in the enterprise. Proven technology is used to automatically check whether the data conforms to regulation rules. In case of non-compliance, we clearly identify the non-compliant data element and provide traceability links to the regulation text being violated.

Shifting the focus from text documents to models helps make compliance management process more agile. Impact of a change in regulation can now be computed automatically and with precision. Furthermore, automatic transformation of these models to an executable form and subsequent automated checking results in highly responsive compliance process.

Risks and mitigation measures captured in the policy, control, and process models can be simulated to play out various what-if and if-what scenarios, enabling analysis of remediation approaches and risk assessment.

Therefore, we argue, the proposed approach is a significant step towards achieving the goal of "staying compliant with minimal risk exposure and optimal cost".

3   Decision-Making in the Face of Uncertainty

3.1   The Problem

Digital technologies like IoT, AI, Cloud, and advances in computing, and connectivity are blurring the operational boundaries of traditional enterprises. These digital forces are shaping Business 4.0 where enterprises are dynamic ecosystems that need to continually adapt to change s that cannot be deduced upfront in order to stay relevant. The critical questions that remain therefore are: How can a complex system of systems survive in an increasingly dynamic environment? How best can enterprises be resilient in the face of constant change? What is the right strategy for adaptation as opposed to a reactive, time-triggered tactical response?

3.2   Current Practice

Industry practice today uses several ad hoc techniques to address some of these adaptation requirements, with various degrees of rigour. Such as linear programming for multi variate optimization, stock-and-flow models for simulation of dynamics, empirical methods, best practices, etc. However, enterprises are socio technical in nature and many problems do not lend themselves to neat analytical specifications. Also, large size and complex interactions within enterprise inhibit knowledge of the overall behavior a-priori. Instead, it is possible to know the behavior only in localized contexts and that too without full certainty. The overall system behavior emerges from these part-behaviors and interactions between the parts. As a result, analytical techniques relying on specification of overall system behavior cannot be used.

Approaches relying on past data are finding good traction these days especially since advance in compute capabilities has made it possible to apply machine learning techniques to industry scale problems. The general idea is to (machine) learn a model of system from past data and use it for predictive analysis. As past data represents only the manifest behaviors amongst the possible system behaviors, any model learnt from it is at best a subset of true model. As a result, inferences derivable from analysis using this model can at best be sub-optimal or at worst incorrect.

Therefore, industry practice is forced to rely on human expertise to impart dynamic adaptation. While experts do come up with interventions for a perturbation, they typically find it rather difficult to explain how the intervention was arrived at. Also, like all humans, experts too are susceptible to the law of bounded rationality, and more often than not their interventions turn out to be sub optimal in hindsight. Thus, it can be said that current industry practice is found wanting in imparting dynamic adaptability to enterprises.

3.3   Our Solution

We propose a simulation-based, data-driven learning-aided approach to decision-making in the face of uncertainty [5]. The approach is based on proven ideas from Modelling & Simulation, Control Theory, and Artificial Intelligence, and builds upon further to be able to use these in an integrated manner as shown in Fig. 2.

Fig. 2. Digital twin centric approach to decision-making

At the core of the approach is the concept of Digital Twin – a virtual, hi-fidelity, machine processable representation of a system or reality that is amenable to quantitative and qualitative analysis.

We have developed an actor-based language[3] to specify a purposive Digital Twin as a set of interacting intentional and autonomous actors. The language provides stochastic constructs to specify uncertainty in actor behavior and interactions. Simulation of the constituent actor behaviors and their interactions leads to emergence of the overall system behavior that Subject Matter Experts can interpret to come up with a candidate set of corrective interventions. To reduce the analysis and synthesis burden on human experts, we bring in Reinforcement Learning (RL) for training a recommendation engine using the Digital Twin. A dynamic adaptation architecture, inspired by model reference adaptive control paradigm, is conceptualized to integrate the Digital Twin, RL agent, and the system to support dynamic adaptation.

The approach and associated toolset support the following key use cases "in silico".

Holding a Mirror: Recreate the real-world situation in digital space to enable "in silico" analysis.

Experimentation Aid: Provide a digital aid to imitate the behaviour of enterprise in response to changes in its input an d/or operating environment thus saving on design of experiment effort that's time-, cost- and intellect-intensive.

Design Aid: Provide a digital aid to "in silico" explore the solution space to identify better states modulo a given set of constraints thus providing a-priori assurances about reaching the desired state.

Transformation Aid: Provide a digital aid to establish a path from current state to the desired state through "in silico" exploration of the solution space and validation of candidate interventions thus leading to a sequence of decisions to be implemented to effect the desired transformation in a tractable evidence-backed manner.

We have so far demonstrated the utility and efficacy of the approach as a "risk free business experimentation aid" for a wide variety of real-world use cases [6, 7].

---

[3] http://www.esl-lang.org.

4 Software Architecture for Continuous Adaptation

4.1 The Problem

Just identifying the right decision (or policy or strategy) is not enough. It also needs to be implemented effectively. Given the pervasiveness of software in enterprises, implementation of the decision will mean suitably modifying the relevant set of software systems that could possibly be distributed across the three planes. Therefore, software needs be designed to adapt to unforeseen changes along various dimensions such as functionality, business processes, technology infrastructure, user experience, goals and operating environment. Moreover, it should do so while being aligned with the enterprise goals and conforming to internal policies & external regulations.

4.2 Current Practice

While considerable progress has been made by [self-]adaptive software community in meeting the adaptation needs pertaining to executing machinery, there is little work reported on adaptation of business functionality and processes. Several conceptual architectures are proposed but they have not been demonstrated to effectively address industry scale problems. State of the art of [self] adaptive software addresses known knowns and known unknowns leaving out unknown knowns and unknown unknowns. Clearly, a new architecture to support continuous adaptation is needed.

4.3 Our Solution

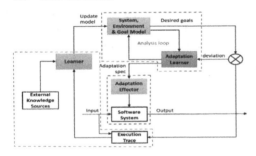

Fig. 3. Learning-native adaptation architecture

We propose a novel architecture for continuous dynamic adaptation of software systems that innovatively integrates proven ideas from software engineering, AI and control theory [8–11] as shown in Fig. 3.

At the heart of the adaptation architecture is a knowledge model manifested in the form of a *System, Environment & Goal Model* (SEG) that symbolizes a hi-fidelity machine-processable representation of the software (i.e., its digital twin). The *Adaptation Learner* component treats SEG as experience generator to learn an adaptation policy using Reinforcement Learning. The *Adaptation Effector* component knows the relationship between the SEG model and the software system, and hence can map the sequence of actions introduced into the SEG model (digital twin) to its underlying system implementation. This is necessary and sufficient information to affect the learnt policy for adaptation. The goal of the second *Learner* component is to continually enhance knowledge by learning from past execution traces and external knowledge sources so as to keep the SEG model in sync with the accessible knowledge.

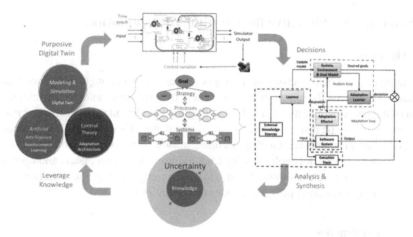

Fig. 4. AI-native adaptive enterprise

5 Bringing It All Together

While point solutions to the challenges listed above are useful in their own right, together they can bring about a significant multiplier effect as regards benefits accruable. Therefore, there is a clear need to develop a holistic approach, architecture, method and toolset in order to be able to integrate the various point solutions and build further upon them to support the vision of AI-native enterprise. Figure 4 depicts a work-in-progress conceptual architecture for AI-native enterprise.

The architecture addresses the two key needs for supporting dynamic adaptation namely decision-making in the face of uncertainty and effecting the decisions into software systems with as little burden on human experts as possible. We rely on the concept of digital twin to meet both these needs. While there is bound to be some uncertainty at any point of time when dealing with open-ended spaces, we use learning techniques to reduce the uncertainty to the extent possible.

6 Summary and Future Work

We argued the need for future enterprises to be dynamically adaptive to unforeseen changes in their environment and goals. We proposed solutions to three critical needs namely regulatory compliance, decision-making in the face of uncertainty, and continuously adaptive software. A few real-world industry-scale application of these solutions were cited. We proposed an innovative architecture to integrate these solutions into a whole.

While we seem to be on the right track, several challenges need to be overcome such as multi-paradigm digital twin, multi-objective reinforcement learning, leveraging knowledge & reasoning, and adaptive agents – to name just a few.

References

1. Sergot, M.J., Sadri, F., Kowalski, R.A., Kriwaczek, F., Hammond, P., Terese Cory, H.: The British Nationality Act as a logic program. Commun. ACM **29**(5), 370–386 (1986)
2. Antoniou, G., Dimaresis, N., Governatori, G.: A system for modal and deontic defeasible reasoning. In: AI 2007: Advances in Artificial Intelligence, 20th Australian Joint Conference on Artificial Intelligence, Gold Coast, Australia, 2–6 December 2007, Proceedings (2007)
3. Roychoudhury, S., Sunkle, S., Kholkar, D., Kulkarni, V.: From natural language to SBVR model authoring using structured English for compliance checking. In: EDOC 2017, pp. 73–78 (2017)
4. Kholkar, D., Sunkle, S., Kulkarni, V.: Applying MDA to rule and data generation for compliance checking. In: Cabello, E., Cardoso, J., Ludwig, A., Maciaszek, L.A., van Sinderen, M. (eds.) ICSOFT 2016. CCIS, vol. 743, pp. 239–263. Springer, Cham (2017). https://doi.org/10.1007/978-3-319-62569-0_12
5. Kulkarni, V., Barat, S., Clark, T.: Towards adaptive enterprises using digital twins. In: WSC 2019, pp. 60–74 (2019)
6. Barat, S., et al.: Reinforcement learning of supply chain control policy using closed loop multi-agent simulation. In: MABS 2019, pp. 26–38 (2019)
7. Barat, S., et al.: An agent-based digital twin for exploring localized non-pharmaceutical interventions to control COVID-19 pandemic. Trans. Indian Nat. Acad. Eng. **6**(2), 323–353 (2021). https://doi.org/10.1007/s41403-020-00197-5
8. Garlan, D.: Software engineering in an uncertain world. In: Proceedings of the FSE/SDP Workshop on Future of Software Engineering Research (Santa Fe, New Mexico, USA) (FoSER 2010), pp. 125–128. Association for Computing Machinery, New York (2010). https://doi.org/10.1145/1882362.1882389
9. Patikirikorala, T., Colman, A.W., Han, J., Wang, L.: A systematic survey on the design of self-adaptive software systems using control engineering approaches. In: Müller, H.A., Baresi, L. (eds.) 7th International Symposium on Software Engineering for Adaptive and Self-Managing Systems, SEAMS 2012, Zurich, Switzerland, 4–5 June 2012, pp. 33–42. IEEE Computer Society (2012). https://doi.org/10.1109/SEAMS.2012.6224389
10. Shevtsov, S., Berekmeri, M., Weyns, D., Maggio, M.: Control-theoretical software adaptation: a systematic literature review. IEEE Trans. Software Eng. **44**(8), 784–810 (2018). https://doi.org/10.1109/TSE.2017.2704579
11. Weyns, D., Usman Iftikhar, M., de la Iglesia, D.G., Ahmad, T.: A survey of formal methods in self-adaptive systems. In: Proceedings of the Fifth International C* Conference on Computer Science and Software Engineering (Montreal, Quebec, Canada) (C3S2E 2012), pp. 67–79. Association for Computing Machinery, New York (2012). https://doi.org/10.1145/2347583.2347592

Presented Papers

Modeling Payments and Linked Obligation Settlements

Glenda Amaral[1([⊠])], Tiago Prince Sales[1], and Giancarlo Guizzardi[1,2]

[1] CORE/KRDB, Free University of Bozen-Bolzano, Bolzano, Italy
{gmouraamaral,tiago.princesales,giancarlo.guizzardi}@unibz.it
[2] Services and Cybersecurity, University of Twente, Enschede, The Netherlands

Abstract. Recently, digital innovation has revolutionized the world of payments and settlement services. Innovative technologies, such as the tokenization of assets, as well as new forms of digital payments, have challenged both current business models and the existing models of regulation. In this scenario, semantic transparency is fundamental not only to adapt regulation frameworks, but also to support information integration and semantic interoperability. In this paper, we deal with these issues by proposing an ontology-based approach for the modeling of payments and linked obligation settlements, that reuses reference ontologies to create ontology-based modeling patterns that are applied to model the domain-related concepts.

Keywords: Economic exchanges · Delivery versus payment · OntoUML · gUFO

1 Introduction

Over the past decades, the financial industry has been disrupted by innovations that have shaken up the world of money, payments, and economic exchanges. These innovations, which include cryptocurrencies, blockchains and distributed ledger technologies, smart contracts [33], programmable money [6], and stablecoins [6], have challenged regulatory frameworks and business models in the financial industry. They have fostered the creation of financial products and services on top of decentralized technologies, giving rise to the concept of Decentralized Finance (DeFi) [33,37]—the decentralized provision of financial products and services.

This disruption, alongside the entry of *big techs* into payments and financial services, pushed central banks to investigate new forms of digital money and prepare the grounds for central bank digital currencies (CBDCs). A CDBC is a form of digital money, denominated in the national unit of account, which is a direct liability of the central bank, such as physical cash and central bank settlement accounts [4]. The development of CBDCs as neutral means of payment and settlement assets enables the improvement of DeFi services and contributes

© Springer Nature Switzerland AG 2022
D. Aveiro et al. (Eds.): EEWC 2021, LNBIP 441, pp. 21–41, 2022.
https://doi.org/10.1007/978-3-031-11520-2_3

to the open finance initiative by serving as a common platform around new payments ecosystems.

Open finance aims at empowering customers to have control over their data, so they can leverage it to have access to a wider range of financial products and services in a more open and competitive market [8]. It relies on standards, data sharing principles, and on a common understanding of key financial concepts to provide interoperability at different levels of DeFi ecosystems. Another important aspect of interoperability is related to the role played by central banks and regulatory authorities, which need to integrate a plethora of information from dynamic and complex decentralized environments to perform advanced analytics. This integrated view allows supervisors and regulatory entities to figure out what is going on, so they can ensure financial stability, manage financial risks, support anti-money laundering, combat the financing of terrorism, etc. Again, data needs to be clearly conceptualized and understood in order to be properly integrated and analyzed.

In this context, interoperability relies upon three interacting "layers" [29, p. 3]:

(i) a *social layer*, in which social actors interact to determine business models, regulatory frameworks and governance models;
(ii) an *information layer*, which supplies data stored both on-chain and off-chain; and
(iii) a *technical layer*, in which social actors interact to create, store, and obtain information via applications, networks, and consensus mechanisms.

In this paper, we deal with issues related to conceptual clarification (interoperability in the social layer) and semantic interoperability (interoperability in the information layer) in DeFi. We focus on the integration of DeFi off-chain data [37] and traditional finance data [37] that could be used in advanced analytics for regulation and supervisory purposes. It is important to note that DeFi ecosystems, as proposed by many countries, are ongoing systems under design, and the outcome is not clear yet. The initiatives around the world are at the stage of experimentation, proof of concept or pilot arrangements. Therefore, research on the integration of DeFi data and traditional finance is still in its infancy. To the best of our knowledge, the semantic-level integration of (DeFi) data and traditional finance data has not yet been addressed in the literature and is still an open issue.

We address this problem by proposing an ontology-driven conceptual modeling approach in which we (i) extract fragments of knowledge from reference ontologies to (ii) create ontology-based modeling patterns, which are (iii) systematically applied to represent concepts in the realm of money, payments, and economic exchanges. We first specify the models grounded on the Unified Foundational Ontology (UFO) [22], via the OntoUML [22] language, thus contributing to improving communication, problem-solving, and meaning negotiation among people. Then, we codify the models in gUFO [2], an implementation of UFO suitable for linked data applications, which contributes to dealing with semantic interoperability issues in heterogeneous scenarios.

We illustrate our approach by modelling payments and linked obligation settlements. Among many innovations in this area, decentralized technologies allow financial and real tradeable assets to be digitally represented by what is known as digital tokens [11,28]. An important aspect in this scenario is the utilization of settlement mechanisms that can prevent the risk that one counterparty irrevocably transfers the ownership of an asset, but does not receive the corresponding payment. A common way to mitigate this risk is to link the delivery and the payment legs, so that the asset moves if and only if the corresponding funds transfer occurs [9]. This settlement mechanism (a.k.a. *Delivery versus Payment*) is an example of a linked obligation settlement, a type of exchange transaction that must be performed atomically.

Although payments and linked obligation settlements have been modeled for decades [10,13,15,19,31], making sense of data in these new decentralized ecosystems is still a challenge. How to properly do analytics on financial data from different sources in decentralized heterogeneous ecosystems? The position defended here is that, in order to properly integrate data, it is necessary to make explicit their underlying ontological commitments. Let us take the example of two different ecosystem participants A and B that record information about payments. A and B may conceptualize the notion of payment in different ways. We cannot assume that just because the same term (e.g., payment) is used in both structures that they mean the same thing. For instance, Payment-A can refer to events, while Payment-B may refer to reified relationships [21]. In this case, the relation between Payment-A and Payment-B is one of manifestation, that is, instances of payment in one case (A) are manifestations of properties of payments as a bundle of relational aspects (B). For this reason, we advocate the use of ontology-based models, so that the nature of real world entities can be properly understood and represented.

This paper is organized as follows. In Sect. 2 we provide an overview of our research baseline, including payments and linked obligation settlements, UFO, the Core Ontology for Economic Exchanges, and the Reference Ontology of Money and Virtual Currencies, the latter two serving as conceptual foundation for our proposal. Then, in Sect. 3, we present our approach and use it to model payments and linked obligation settlements. In Sect. 4, we demonstrate our approach by modelling an application example. We present some related work on Sect. 5 and conclude in Sect. 6 with some final considerations.

2   Background

2.1   Linked Obligation Settlements

In general, transactions involving the acquisition of goods, financial assets, or services have two settlement components: (i) the delivery of the good or service; and (ii) the transfer of funds [16]. According to the European Central Bank (ECB) [16], a payment is "a transfer of funds which discharges an obligation on the part of a payer vis-à-vis a payee". In this case, the payer is the party to a payment transaction which issues the payment order or agrees to the transfer of funds to the payee, while the payee is the final recipient of funds. When a payment is successfully made, the obligation between the payer and the payee is discharged. In the context of payments, settlement is an act that discharges obligations between two or more agents. For a payment instruction in a payment system, settlement occurs when funds are transferred from the payer's bank to the payee's bank. According to the ECB [16] "settlement discharges the obligation of the payer's bank vis-à-vis the payee's bank in respect of the transfer".

As explained in [7], a financial transaction involving two linked obligations may be settled by different mechanisms:

– **Payment versus Payment (PvP).** A settlement mechanism that ensures that the payment in one currency occurs if and only if the counterpart payment in another currency occurs as well [7]. This mechanism is typically used to mitigate settlement risk in foreign exchanges, which is the risk of delivering the currency sold without receiving the currency purchased (or vice versa).
– **Delivery versus Payment (DvP).** A settlement mechanism that links a securities transfer and a funds transfer in such a way as to ensure that delivery occurs if and only if the corresponding payment occurs [7].
– **Delivery versus Delivery (DvD).** A settlement mechanism that links two securities transfers in such a way as to ensure that the delivery of one security occurs if and only if the security in the other transfer is also delivered [7].

Recently, the European Central Bank and the Bank of Japan conducted a proof-of-concept, in the context of Project Stella [17], to explore how the settlement of two linked obligations, such as DvP, could be conceptually designed and operated in an environment based on the distributed ledger technology (DLT). In fact, such DLT-based Delivery versus Payment settlement can be applied not only in the context of financial assets but rather for all DLT use cases where assets, such as immovable property, goods, or services, are bought with money or exchanged with other assets.

2.2   The Unified Foundational Ontology (UFO)

The Unified Foundational Ontology (UFO) is an axiomatic domain-independent formal theory built on top of theories from formal ontology, philosophical logic, philosophy of language, linguistics, and cognitive psychology. It is organized in three main components: UFO-A, an ontology of endurants (objects) [22], UFO-B, an ontology of perdurants (events) [1], and UFO-C, an ontology of social entities [23].

UFO is formally connected to a conceptual modeling language (OntoUML). OntoUML was designed such that its modeling primitives reflect the ontological distinctions put forth by UFO, and its grammatical constraints follow UFO axiomatization. In fact, OntoUML is formally a pattern-language whose modeling primitives are *ontological design patterns*, representing UFO's constituting (micro)theories. Over the past decade, a number of ontology patterns have been derived from UFO, using OntoUML as a pattern language. An ontology pattern

(OP) describes a particular recurring modeling problem that arises in specific ontology development contexts and presents a well-proven solution for the problem [18]. OPs are reused by analogy, i.e., by establishing a structural correspondence (or structural transfer) between the structure of the pattern and the one of the problem at hand. In this article, we focus on the use of domain-related ontology patterns, which are modeling fragments extracted of core/domain reference ontologies, containing pieces of knowledge that can be reused.

Furthermore, the "OntoUML Toolkit" contains several ontology engineering tools, such as ontological design patterns and anti-patterns, visual model simulation, and transformations for codification technologies. UFO has a partial translation to OWL termed gUFO [2], which is suitable for knowledge graph applications.

2.3   The Core Ontology for Economic Exchanges (COEX)

The Core Ontology for Economic Exchanges[1] (COEX) [32] is a well-founded reference ontology, specified in OntoUML, that formally characterizes the concept of economic exchanges based on the Action Theory of Economic Exchanges [30]. In this theory, an economic exchange is based on an agreement in which agents commit to performing certain reciprocal actions. This allows it to elegantly accommodate exchanges involving both products and services.

In COEX, when an Offeree accepts an Economic Offering proposed by an Offeror, the event of the offering founds a new relator of Economic Agreement between the two agents. This new relator has as parts the unconditional commitments of the agents (Offeror Unconditional Agreement and Offeree Unconditional Agreement) to fulfill the promised courses of actions. These agreements refer to types of actions, namely Offered Contribution Type and Counterpart Contribution Type. The actual event of Economic Exchange is required then to have as parts the event (action) of fulfillment of the offerer commitments as well as the event (action) of the fulfillment of the requested counterparts. Those events are of the right type, i.e. the Offered Contribution and the Counterpart Contribution match the type in Offered Contribution Type and Counterpart Contribution Type (respectively), cf. the relation instantiation. The relation participation models the fact that the offeror participates in the Offered Contribution event and the offeree participates in the Counterpart Contribution event. Figure 1[2] depicts a COEX diagram in OntoUML, which captures the aforementioned ontological notions.

---

[1] The complete version of COEX in OntoUML and its implementation in OWL are available at http://purl.org/krdb-core/economic-exchanges-ontology.

[2] We adopt the following color coding in the OntoUML diagrams: types are represented in purple, objects in pink, qualities and modes in blue, relators in green, events in yellow, and datatypes in white.

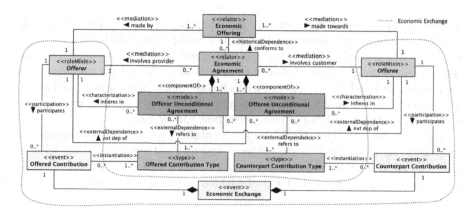

Fig. 1. A fragment of COEX [32] depicting economic exchanges. (Color figure online)

2.4 The Reference Ontology of Money and Virtual Currencies (ROME)

The Reference Ontology of Money and Virtual Currencies[3] (ROME) [5] is a reference model, grounded on the UFO [22], that formalizes the characterization of money, currency, and virtual currencies (VC). The ontological distinctions between money and virtual currencies provided by ROME are important here because different rules and controls may apply to official money and VCs in activities such as issuance, risk assessment, risk mitigation, tax calculation, the elaboration of regulatory responses, among others. For this reason, we focus here on the representation of both currencies and VCs.

Nowadays, the status of money is supported by law, which specifies both the currency and the objects that are considered money in a particular country or region. It also defines a structure for the currency value domain. An example of structure is the one-dimensional structure of numbers with two decimal places defined for euros [25]. In Fig. 2, we present a fragment of ROME that depicts the concept of Money Status Function Description, which defines a Currency and the Monetary Object Types that have the status of money. For example, the "Treaty on the Functioning of the European Union" [35] is an example of Money Status Function Description, which gives to euro banknotes and coins the status of money in the countries of the euro area. In this case, "euro" is the Currency, while "euro banknote" and "euro coin" are Monetary Object Types. The Money Status Function Description also defines a Currency Quality Space Structure for the Currency Quality Space. The former corresponds to a Social Object that prescribes a structure for the domain of values (e.g. number with two decimal places), while the latter corresponds to the value domain itself (see [22] for quality spaces).

---

[3] The complete version of ROME in OntoUML and its implementation in OWL are available at http://purl.org/krdb-core/money-ontology.

Virtual currencies are similar to money within their user community. They also have their value grounded on a status function, which is defined in their underlying virtual currency scheme. Figure 2 presents a fragment of ROME that depicts the concept of Virtual Currency Scheme Description. An instance of such a description defines a Virtual Currency, a Virtual Currency Token Type, a Virtual Currency Quality Space Structure, and a Virtual Currency Quality Space. Examples of Virtual Currency include frequent flyer program points and privately-issued cryptocurrencies such as ETH (of the Ethereum blockchain platform). For an extensive discussion on money, currency and virtual currencies, please refer to [5].

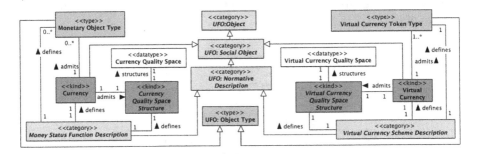

Fig. 2. A fragment of ROME [5] depicting currency and virtual currency.

3 Ontology-Based Modeling of Payments and Linked Obligation Settlements

3.1 The Ontology-Based Modeling Approach

In this section we present our ontology-based modeling approach and apply it to represent payments and linked obligation settlements, aiming at providing conceptual clarification and supporting semantic interoperability in the integration of DeFi off-chain data and traditional finance data. The three activities that compose our approach are described below.

1. **Extract knowledge fragments from reference ontologies:** In this step, we identify and extract fragments of core/domain reference ontologies, containing pieces of knowledge that describe the portion of reality that is intended to be represented, and that constitutes a well-proven modeling solution for the problem.
2. **Create ontology-based modeling patterns:** According to Buschmann et al. [14], "a pattern describes a particular recurring design problem that arises in specific design contexts and presents a well-proven solution for the problem". In this step, we reuse the model fragments extracted in step 1 to create ontology-based modeling patterns to represent recurrent structures in the domain.

3. **Apply the ontology-based modeling patterns to represent specific concepts in a particular domain:** In this step, we effectively apply the ontology-based modeling patterns identified in step 2 to model the problem at hand.

Our approach was inspired in the NeOn Methodology Framework [34]. NeOn provides guidance for the main activities in ontology engineering, making available detailed processes, guidelines and different scenarios for collaboratively building ontologies. In particular, we applied some of NeOn methodological guidelines regarding reusing and reengineering ontological resources, which in our case are reference ontologies. One of the benefits of this approach is that pieces of knowledge from reference ontologies can be reused as needed: whole or extracts of it.

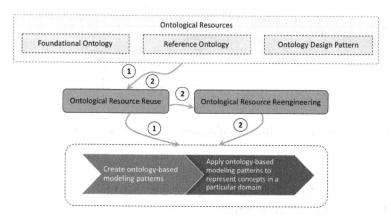

Fig. 3. Overview of the ontology-based modeling approach inspired in the NeOn methodology (adapted from [34])

Figure 3 presents the customized version of the NeOn [3] methodology, suited to our particular context and needs. We defined two flexible scenarios, in which we applied some methodological directions of NeOn for reusing and reengineering ontological resources, namely reference ontologies.

3.2 Modeling Payments and Linked Obligation Settlements

For the modeling of payments and linked obligation settlements, we reuse concepts and relations defined in COEX [32] and ROME [4,5] (step 1). As a result, we propose two ontology patterns (step 2) and apply them to model payments and different types of linked obligation settlements [9] (step 3), namely, Delivery versus Payment, Delivery versus Delivery and Payment versus Payment. We extend the notion of Delivery versus Payment and Delivery versus Delivery to consider not only financial assets (securities), but also any digital representation of assets (such as a share in a company, ownership of a piece of real estate, ownership of a car, or participation in an investment fund), which we name here *digital asset*. An example of digital asset is a token created on top of a blockchain network to represent the ownership of a real tradeable asset.

We start by defining a *digital transfer* as an event (action), in which the ownership of a digital object is transferred from one agent to another agent. By a *digital object* we mean a monetary amount or a digital asset [27]. For example, a digital payment is a digital transfer, in which a monetary amount is transferred from one agent to another. Similarly, a digital asset transfer is a digital transfer, in which a digital asset is transferred from a sender to a receiver. We define *digital exchanges* as events that have as parts two or more digital transfer events of: transferring a digital object to fulfill a commitment and transferring back another digital object to fulfill the requested counterpart. Confronting this view with COEX, we can see that this aspect is captured by the occurrence of an `Economic Exchange` event (Fig. 1), which is composed of two events that represent the fulfillment of an economic agreement, namely the `Offered Contribution` and `Counterpart Contribution` (Fig. 1). Moreover, what is brought about in digital transfers is the transferring of ownership of a digital object, which is in fact an event, see [6]. This is indeed a specific type of action, which can be straightforwardly accounted by either an `Offered Contribution` or a `Counterpart Contribution` in COEX. Therefore, digital exchanges can be seen as a specific type of economic exchange, in which the `Offered Contribution` and `Counterpart Contribution` are digital transfers between agents. This fragment of knowledge can be retrieved by isolating a part of the OntoUML [22] model that represent economic exchanges in COEX (area circled in green dotted lines, in Fig. 1).

Based on these considerations, in Fig. 4, we propose the Digital Transfer Pattern, represented in OntoUML [22]. In this pattern, a `Digital Transfer` is modeled as an event, which represents the action of transferring the ownership of a digital object (`Exchanged Digital Object`) from a `Sender` to a `Receiver`. As in COEX (Fig. 1), both the `Sender` and the `Receiver` are UFO *agents* [22]. According to UFO, agent can be categorized into *human* (i.e. a person), *artificial* (i.e. artificial systems, such as information systems, cyber-physical systems, etc.) and *institutional* (i.e. organization). For reasons of space, we do not include a figure showing this agent categorization, but we refer the reader to [24] (chap.3), for details. In the Digital Transfer Pattern, `Sender` and `Receiver` are modelled as *rolemixins* because they represent roles played by entities of different kinds (e.g., information systems and organizations). The same goes for `Exchanged Digital Objects`, which represent roles that can be played either by monetary amounts or by different kinds of digital assets. In Fig. 5, we use the Digital Transfer Pattern to construct the Digital Exchange Pattern, which represents digital exchanges. It consists of a `Digital Exchange` event, composed of two or more `Digital Transfer` events.

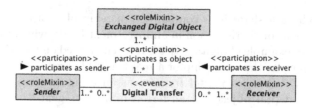

Fig. 4. The digital transfer pattern.

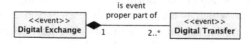

Fig. 5. The digital exchange pattern.

In the sequel, we systematically apply and reuse both the Digital Transfer Pattern and the Digital Exchange Pattern to build a set of models that characterize the concepts and relations involved in the representation of payments and linked obligation settlements. Firstly, we specify the models using the OntoUML language [22]. Then, we generate their representation in gUFO.

Digital Asset Transfer. Digital asset transfer concerns the execution of actions aiming at transferring some sort of ownership rights to an asset from an agent to another agent. In Fig. 6 we use the Digital Transfer Pattern (Fig. 4) to model a `Digital Asset Transfer` as an action (an UFO event [1]), in which a `Sender` agent transfers the ownership of a `Digital Asset` to a `Receiver` agent. The Turtle[4] fragment in Listing 1 shows the representation of a digital asset transfer in gUFO. This representation reproduces, with the limitations imposed by the expressiveness of the OWL language, the concepts presented in the OntoUML model in Fig. 6. Figure 7 presents an instantiation example of the OntoUML model.

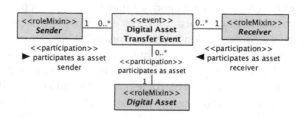

Fig. 6. Digital asset transfer in OntoUML.

---

[4] https://www.w3.org/TR/turtle/.

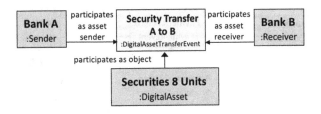

Fig. 7. Instantiation example of digital asset transfer.

Listing 1. Digital asset transfer represented in gUFO.

```
:DigitalAsset                  rdf:type gufo:RoleMixin ;
                               rdfs:subClassOf gufo:FunctionalComplex .

:DigitalAssetTransferEvent     rdf:type gufo:EventType ,
                               rdfs:subClassOf gufo:Event .

:Receiver                      rdf:type gufo:RoleMixin ;
                               rdfs:subClassOf gufo:FunctionalComplex .

:Sender                        rdf:type gufo:RoleMixin ;
                               rdfs:subClassOf gufo:FunctionalComplex .

:participatesAsAssetSender     rdfs:subPropertyOf gufo:participatedIn ;
                               rdfs:domain :Sender ;
                               rdfs:range  :DigitalAssetTransferEvent .

:participatesAsAssetReceiver   rdfs:subPropertyOf gufo:participatedIn ;
                               rdfs:domain :Receiver ;
                               rdfs:range  :DigitalAssetTransferEvent .

:participatesAsObject          rdfs:subPropertyOf gufo:participatedIn ;
                               rdfs:domain :DigitalAsset ;
                               rdfs:range  :DigitalAssetTransferEvent .
```

Payment. Payment concerns the transfer of a monetary amount in one currency
from an agent to another. As explained in the modeling of Monetary Amount
(Fig. 10), we are considering here payments made both in official currencies and
in virtual currencies.

In Fig. 8 we use the Digital Transfer Pattern (Fig. 4) to model a `Payment` as
an action (an UFO event [1]), in which a `Sender` agent transfers a `Monetary
Amount` to a `Receiver` agent. Figure 9 presents an instantiation example of this
model. The Turtle fragment in Listing 2 shows the representation of a payment
in gUFO.

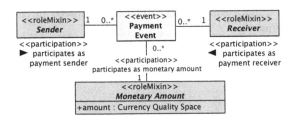

Fig. 8. Payment model in OntoUML.

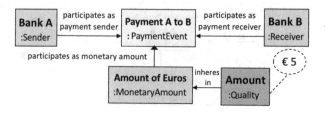

Fig. 9. Instantiation example of payment.

Listing 2. Payment represented in gUFO.

```
:MonetaryAmount              rdf:type gufo:RoleMixin ;
                             rdfs:subClassOf gufo:FunctionalComplex .

:Receiver                    rdf:type gufo:RoleMixin ;
                             rdfs:subClassOf gufo:FunctionalComplex .

:PaymentEvent                rdf:type gufo:EventType ;
                             rdfs:subClassOf gufo:Event .

:Sender                      rdf:type gufo:RoleMixin ;
                             rdfs:subClassOf gufo:FunctionalComplex .

:participatedsAsPaymentSender   rdfs:subPropertyOf gufo:participatedIn ;
                             rdfs:domain :Sender ;
                             rdfs:range :PaymentEvent .

:participatesAsPaymentReceiver  rdfs:subPropertyOf gufo:participatedIn ;
                             rdfs:domain :Receiver ;
                             rdfs:range :PaymentEvent .

:participatedsAsMonetaryAmount  rdfs:subPropertyOf gufo:participatedIn ;
                             rdfs:domain :DigitalAsset ;
                             rdfs:range :PaymentEvent .
```

Monetary Amount. To cope with the wide range of public and private payment means that emerged in recent times, our proposal considers not only payments made with real money and thus denominated in an official currency (e.g. Euro), but also payments using virtual currencies (e.g. privately-issued cryptocurrencies like ETH). We rely on the notions of money, currencies, and virtual currencies defined in ROME [5] (Sect. 2.4) and on the concept of monetary amount defined in the Financial Industry Business Ontology (FIBO) [15]. According to FIBO, monetary amount corresponds to an amount of money specified in a currency. We extend FIBO's definition of monetary amount to consider also amounts specified in virtual currencies. Figure 10 shows an OntoUML diagram depicting the main concepts and relations involved in the representation of monetary amount.

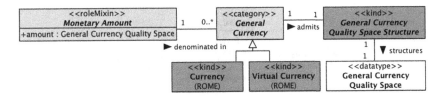

Fig. 10. Monetary amount in OntoUML.

Fig. 11. Instantiation example of monetary amount.

In `Monetary Amount`, the property `amount` represents the quantity, which has a value in a `Currency Quality Space` [5] (cf. Sect. 2.4). For example, euro has a measurable value in one-dimensional structure of numbers with two decimal places. A Monetary Amount is denominated in a General Currency, which is specialized into Currency [5] and Virtual Currency [5]. For an extensive discussion on money, currency and virtual currencies, please refer to [5]. Figure 11 presents an instantiation example of the OntoUML model. The Turtle fragment in Listing 3 shows the representation of monetary amount in gUFO.

Listing 3. Monetary amount represented in gUFO.

```
:MonetaryAmount        rdf:type gufo:RoleMixin ;
                       rdfs:subClassOf gufo:FunctionalComplex.

:GeneralCurrency       rdf:type gufo:Category ;
                       rdfs:subClassOf gufo:FunctionalComplex.

rome:Currency          rdf:type gufo:Kind ;
                       rdfs:subClassOf :GeneralCurrency .

rome:VirtualCurrency   rdf:type gufo:Kind ;
                       rdfs:subClassOf :GeneralCurrency .

:amount                rdfs:domain :MonetaryAmount ;
                       rdf:type owl:DatatypeProperty ;
                       rdfs:subPropertyOf gufo:hasQualityValue .

:denominatedIn         rdf:type owl:ObjectProperty ;
                       rdfs:domain :MonetaryAmount ;
                       rdfs:range :GeneralCurrency .
```

Delivery versus Payment. DvP can be seen as a specific type of digital exchange, in which the linked obligations are one or more digital asset transfers and the corresponding payment (or payments).

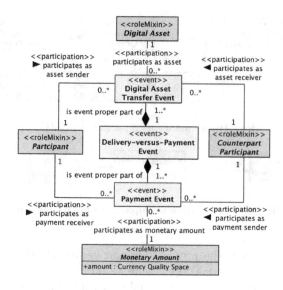

Fig. 12. Delivery versus Payment in OntoUML.

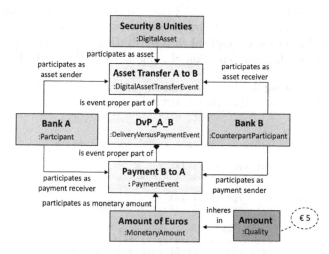

Fig. 13. Instantiation example of Delivery versus Payment.

In Fig. 12 we use the Digital Exchange Pattern (Fig. 5) to model the Delivery versus Payment as an action (an UFO event [1]), composed of one or more Digital Asset Transfers (Fig. 6) and one or more Payments (Fig. 8). Figure 13 presents an instantiation example of this model. The Turtle fragment in Listing 4 shows the representation of the Delivery versus Payment in gUFO.

Listing 4. Delivery versus Payment represented in gUFO.

```
:DeliveryVersusPaymentEvent      rdfs:subClassOf gufo:Event .

:DigitalAssetTransferEvent       rdfs:subClassOf gufo:Event ;
                   gufo:isEventProperPartOf :DeliveryVersusPaymentEvent .

:PaymentEvent                    rdfs:subClassOf gufo:Event ;
                   gufo:isEventProperPartOf :DeliveryVersusPaymentEvent .

:DigitalAsset                    rdf:type gufo:RoleMixin ;
                                 rdfs:subClassOf gufo:FunctionalComplex .

:MonetaryAmount                  rdf:type gufo:RoleMixin ;
                                 rdfs:subClassOf gufo:FunctionalComplex .

:Partcipant                      rdf:type gufo:RoleMixin ;
                                 rdfs:subClassOf gufo:FunctionalComplex .

:CounterpartParticipant          rdf:type gufo:RoleMixin ;
                                 rdfs:subClassOf gufo:FunctionalComplex .

:participatesAsAssetSender       rdfs:subPropertyOf gufo:participatedIn ;
                                 rdfs:domain :Partcipant ;
                                 rdfs:range :DigitalAssetTransferEvent .

:participatesAssetReceiver       rdfs:subPropertyOf gufo:participatedIn ;
                                 rdfs:domain :CounterpartParticipant ;
                                 rdfs:range :DigitalAssetTransferEvent .

:participatesAsAsset             rdfs:subPropertyOf gufo:participatedIn ;
                                 rdfs:domain :DigitalAsset ;
                                 rdfs:range :DigitalAssetTransferEvent .

:participatesAsPaymentSender     rdfs:subPropertyOf gufo:participatedIn ;
                                 rdfs:domain :CounterpartParticipant ;
                                 rdfs:range :PaymentEvent .

:participatesAsPaymentReceiver   rdfs:subPropertyOf gufo:participatedIn ;
                                 rdfs:domain :Participant ;
                                 rdfs:range :PaymentEvent .

:participatesAsMonetaryAmount    rdfs:subPropertyOf gufo:participatedIn ;
                                 rdfs:domain :DigitalAsset ;
                                 rdfs:range :PaymentEvent .
```

Payment versus Payment. PvP can be seen as specific type of digital exchanges, in which the linked obligations are two payments. In Fig. 14 we use the Digital Exchange Pattern (Fig. 5) to model the **Payment versus Payment** as an action composed of two **Payments** (Fig. 8). Figure 15 presents an instantiation example of this model. The representation of PvP in gUFO is analogous to the representation of DvP (Listing 4).

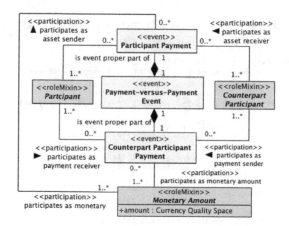

Fig. 14. Payment versus Payment in OntoUML.

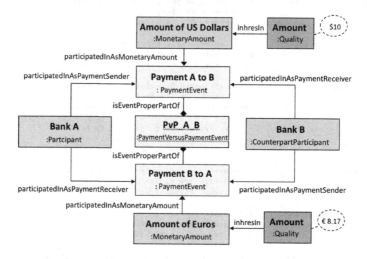

Fig. 15. Instantiation example of Payment versus Payment.

Delivery versus Delivery. DvD can be seen as specific type of digital exchanges, in which the linked obligations are two digital asset transfers. In Fig. 16 we use the Digital Exchange Pattern (Fig. 5) to model the Delivery versus Delivery as an action composed of two Digital Asset Transfers (Fig. 6). Figure 17 presents an instantiation example of this model. The representation of DvD in gUFO is analogous to the representation of DvP (Listing 4).

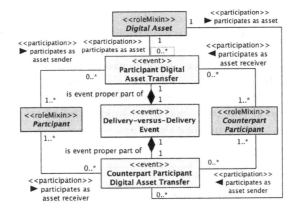

Fig. 16. Delivery versus Delivery in OntoUML.

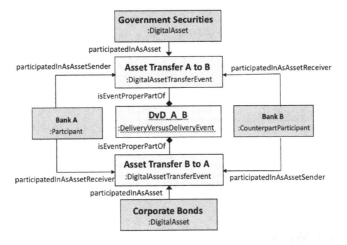

Fig. 17. Instantiation example of Delivery versus Delivery.

4 Application Example

A major concern of regulators is the use of digital money for illegitimate activities, like money laundering, terrorist financing, and tax evasion. Digital solutions for anti-money laundering and counter financing of terrorism based on artificial intelligence and data analytics can potentially help to identify risks and respond to, communicate, and monitor suspicious activity. Semantic interoperability is a fundamental aspect for applications in this context, as information from multiple and heterogeneous sources must be analyzed to detect unusual patterns, such as large amounts of cash flow at certain periods by particular groups of agents. Let us take as an example the assessment of a company named "Orange Corporate" regarding suspicious transactions. In order to detect unusual patterns, it is important to analyze all payment transfers performed by Orange Corporate. As the company operates in multiple ecosystems, it may be necessary to integrate DeFi on-chain and/or off-chain data with traditional finance data. Furthermore, from the perspective of the prevention of tax evasion, it is also important to be able to distinct payment transfers denominated in official currencies from the ones denominated in virtual currencies as different controls and rules may apply in each case. Figure 18 illustrates the application of the Payment and the Monetary Amount models (Listing 2 and 3) to support information integration in data analytics, for the example just described.

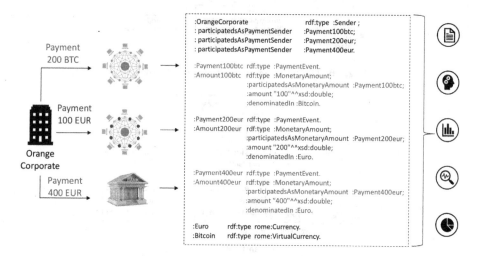

Fig. 18. Regulatory data analytics example.

5   Related Work

The notions of payments and settlement services have been addressed by financial standards such as the Financial Industry Business Ontology (FIBO) [15], which includes the modeling of payments and monetary amounts. However, these standards usually represent only payments made in official currencies. Payments made in virtual currencies such as privately-issued cryptocurrencies are not considered in their models.

Economic exchanges are a central notion in the Resource-Event Action (REA) ISO Standard [31]. In fact, as shown in [32], REA can be seen as subsumed by the Common Ontology for Economic Exchanges (COEX), on which our proposal is based. However, REA does not address the particularities of linked obligation settlement mechanisms (DvP, DvD and PvP) nor does it provide an ontological account of payments.

Another approach related to the notion of economic exchange is e3-value [20], an ontology-based methodology, commonly used for the modeling value exchanges. It adopts the economic value perspective by representing what is exchanged and by whom. The e3value ontology is based on the principle of reciprocity, denoting that every actor offers something of value, such as money, goods, services, etc., and gets a value in return. However, e3-value focuses on the exchanged value among actors in a generic way, leaving out the particularities of linked obligation settlement mechanisms as well as the ontological distinctions between assets and payments.

Fischer-Pauzenberger and Schwaiger [19] proposed the OntoREA Accounting and Finance Model, which constitutes an ontology-based conceptualization of the accounting and finance domain, grounded on UFO. Similarly, Blums and Weigand [13] proposed a Reference Ontology of Complex Economic Exchanges for Accounting Information Systems, grounded on UFO, which is a commitment-based economic exchange ontology, whose conceptualization is based on the establishment and fulfillment of commitments and claims between exchange participants (enterprise and counterparty) along the exchange life-cycle. In [36], the same authors proposed a comprehensive approach for implementing economic exchanges in DLT. These three approaches are similar to ours in the sense that it uses a well-founded language to represent concepts in the realm of economic exchanges. However, they differ from our work as they do not consider the ontological distinctions between money and virtual currencies in the modeling of payments.

Finally, the Project Ellipse, launched by the Bank for International Settlements Innovation Hub [10] proposes the creation of an integrated regulatory data and analytics platform to support regulatory oversight. Although they rely on "common data models" to provide a common understanding and properly integrate information, their models do not consider the ontological distinctions between the concepts.

6   Final Remarks

In this paper, we proposed and ontology-based approach for the modeling of payments and linked obligation settlements, aiming at providing conceptual clarification and supporting semantic interoperability. Firstly, we created two domain-related ontology patterns by reusing pieces of knowledge extracted from reference ontologies. Then, we applied these patterns to model payments and linked obligations settlements in OntoUML. Finally, we exported the models to OWL using gUFO. These gUFO/OWL concrete artifacts can contribute to semantic web related initiatives in finances [12], as well as to the goal of transparency of financial data exchange according to FAIR principles [26].

This work is part of a broader research initiative in the domains of finance and economics. We have been working with concepts like money, value, risk, trust and economic exchanges, creating a federation of reference conceptual models which are now becoming a kind of network of models in economics and finance. This paper, in particular, is an application example of two of these ontologies: the ontology of money and the ontology of economic exchanges. One of our objectives is to raise awareness of the importance of making explicit the ontological commitments of financial data, so that data from different sources in decentralized heterogeneous ecosystems can be properly and safely integrated.

As future work, we plan to validate our models in practice, to support information integration between multiple DLT/blockchain networks and traditional finance datasets. We also plan to expand our analysis to different types of settlement agreements, including those involving more than two participants.

Acknowledgments. This work is partially supported by CAPES (PhD grant# 88881.173022/2018-01) and NeXON project (UNIBZ).

References

1. Almeida, J.P.A., Falbo, R.A., Guizzardi, G.: Events as entities in ontology-driven conceptual modeling. In: Laender, A.H.F., Pernici, B., Lim, E.-P., de Oliveira, J.P.M. (eds.) ER 2019. LNCS, vol. 11788, pp. 469–483. Springer, Cham (2019). https://doi.org/10.1007/978-3-030-33223-5_39
2. Almeida, J., Guizzardi, G., Sales, T.P., Falbo, R.: gUFO: a lightweight implementation of the unified foundational ontology (UFO). Technical report, Ontology & Conceptual Modeling Research Group (NEMO) - Federal University of Espirito Santo (2020)
3. Almeida Falbo, R.: SABiO: systematic approach for building ontologies. In: ONTO.COM/ODISE@ FOIS (2014)
4. Amaral, G., Sales, T.P., Guizzardi, G.: Towards ontological foundations for central bank digital currencies. In: 15th Value Modelling and Business Ontologies Workshop (2021)
5. Amaral, G., Prince Sales, T., Guizzardi, G., Porello, D.: A reference ontology of money and virtual currencies. In: Grabis, J., Bork, D. (eds.) PoEM 2020. LNBIP, vol. 400, pp. 228–243. Springer, Cham (2020). https://doi.org/10.1007/978-3-030-63479-7_16
6. Arner, D.W., Auer, R., Frost, J.: Stablecoins: risks, potential and regulation. Financ. Stab. Rev. (39) (Autumm 2020), 95–123 (2020)
7. Bank for International Settlements: A glossary of terms used in payments and settlement systems (2016)
8. Bank for International Settlements: Enabling open finance through APIs (2020)
9. Bank for International Settlements/International Organization of Securities Commissions: Principles for financial market infrastructures (2012)
10. Bank of International Settlements: Ellipse: regulatory reporting and data analytics platform (2021). https://www.bis.org/about/bisih/topics/suptech_regtech/ellipse.htm. Accessed 16 Dec 2021
11. Bech, M.L., Hancock, J., Rice, T., Wadsworth, A.: On the future of securities settlement. BIS Q. Rev. (2020)
12. Bennett, M.: The financial industry business ontology: best practice for big data. J. Bank. Regul. **14**(3), 255–268 (2013)
13. Blums, I., Weigand, H.: Financial reporting by a shared ledger. In: JOWO (2017)
14. Buschmann, F., Henney, K., Schmidt, D.C.: Pattern-Oriented Software Architecture, on Patterns and Pattern Languages, vol. 5. Wiley (2007)
15. Enterprise Data Management Council: Financial Industry Business Ontology (2015)
16. European Central Bank: The payment system - payments, securities and derivatives, and the role of the Eurosystem. European Central Bank (2010)

17. European Central Bank, Bank of Japan: Securities settlement systems: delivery-versus-payment in a distributed ledger environment - Stella project report phase 2. ECB (2018)
18. Falbo, R.D.A., Guizzardi, G., Gangemi, A., Presutti, V.: Ontology patterns: clarifying concepts and terminology. In: 4th Workshop on Ontology and Semantic Web Patterns (2013)
19. Fischer-Pauzenberger, C., Schwaiger, W.S.A.: The OntoREA accounting and finance model: ontological conceptualization of the accounting and finance domain. In: Mayr, H.C., Guizzardi, G., Ma, H., Pastor, O. (eds.) ER 2017. LNCS, vol. 10650, pp. 506–519. Springer, Cham (2017). https://doi.org/10.1007/978-3-319-69904-2_38
20. Gordijn, J., Akkermans, H.: Designing and evaluating e-business models. IEEE Intell. Syst. **16**(04), 11–17 (2001)
21. Guarino, N., Guizzardi, G.: Relationships and events: towards a general theory of reification and truthmaking. In: Adorni, G., Cagnoni, S., Gori, M., Maratea, M. (eds.) AI*IA 2016. LNCS (LNAI), vol. 10037, pp. 237–249. Springer, Cham (2016). https://doi.org/10.1007/978-3-319-49130-1_18
22. Guizzardi, G.: Ontological Foundations for Structural Conceptual Models. Telematica Instituut Fundamental Research Series, No. 15 (2005). ISBN 90-75176-81-3
23. Guizzardi, G., Falbo, R.A., Guizzardi, R.S.S.: Grounding software domain ontologies in the Unified Foundational Ontology (UFO). In: 11th Ibero-American Conference on Software Engineering (CIbSE), pp. 127–140 (2008)
24. Guizzardi, R.: Agent-oriented constructivist knowledge management. Ph.D. thesis, University of Twente, Netherlands (2006)
25. ISO: Codes for the representation of currencies - ISO 4217:2015 (2015)
26. Jacobsen, A., et al.: FAIR principles: interpretations and implementation considerations. Data Intell. **2**(1–2), 10–29 (2020)
27. Kud, A.: Substantiation of the term "Digital Asset": economic and legal aspects. Int. J. Educ. Sci. **2**(1), 41–52 (2019)
28. Laurent, P., Chollet, T., Burke, M., Seers, T.: The tokenization of assets is disrupting the financial industry. Are you ready? Inside Mag. **19**, 62–67 (2018)
29. Lemieux, V.L., Feng, C. (eds.): Building Decentralized Trust. Springer, Cham (2021). https://doi.org/10.1007/978-3-030-54414-0
30. Massin, O., Tieffenbach, E.: The metaphysics of economic exchanges. J. Soc. Ontol. **3**(2), 167–205 (2016)
31. McCarthy, W.: ISO 15944-4 - REA Ontology. ISO, June 2007
32. Porello, D., Guizzardi, G., Sales, T.P., Amaral, G.: A core ontology for economic exchanges. In: Dobbie, G., Frank, U., Kappel, G., Liddle, S.W., Mayr, H.C. (eds.) ER 2020. LNCS, vol. 12400, pp. 364–374. Springer, Cham (2020). https://doi.org/10.1007/978-3-030-62522-1_27
33. Schär, F.: Decentralized finance: on blockchain-and smart contract-based financial markets. FRB of St. Louis Review (2021)
34. Suárez-Figueroa, M.C., Gómez-Pérez, A., Motta, E., Gangemi, A. (eds.): Ontology Engineering in a Networked World. Springer, Heidelberg (2012). https://doi.org/10.1007/978-3-642-24794-1
35. Treaty on the functioning of the European Union: Off. J. Eur. Union **C326**, 47–390 (2012)
36. Weigand, H., Blums, I., de Kruijff, J.: Shared ledger accounting-implementing the economic exchange pattern. Inf. Syst. **90**, 101437 (2020)
37. Zetzsche, D.A., Arner, D.W., Buckley, R.P.: Decentralized finance (DeFi). IIEL Issue Brief 2 (2020)

Towards an Ontology Network in Finance and Economics

Glenda Amaral[1]([✉]), Tiago Prince Sales[1], and Giancarlo Guizzardi[1,2]

[1] CORE/KRDB, Free University of Bozen -Bolzano, Bolzano, Italy
{gmouraamaral,tiago.princesales,giancarlo.guizzardi}@unibz.it
[2] Services & Cybersecurity, University of Twente, Enschede, The Netherlands

Abstract. Finance and economics are wide domains, where ontologies are useful instruments for dealing with semantic interoperability and information integration problems, as well as improving communication and problem solving among people. In particular, reference ontologies have been widely recognized as powerful tools for representing a model of consensus within a community to support communication, meaning negotiation, consensus establishment, as well as semantic interoperability and information integration. In domains like economics and finance, which are too large and complex to be represented as a single, large and monolithic ontology, it is necessary to create an ontological framework, built incrementally and in an integrated way, as a network. Therefore, in this paper we introduce OntoFINE, an Ontology Network in Finance and Economics that organizes and integrates knowledge in the realm on finance and economics, serving as a basis to several applications. We discuss the development of OntoFINE and present some of its applications.

Keywords: Ontology Network · Money · Value · Trust · Risk · Economic Exchanges

1 Introduction

In the last years, there has been a growing interest, within the financial sector, in the adoption of ontology-based conceptual models [44] to make the nature of the conceptualizations explicit, as well as to safely establish the correct relations between them, thereby supporting semantic interoperability. Naturally, having a clear understanding of the ontological nature of the concepts is fundamental not only to proper address semantic interoperability but also to understand the evolution of the economy before innovations in the financial industry, such as the introduction of cryptocurrencies and blockchain networks, the development of smart contracts, the release of stablecoins, the development of central bank digital currencies and the emergence of decentralized finance—the decentralized provision of financial products and services.

Reference ontologies have been widely recognized as a powerful tool for representing a model of consensus within a community. They are used for establishing a common conceptualization of the domain of interest to support communication, meaning negotiation, consensus establishment, as well as semantic interoperability and information

© Springer Nature Switzerland AG 2022
D. Aveiro et al. (Eds.): EEWC 2021, LNBIP 441, pp. 42–57, 2022.
https://doi.org/10.1007/978-3-031-11520-2_4

integration. However, some domains are often too large and complex to be represented as a single, large and monolithic ontology. This is the case of *finance* and *economics*. We believe that an integrated ontological framework, built incrementally and in an integrated way, as a network, can improve ontology-based applications in finance and economics, as well as improve communication among the different actors in these sectors.

This research aims at tackling these issues by investigating the conceptual foundations of some intertwined concepts in finance and economics, namely those of money, trust, value, risk and economic exchanges, to propose an Ontology Network in Finance and Economics (OntoFINE)[1], grounded in the Unified Foundational Ontology (UFO) [26], based on the literature review of the most relevant economic theories and considering recent innovations in the financial industry. The reason why we have chosen these subdomains is threefold. Firstly, because of their ubiquitous presence in the realm of finance and economics. Secondly because they are related to recent challenges faced by the financial industry, which involve new forms of money and trust, as well as new business models for digital exchanges. And finally, because they have been little explored by other initiatives in the same direction.

This paper is organized as follows. Section 2 provides an overview of our research baseline, including ontologies and their classifications, ontology networks and the Unified Foundational Ontology. Section 3 elaborates on the research method adopted. Section 4 presents OntoFINE and how it builds up from foundational to core and domain ontologies. Section 5 reports the application of OntoFINE in several initiatives. Section 6 discusses related works. Finally, Sect. 7 presents our final considerations.

2 Background

2.1 Ontologies and Their Classifications

There are different classifications of ontologies in the literature. In the context of this research, we are interested in the ones that classify ontologies according to their generality levels and intended application. Regarding the generality level, ontologies can be classified into foundational, core and domain ontologies [43]. At the highest level of generality, there are the foundational ontologies. Foundational ontologies span across many fields and model the very basic and general concepts and relations that make up the world, such as object, event, parthood relation etc. [15,25,26]. Domain ontologies, in turn, describe the conceptualization related to a given domain, such as electrocardiogram in medicine [25]. With a level of generality between that of foundational and domain ontologies, there are core ontologies. Core ontologies provide a precise definition of structural knowledge in a specific field that spans across different application domains in this field. These ontologies are built based on foundational ontologies and provide a refinement to them by adding detailed concepts and relations in their specific field [43]. The different generality levels do not amount to a discrete classification, but to a continuum [3], ranging from foundational ontologies that are totally domain-independent (such as DOLCE [15] and UFO [26]), to domain ontologies, for a very particular domain. Finally, core ontologies, despite being more general than domain

---

[1] The current specification of OntoFINE is available at http://purl.org/krdb-core/ontofine.

ontologies, are also domain-dependent. Higher-level ontologies can be used to support the development of lower-level ontologies, e.g., foundational ontologies can be used as basis for building core and domain ontologies, and core ontologies can support the development of domain ontologies. In fact, considering the continuous nature of the aforementioned classification, some ontologies can be used for supporting the development of more specific ontologies even within the same level of generality. For example, UFO-A (an ontology of endurants) [26] and UFO-B (an ontology of events) [30], both of which are foundational ontologies, have been used as basis for building UFO-C (an ontology of social entities) [28]. The latter, albeit being more specific, is still considered to be a foundational ontology. ROME (a core reference ontology on money) [12] is grounded in UFO-C, while an electrocardiogram ontology in medicine is an example of domain ontology.

Another relevant classification criterion concerns the intended application of ontologies. Guizzardi [26] makes an important distinction between ontologies as conceptual models, known as reference ontologies, and ontologies as coding artifacts, called here operational ontologies. A reference domain ontology is constructed with the goal of making the best possible description of the domain in reality. It is a special kind of conceptual model, an engineering artifact with the additional requirement of representing a model of consensus within a community [26]. On the other hand, once users have already agreed on a common conceptualization, operational versions of a reference ontology can be created. Contrary to reference ontologies, operational ontologies are designed with the focus on guaranteeing desirable computational properties. In other words, when developing a reference ontology, the focus is on expressivity of the representation and truthfulness to the domain being represented (domain appropriateness), even at the expenses of computational characteristics such as tractability and decidability [27]. In summary, in the view employed here, a reference ontology is a particular kind of conceptual model, namely, a reference conceptual model capturing the shared consensus of a given community.

2.2 Ontology Networks

Ontologies have been widely recognized as a key enabling technology for knowledge management. They are used for establishing a common conceptualization of the domain of interest to support knowledge representation, integration, storage, search and communication [40]. However, some domains are often too large and complex to be represented as a single ontology. This is the case of finance and economics. If we try to represent the whole domain as a single ontology, we will achieve a large and monolithic ontology that is hard to manipulate, use, and maintain [46]. On the other hand, representing each subdomain separately would be too costly, fragmented, and again hard to handle.

D'Aquin and Gangemi [19] point out a set of characteristics that are presented in "beautiful ontologies", from which we detach the following ones: having a good domain coverage; being modular or embedded in a modular framework; being formally rigorous; capturing also non-taxonomic relations; and reusing foundational ontologies. We believe that an integrated ontological framework, built considering them, can improve ontology-based applications in finance and economics. In such integrated ontological framework, there must be ways for creating, integrating and evolving related ontologies. Thus, we advocate that these ontologies should be built incrementally and in an integrated way, as a network. An Ontology Network is a collection of ontologies related together through a variety of relationships, such as alignment, modularization, and dependency. A networked ontology, in turn, is an ontology included in such a network, sharing concepts and relations with other ontologies [46]. One of the most common ways for two ontologies to relate is to be dependent on each other. More precisely, it is often the case that in order to define its own model, an ontology refers to the definitions included in another ontology. Large, monolithic ontologies are hard to manipulate, use, and maintain. Modular ontologies on the contrary divide the ontological model in self-contained, interlinked components, which can be considered independently, while at the same time participate to the definition of a specific aspect of an ontology.

2.3   The Unified Foundational Ontology (UFO)

This research intends to provide conceptual foundations for modeling information in finance and economics, grounded on the Unified Foundational Ontology (UFO). UFO is an axiomatic domain independent formal theory developed based on a number of theories from Formal Ontology, Philosophical Logics, Philosophy of Language, Linguistics and Cognitive Psychology. Other examples of foundational ontologies include DOLCE [15] and GFO [32]. UFO, however, was created with the specific purpose of providing foundations for conceptual modeling. For example, unlike these other ontologies, UFO includes a rich ontology of relations [24], and an expressive system of formal distinctions among types of universals [29]. Furthermore, it provides an ontological treatment of higher-order domain types and the multi-level structures involving them [26]. Finally, again unlike DOLCE and GFO, UFO is formally connected to a set of engineering tools including a modeling language (OntoUML), as well as a number of methodological (e.g., patterns, anti-patterns) and computational tools [31].

UFO is divided into three incrementally layered compliance sets: UFO-A [26], an ontology of endurants (objects), UFO-B [30], an ontology of perdurants (events), and UFO-C [28], an ontology of social entities built on the top of UFO-A and UFO-B, which addresses terms related to the spheres of intentional and social things. For an in-depth discussion and formalization, one should refer to [26,30]. UFO is the theoretical basis of OntoUML, a language for Ontology-driven Conceptual Modeling that has been successfully employed in a number of academic and industrial projects in several domains, such as services, value, petroleum and gas, media asset management, telecommunications, and government [31].

The "OntoUML Toolkit" contains a number set of tools to facilitate the ontology engineering process, such as ontological design patterns and anti-patterns, visual model simulation, and transformations for codification technologies [1]. UFO has a partial translation to OWL termed gUFO [1], which is suitable for knowledge graph applications. These gUFO/OWL concrete artifacts can contribute to semantic web related initiatives in finance [13], as well as to the goal of transparency of financial data exchange according to FAIR principles [35].

3   Methodological Aspects

For building OntoFINE, we followed some directions of the NeOn Methodology Framework [46]. NeOn provides guidance for engineering networked ontologies, making available detailed processes, guidelines and different scenarios for collaboratively building networked ontologies. In our work we have applied some of the NeOn methodological guidelines regarding ontology modularization, reusing and reengineering ontological resources.

In the development of each ontology we follow a customized version of the SABiO [2] methodology, suited to our particular context and needs. SABiO defines a process that starts with the development of a reference conceptual model, which is then used to develop a data model. We adhere to the general steps proposed in the methodology, up to the point of developing a reference ontology. These general steps are depicted in Fig. 1. The process starts with the specification of the purpose of the ontology and then enters an iterative loop of knowledge acquisition, ontology formalization, and ontology evaluation.

By combining NeOn Methodology's guidelines with a customized version of SABiO, we defined three flexible scenarios for building ontologies in the context of OntoFINE (Fig. 1). In the first scenario, the ontology is developed following just the customized version of SABiO. In the second and third scenarios, during the step "Ontology Formalization", defined in SABiO, we applied some methodological directions of NeOn for reusing and reenginnering ontological resources, such as foundational and core ontologies, and ontology design patterns.

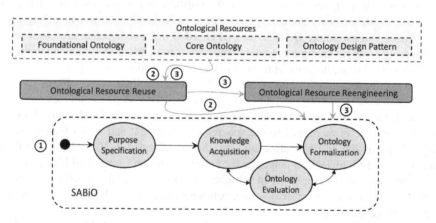

Fig. 1. Overview of the ontology development method (adapted from [46] and [2])

4   The Ontology Network in Finance and Economics (OntoFINE)

OntoFINE is part of a long term research program of providing a solid ontological foundation on finance and economics. It rises with three main premises: (i) being based on

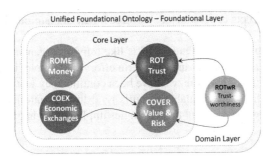

Fig. 2. OntoFINE: the network view

a well-founded grounding for ontology development; (ii) offering mechanisms to easy building and integrating new subdomain ontologies to the network; and (iii) promoting integration by keeping a consistent semantics for concepts and relations along the whole network. OntoFINE architecture is organized considering three ontology generality levels (Fig. 2):

Foundational Layer: The Unified Foundational Ontology lies in the foundational layer, providing the common grounding for all the networked ontologies. UFO's ontological distinctions are used for classifying OntoFINE concepts, e.g., as objects, events, commitments, agents, roles, goals and so on.

Core Layer. In the center of the ontology network, core reference ontologies are used to represent the general domain knowledge, being the basis for the subdomain networked ontologies. In its current version, OntoFINE includes four core reference ontologies:

- The Common Ontology of Value and Risk (COVER) [42];
- The Reference Ontology of Trust (ROT) [11], which reuses concepts from COVER;
- The Reference Ontology of Money and Virtual Currencies (ROME) [12], which reuses concepts from ROT; and
- The Core Ontology for Economic Exchanges (COEX) [41], which reuses concepts from COVER.

Domain-specific Layer. Over the foundational and core layers, OntoFINE places the domain ontologies. Each networked ontology is grounded in one or more core reference ontologies of the core layer and also in UFO, and encompasses a subdomain of OntoFINE. Currently, this layer contains the Reference Ontology of Trustworthines Requirements [5], which reuses concepts from ROT and COVER.

Figure 2 shows the current status of OntoFINE. Each circle represents an ontology. They are described further in this Section. Arrowed lines denote dependencies between networked ontologies.

It is important to notice that, even adopting a layered architecture, OntoFINE is a network and each new added node contributes for the whole network. When a new ontology is added, it should reuse existing elements (from a higher or the same layer). Other ontologies, in turn, may be adapted to keep consistency and share the same semantics along the whole network. Even the core ontologies can evolve to adapt or incorporate new concepts or relations discovered when domain ontologies are created or integrated.

Being an ontology network, OntoFINE is like a living organism and is constantly evolving. It requires a continuous and long-term effort with ontologies being added and integrated incrementally. Therefore, we have been continuously working on OntoFINE. OntoFINE specifications are available at purl.org/krdb-core/ontofine, where machine processable lightweight versions of the ontologies implemented in gUFO/OWL are also available.

4.1   The Reference Ontology of Trust (ROT)

The Reference Ontology of Trust[2] (ROT) [11] is a UFO-based ontology that formally characterizes the concept of trust, clarifies the relation between trust and risk, and represents how risk emerges from trust relations. ROT makes the following ontological commitments about the nature of trust:

Trust is Relative to a Goal. An agent, the trustor, trusts someone or something, the trustee, only relative to a goal, for the achievement of which she counts upon the trustee.

Trust is a Complex Mental State of a Trustor Regarding a Trustee and her Behavior. It is composed of: (i) a trustor's intention, whose propositional content is a goal of the trustor; (ii) the belief that the trustee has the capability to perform the desired action or exhibit the desired behavior; and (iii) the belief that the trustee's vulnerabilities will not prevent her from performing the desired action or exhibiting the desired behavior. When the role of trustee is played by an agent, trust is also composed of the trustor's belief that the trustee has the intention to exhibit the desired behavior.

The Trustor is Necessarily an "Intentional Entity". Briefly put, the trustor is a cognitive agent, an agent endowed with goals and beliefs [18].

The Trustee is not Necessarily a Cognitive System. The trustee is an entity capable of having a (hopefully positive) impact on a goal of the trustor by the outcome of its behavior [18]. A trustee may be a person, an animal, a car, a vaccine, etc.

Trust is Context Dependent. The trustor may trust the trustee for a given goal in a given context, but not do so for the same goal in a different context. We assume trust relations to be highly dynamic [18].

Trust Implies Risk. By trusting, the trustor accepts to become vulnerable to the trustee in terms of potential failure of the expected behavior and result, as the trustee may not exhibit the expected behavior or it may not have the desired result [37, p 21].

The reader interested in an in-depth description of the complete version of ROT is referred to [8, 11].

---

[2] The complete version of ROT in OntoUML and its implementation in OWL are available at http://purl.org/krdb-core/trust-ontology.

4.2 The Reference Ontology of Money and Virtual Currencies (ROME)

The Reference Ontology of Money and Virtual CurrEncies[3] (ROME) [12] is a reference model, grounded on the UFO, that formalizes the characterization of money, currency and virtual currencies, as well as its embedded concepts and relations. Some of ROME main ontological commitments on the nature of money are listed below:

Money Depends on the Collective Acceptance or Recognition of its Status as Money. [34,36,45]. In contemporary society the status function of money is supported by law, which specifies both the currency and the objects that are considered money in a particular country or region. It also defines a structure for the currency value domain.

Monetary Objects have a Nominal Value. This value is denominated in the currency defined in the law that describes its status function.

Physical Monetary Objects can be Considered Either Valid or not Valid. For example damaged banknotes fulfilling certain criteria defined in law are not considered valid. Obviously, only valid monetary objects can be exchanged for goods and services in the economy.

Money Presupposes the Existence of a Credit/Debt Relation. [34,38]. Monetary objects establish this relation between the agent holding control of them and the central bank. As for central bank deposits and commercial bank deposits, they correspond to an electronic monetary credit denominated in a certain currency and represent a claim on the central bank or the issuing bank, respectively.

Monetary Objects and Electronic Monetary Credits have an Associated Exchange Value. Agents holding control of monetary objects or owing electronic monetary credits are endowed with the capacity of making economic transactions in the amount corresponding to their exchange value. The exchange power resulting from the total of electronic monetary credits and monetary objects controlled by an agent stands for an aggregated exchange power that corresponds to the total value in economic transactions the agent is capable to carry out.

The Aggregated Exchange Power of an Agent has a Correspondent Purchasing Power. Simply put, the purchasing power describes the quantity of goods an amount of money can buy. As the price of goods and services can change, the purchasing power of an agent can vary, but its aggregated exchange power remains the same.

Money Depends on Trust. A precondition for the functioning of any monetary system is trust that the monetary objects and credits will be generally accepted, as well as that both price and financial stability will be maintained.

The reader interested in an in-depth description of the complete version of ROME is referred to [9,12].

---

[3] The complete version of ROME in OntoUML and its implementation in OWL are available at http://purl.org/krdb-core/money-ontology.

4.3 The Core Ontology for Economic Exchanges (COEX)

The Core Ontology for Economic Exchanges[4] (COEX) [41] is a well-founded reference ontology, specified in OntoUML, that formally characterizes the concept of economic exchanges based on the Action Theory of Economic Exchanges [39]. In this theory, an economic exchange is based on an agreement in which agents commit to performing certain reciprocal actions. This allows it to elegantly accommodate exchanges involving both products and services. The core assumption made by the Action Theory of Exchanges [39] is that, in any economic transaction, the "object" of the transaction is a pair of actions to be performed by the relevant agents involved in it. By viewing the object of transactions as actions, the ATE is capable of accounting for economic transactions about goods as well as services. In the case of services, the agreement is about the respective actions to be performed by the relevant parties. ATE's mechanism for explaining why economic transactions happen works by turning a conditional commitment into an unconditional commitment, under the suited conditions. For this reason, ATE also provides an explanation of why and under which circumstances an economic exchange happens.

The reader interested in an in-depth description of the complete version of COEX is referred to [41].

4.4 The Common Ontology of Value and Risk (COVER)

The Common Ontology of ValuE and Risk[5] (COVER) [42], a well-founded ontology that makes the deep connections between the concepts of value and risk explicit. COVER is grounded on several theories from marketing, service science, strategy and risk management. It is specified in OntoUML. COVER proposes an ontological analysis of notions such as value, risk, risk event (threat event, loss event) and vulnerability, among others. This ontology characterizes and integrates different perspectives of value and risk.

COVER makes the following ontological commitments on the nature of value:

Value emerges from impacts on goals: value emerges from events that affect the degree of satisfaction of one or more goals of an agent.

Value is relative: the same object or experience may be valuable to a person and of no value to another.

Value is experiential: even though value can be ascribed to objects, it is ultimately grounded on experiences. For instance, in order to explain the value of a smartphone, one must refer to the experiences enabled by it.

Value is contextual: the value of an object can vary depending on the context in which it is used.

As for risk, COVER makes the following ontological commitments:

---

[4] The complete version of COEX in OntoUML and its implementation in OWL are available at http://purl.org/krdb-core/economic-exchanges-ontology.

[5] The complete version of COVER in OntoUML and its implementation in OWL are available at http://purl.org/krdb-core/value-and-risk-ontology.

Risk is relative: this means that an event might be simultaneously considered as a risk by one agent and not as a risk by another (it may even be considered as an opportunity by such an agent).

A risk is perceived according to its impact on goals: in order to talk about risk, one needs to account for which goals are "at stake".

Risk is experiential: this means that we ultimately ascribe risk to events, not objects.

Risk is contextual: thus, the risk an object is exposed to may vary even if all its intrinsic properties (e.g. its vulnerabilities) are the same.

Risk is grounded on uncertainty about events and their outcomes.

The reader interested in an in-depth description of the complete version of COVER is referred to [42].

4.5   The Reference Ontology of Trustworthiness Requirements (ROTwR)

The Reference Ontology of Trustworthiness Requirements[6] (ROTwR) [5], is a reference domain ontology grounded on UFO [9], and based on the trust-related concepts defined in ROT. In ROTwR, trustworthiness requirements are defined as non-functional requirements, where the desired states-of-affairs are stakeholder mental states that include an attitude of trust towards the system-to-be. Trustworthiness requirements are related to an intention that is part of a trust relation between a stakeholder (the trustor) and the system-to-be (the trustee). According ROTwR, the system can emit trust-warranting signals to ensure trustworthy behavior. For example, information about how privacy and security measures are implemented could be provided as signals of the trustworthiness of a system. The reader interested in an in-depth description of the complete version of ROTwR is referred to [5].

5   OntoFINE Applications

In this section, we demonstrate the relevance of OntoFINE by presenting some of its applications (Fig. 3).

Modeling Capability Agreements and Risk [4, 11]: In this initiative, COVER and ROT were used to analyze the emergence of value and risk from trust, in delegation relations. Briefly speaking, the decision to delegate depends largely on the degree of trust. This decision may create value, as the trustor is endowed with new capabilities, but also implies some risk, as the trustor becomes dependent on the trustee, and consequently, more vulnerable. Having a clear understanding of the influence of these forces over delegation networks is fundamental both for the management of risks and for the awareness of the value created through the complex network of interdependencies.

Trust Pattern Language for ArchiMate [10]: Driven by the need to align the vision and strategic goals of enterprises with their business architectures, we specified a pattern language for trust modeling in ArchiMate, based on ROT and COVER, which can

---

[6] The complete version of ROTwR in OntoUML and its implementation in OWL are available at http://purl.org/krdb-core/trustworthiness-requirements-ontology.

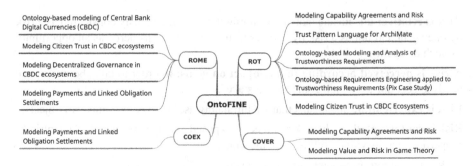

Fig. 3. OntoFINE applications

be used to model trust in the context of Enterprise Architecture (EA). The advantage of a pattern language [16] is that it offers a context in which related patterns can be combined, thus, reducing the space of design choices and design constraints [22]. In ROT, trust is modeled as a complex mental state of a trustor, composed of a set of beliefs about a trustee and her behavior. In the specification of the trust pattern language, we focused on the modeling and on the assessment of the beliefs that compose trust relations, in order to identify potential risks that can emerge from these relations. These models can be used, for example, in risk management to address the gap between trust concerns and the components that integrate the different layers of the enterprise architecture.

Ontology-based Modeling and Analysis of Trustworthiness Requirements [5]: We proposed a novel methodology for ontology-based requirements engineering, which applied ROT in a case illustration. In this work, we relied on ROT to define the class of trustworthiness requirements for software systems and their relation to concepts such as trust, capability, vulnerability and risk, among others.

Ontology-based Requirements Engineering Applied to Trustworthiness Requirements (Pix Case Study) [6]: We conducted a real case study to verify if ROT is capable of properly representing real world situations. In this study, ROT was applied to help with the elicitation of trustworthiness requirements of software systems by analyzing the case of Pix, the Brazilian Instant Payments Ecosystem created and managed by the Central Bank of Brazil.

Ontology-based Modeling of Central Bank Digital Currencies [9]: We applied ROME to provide an ontological account for the concept of Central Bank Digital Currencies (CBDC) and represent its embedded concepts and relations.

Modeling Value and Risk in Game Theory [7]: We conducted an ontological analysis characterizing some basic concepts in game theory, which made clear the emergence of value and risks from game outcomes. We made use of the concepts and relations defined in COVER to analyze the payoffs of a game in terms of value and risk, as well as how they emerge from outcomes in game theory. We formalized our analysis by means of an ontologically well-founded model, specified in OntoUML. In addition, we applied these results to represent the emergence of value and risk from game outcomes in enterprise architecture models in ArchiMate.

Modeling Payments and Linked Obligation Settlements: We proposed and ontology-based approach for the modeling of payments and linked obligation settlement mechanisms, aiming at providing conceptual clarification and supporting semantic interoperability in decentralized finance ecosystems. Firstly, we created two domain-related ontology patterns by reusing pieces of knowledge extracted from COEX and ROME. Then, we systematically applied these patterns to model payments and linked obligations in OntoUML. Finally, we exported the models to OWL using gUFO.

Modeling Decentralized Governance in CBDC Ecosystems: ROME is being applied to support an ontological approach for decentralized governance in CBDC ecosystems. To define a proper governance model for CBDCs it is necessary to make explicit the notion of CBDC and its associated concepts and relations, which is provided by ROME.

Modeling Citizen Trust in CBDC Ecosystems: ROME and ROT are also being applied to support the modeling and analysis of citizens' trust in CBDC ecosystems.

6   Related Work

There exists in the literature a number of initiatives aiming at the creation of an unified view of the reality related to finance and economics. These works include vocabularies relevant to the financial sector, semi-structured data schemas and ontologies.

The Financial Industry Business Ontology (FIBO) [20] is an industry standard resource for the definition of business concepts in the financial services industry. It is developed and hosted by the Enterprise Data Management Council (EDMC) and is published in a number of formats for operational use and business definitions. It is also standardized through the Object Management Group (OMG). FIBO is developed as a series of ontologies and, in general, can be seen as a kind of ontology network. Despite presenting some definitions in the domains of money, FIBO is considerably less comprehensive than OntoFINE regarding this topic. For example, concepts related to digital currencies and cryptocurrencies are not present in this ontology. Furthermore, FIBO does not explore concepts related to trust.

The Financial Industry Regulatory Ontology (FIRO) [21] is an ontology model composed of relevant and interlinked ontologies in the financial industry regulatory domain. FIRO captures regulatory vocabularies, compliance imperatives and rules into the Description Logic-based Web-Ontology Language (OWL-DL). Basically, the objective of FIRO is to enable efficient access and smarter consumption of the wide and complex spectrum of legislation and regulatory rules governing the financial industry globally. It is focused on the legislation and regulation domains and does not address the notions of money, trust, value, risk and economic exchanges.

The Financial Regulation Ontologie (FRO) [47] is a set of linked ontologies to implement "semantic compliance" in the financial industry. Regulatory compliance combines the domains of legal and finance. Therefore, FRO imports the FIBO [20] and the Legal Knowledge Interchange Format [33], which represent information in the finance and in the legal domain, respectively. In addition, FRO integrates three operational ontologies, namely: the Bank Regulation Ontology, the Fund Regulation

Ontology, the Hedge Fund Regulation Ontology and the Insurance Regulation Ontology. Although the purpose of FRO is strongly related to OntoFINE, it has a different objective, focusing on regulatory compliance aspects.

The Financial Industry Operational Risk Ontology (FiORO) [17] aims at enabling the systematic identification, assessment, management, mitigation and regulatory compliance reporting of operational risks in a financial services organization. It is expressed using in OWL. Although FiORO is focused on risks, it addresses only operational risks. It does not provide support for the modeling of other types of financial risk nor for the modeling of systemic risk.

In [23] Fischer-Pauzenberger and Schwaiger proposed the OntoREA Accounting and Finance Model, which constitutes an ontology-based conceptualization of the accounting and finance domain, grounded on the UFO. This proposal is similar to OntoFINE in the sense that it uses a well-founded language to represent concepts on economic exchanges, value and risk, however, it does not provide ontological distinctions for the concept of money and trust. Similarly, Blums and Weigand [14] proposed a Reference Ontology of Complex Economic Exchanges for accounting information systems, grounded on UFO, which covers concepts in the realm of economic exchanges, but does not provide ontological foundations neither on money nor on trust.

7   Final Considerations

Knowledge in economics and finance is diverse, interlinked and highly influenced by technology innovations. For dealing with richer scenarios, addressing several subdomains in finance and economics, we need integrated ontologies. An ontology network can provide such integrated solution. Some benefits of ontology networks are: (i) knowledge is organized and structured and can be used as needed: whole or extracts of it; (ii) it is easier to reuse and extend; (iii) it is easier to figure out the "big picture" and at the same time have an understanding of each subdomain separately.

Thus, in this paper, we presented OntoFINE, an Ontology Network in Finance and Economics. In its current version, OntoFINE includes core reference ontologies on money, value, trust, risk and economic exchanges. Diverse initiatives can benefit from the use of OntoFINE, especially the ones in which the focus is improving communication among different actors, semantic interoperability and information integration. We have experienced the benefits of ontology networks by using OntoFINE in applications as the ones mentioned in Sect. 5.

In the future, other core and domain ontologies in economics and finance should be developed and integrated to OntoFINE to enlarge its coverage. We also plan to use OntoFINE in new application scenarios, such as trust aspects in decentralized finance ecosystems and privacy issues in the context of open finance.

Acknowledgments. CAPES (PhD grant# 88881.173022/2018-01) and NeXON project (UNIBZ).

References

1. Almeida, J., Guizzardi, G., Sales, T.P., Falbo, R.: gUFO: a lightweight Implementation of the Unified Foundational Ontology (UFO). Technical Report, Ontology & Conceptual Modeling Research Group (NEMO) - Federal University of Espirito Santo (2020)
2. Almeida Falbo, R.: Sabio: Systematic approach for building ontologies. In: ONTO. COM/ODISE@ FOIS (2014)
3. de Almeida Falbo, R., Barcellos, M.P., Nardi, J.C., Guizzardi, G.: Organizing ontology design patterns as ontology pattern languages. In: Cimiano, P., Corcho, O., Presutti, V., Hollink, L., Rudolph, S. (eds.) ESWC 2013. LNCS, vol. 7882, pp. 61–75. Springer, Heidelberg (2013). https://doi.org/10.1007/978-3-642-38288-8_5
4. Amaral, G., Guizzardi, G., Guarino, N., Porello, D., Sales, T.P.: Capability agreements and risk. In: 13th International Workshop on Value Modelling and Business Ontologies (2019)
5. Amaral, G., Guizzardi, R., Guizzardi, G., Mylopoulos, J.: Ontology-based modeling and analysis of trustworthiness requirements: preliminary results. In: Dobbie, G., Frank, U., Kappel, G., Liddle, S.W., Mayr, H.C. (eds.) ER 2020. LNCS, vol. 12400, pp. 342–352. Springer, Cham (2020). https://doi.org/10.1007/978-3-030-62522-1_25
6. Amaral, G., Guizzardi, R., Guizzardi, G., Mylopoulos, J.: Trustworthiness requirements: the pix case study. In: Ghose, A., Horkoff, J., Silva Souza, V.E., Parsons, J., Evermann, J. (eds.) ER 2021. LNCS, vol. 13011, pp. 257–267. Springer, Cham (2021). https://doi.org/10.1007/978-3-030-89022-3_21
7. Amaral, G., Porello, D., Sales, T.P., Guizzardi, G.: Modeling the emergence of value and risk in game theoretical approaches. In: Aveiro, D., Guizzardi, G., Pergl, R., Proper, H.A. (eds.) EEWC 2020. LNBIP, vol. 411, pp. 70–91. Springer, Cham (2021). https://doi.org/10.1007/978-3-030-74196-9_5
8. Amaral, G., Sales, T.P., Guizzardi, G.: Ontological foundations for trust management: extending the reference ontology of trust. In: 15th International Workshop on Value Modelling and Business Ontologies (VMBO) (2021)
9. Amaral, G., Sales, T.P., Guizzardi, G.: Towards ontological foundations for central bank digital currencies. In: 15th Value Modelling and Business Ontologies Workshop (2021)
10. Amaral, G., Sales, T.P., Guizzardi, G., Almeida, J.P.A., Porello, D.: Modeling trust in enterprise architecture: a pattern language for ArchiMate. In: Grabis, J., Bork, D. (eds.) PoEM 2020. LNBIP, vol. 400, pp. 73–89. Springer, Cham (2020). https://doi.org/10.1007/978-3-030-63479-7_6
11. Amaral, G., Sales, T.P., Guizzardi, G., Porello, D.: Towards a reference ontology of trust. In: Panetto, H., Debruyne, C., Hepp, M., Lewis, D., Ardagna, C.A., Meersman, R. (eds.) OTM 2019. LNCS, vol. 11877, pp. 3–21. Springer, Cham (2019). https://doi.org/10.1007/978-3-030-33246-4_1
12. Amaral, G., Prince Sales, T., Guizzardi, G., Porello, D.: A reference ontology of money and virtual currencies. In: Grabis, J., Bork, D. (eds.) PoEM 2020. LNBIP, vol. 400, pp. 228–243. Springer, Cham (2020). https://doi.org/10.1007/978-3-030-63479-7_16
13. Bennett, M.: The financial industry business ontology: best practice for big data. J. Banking Regul. **14**(3), 255–268 (2013)
14. Blums, I., Weigand, H.: Towards a reference ontology of complex economic exchanges for accounting information systems. In: 2016 IEEE 20th International Enterprise Distributed Object Computing Conference (EDOC), pp. 1–10. IEEE (2016)
15. Borgo, S., Masolo, C.: Foundational choices in DOLCE. In: Staab, S., Studer, R. (eds.) Handbook on Ontologies. IHIS, pp. 361–381. Springer, Heidelberg (2009). https://doi.org/10.1007/978-3-540-92673-3_16

16. Buschmann, F., Henney, K., Schmidt, D.C.: Pattern-oriented Software Architecture, on Patterns and Pattern Languages, vol. 5. Wiley, Hoboken (2007)

17. Butler, T., Naz, T., Ceci, M.: Introducing FiORO: the financial industry operational risk ontology (2017)

18. Castelfranchi, C., Falcone, R.: Trust Theory: A Socio-Cognitive and Computational Model, vol. 18. Wiley, Hoboken (2010)

19. d'Aquin, M., Gangemi, A.: Is there beauty in ontologies? Appl. Ontology 6(3), 165–175 (2011)

20. Enterprise data management council: financial industry business ontology (2015). https://spec.edmcouncil.org/fibo/. Accessed 16 Dec 2021

21. Espinoza, A., Abi-Lahoud, E., Butler, T.: Ontology-driven financial regulatory change management: an iterative development process. In: 2nd Semantic Web and Linked Open Data workshop (SW-LOD). Anais (2014)

22. Falbo, R., Barcellos, M., Ruy, F., Guizzardi, G., Guizzardi, R.: Ontology pattern languages. In: Ontology Engineering with Ontology Design Patterns: Foundations and Applications. IOS Press (2016)

23. Fischer-Pauzenberger, C., Schwaiger, W.S.A.: The OntoREA accounting and finance model: ontological conceptualization of the accounting and finance domain. In: Mayr, H.C., Guizzardi, G., Ma, H., Pastor, O. (eds.) ER 2017. LNCS, vol. 10650, pp. 506–519. Springer, Cham (2017). https://doi.org/10.1007/978-3-319-69904-2_38

24. Fonseca, C.M., Porello, D., Guizzardi, G., Almeida, J.P.A., Guarino, N.: Relations in ontology-driven conceptual modeling. In: Laender, A.H.F., Pernici, B., Lim, E.-P., de Oliveira, J.P.M. (eds.) ER 2019. LNCS, vol. 11788, pp. 28–42. Springer, Cham (2019). https://doi.org/10.1007/978-3-030-33223-5_4

25. Guarino, N.: Formal ontology in information systems: In: Proceedings of the First International Conference (FOIS 1998), 6–8 June, Trento, Italy, vol. 46. IOS press (1998)

26. Guizzardi, G.: Ontological foundations for structural conceptual models. Telematica Instituut Fundamental Research Series, No. 15, ISBN 90-75176-81-3 (2005)

27. Guizzardi, G.: On ontology, ontologies, conceptualizations, modeling languages, and (meta) models. Front. Artif. Intell. Appl. 155, 18 (2007)

28. Guizzardi, G., Falbo, R.A., Guizzardi, R.S.S.: Grounding software domain ontologies in the Unified Foundational Ontology (UFO). In: 11th Ibero-American Conference on Software Engineering (CIbSE), pp. 127–140 (2008)

29. Guizzardi, G., Fonseca, C.M., Benevides, A.B., Almeida, J.P.A., Porello, D., Sales, T.P.: Endurant types in ontology-driven conceptual modeling: towards OntoUML 2.0. In: Trujillo, J.C., et al. (eds.) ER 2018. LNCS, vol. 11157, pp. 136–150. Springer, Cham (2018). https://doi.org/10.1007/978-3-030-00847-5_12

30. Guizzardi, G., Wagner, G., de Almeida Falbo, R., Guizzardi, R.S.S., Almeida, J.P.A.: Towards ontological foundations for the conceptual modeling of events. In: Ng, W., Storey, V.C., Trujillo, J.C. (eds.) ER 2013. LNCS, vol. 8217, pp. 327–341. Springer, Heidelberg (2013). https://doi.org/10.1007/978-3-642-41924-9_27

31. Guizzardi, G., et al.: Towards ontological foundations for conceptual modeling: the Unified Foundational Ontology (UFO) story. Appl. Ontology 10(3–4), 259–271 (2015)

32. Herre, H.: General Formal Ontology (GFO): a foundational ontology for conceptual modelling. In: Poli, R., Healy, M., Kameas, A. (eds.) Theory and Applications of Ontology: Computer Applications, pp. 297–345. Springer, Dordrecht (2010). https://doi.org/10.1007/978-90-481-8847-5_14

33. Hoekstra, R., Breuker, J., Di Bello, M., Boer, A., et al.: The LKIF core ontology of basic legal concepts. LOAIT 321, 43–63 (2007)

34. Innes, A.M.: What is money. Banking Law J. 30, 377 (1913)

35. Jacobsen, A., et al.: FAIR principles: interpretations and implementation considerations. Data Intell. **2**(1–2), 10–29 (2020)
36. Knapp, G.F.: The state theory of money. McMaster University Archive for the History of Economic Thought, Technical Report (1924)
37. Luhmann, N.: Trust and Power. Wiley, Hoboken (2018)
38. Macleod, H.: The Theory of Credit, vol. 2. Green, and Company, Longmans (1890)
39. Massin, O., Tieffenbach, E.: The metaphysics of economic exchanges. J. Soc. Ontology **3**(2), 167–205 (2016)
40. O'Leary, D.E.: Using AI in knowledge management: knowledge bases and ontologies. IEEE Intell. Syst. Their Appl. **13**(3), 34–39 (1998)
41. Porello, D., Guizzardi, G., Sales, T.P., Amaral, G.: A core ontology for economic exchanges. In: Dobbie, G., Frank, U., Kappel, G., Liddle, S.W., Mayr, H.C. (eds.) ER 2020. LNCS, vol. 12400, pp. 364–374. Springer, Cham (2020). https://doi.org/10.1007/978-3-030-62522-1_27
42. Sales, T.P., Baião, F., Guizzardi, G., Almeida, J.P.A., Guarino, N., Mylopoulos, J.: The common ontology of value and risk. In: Trujillo, J.C., et al. (eds.) ER 2018. LNCS, vol. 11157, pp. 121–135. Springer, Cham (2018). https://doi.org/10.1007/978-3-030-00847-5_11
43. Scherp, A., Saathoff, C., Franz, T., Staab, S.: Designing core ontologies. Appl. Ontology **6**(3), 177–221 (2011)
44. Scholes, M., et al.: Regulating Wall Street: The Dodd-Frank Act and the New Architecture of Global Finance, vol. 608. John, Hoboken (2010)
45. Searle, J.: The Construction of Social Reality. Free Press, New York (1995)
46. Suárez-Figueroa, M.C., Gómez-Pérez, A., Fernández-López, M.: The NeOn methodology for ontology engineering. In: Suárez-Figueroa, M.C., Gómez-Pérez, A., Motta, E., Gangemi, A. (eds.) Ontology Engineering in a Networked World, pp. 9–34. Springer, Heidelberg (2012). https://doi.org/10.1007/978-3-642-24794-1_2
47. Ziemer, J.: Financial regulation ontology. http://finregont.com/fro/html_widoco/index-en.html. Accessed 16 Dec 2021

Flexible Enterprise Optimization with Constraint Programming

Sytze P. E. Andringa[✉][iD] and Neil Yorke-Smith[iD]

Algorithmics Group, Delft University of Technology, Delft, The Netherlands
{s.p.e.andringa,n.yorke-smith}@tudelft.nl

Abstract. Simulation–optimization is often used in enterprise decision-making processes, both operational and tactical. This paper shows how an intuitive mapping from descriptive problem to optimization model can be realized with Constraint Programming (CP). It shows how a CP model can be constructed given a simulation model and a set of business goals. The approach is to train a neural network (NN) on simulation model inputs and outputs, and embed the NN into the CP model together with a set of soft constraints that represent business goals. We study this novel simulation–optimization approach through a set of experiments, finding that it is flexible to changing multiple objectives simultaneously, allows an intuitive mapping from business goals expressed in natural language to a formal model suitable for state-of-the-art optimization solvers, and is realizable for diverse managerial problems.

Keywords: Enterprise simulation · Constraint Programming · Deep learning · Simulation–optimization

1 Introduction

Simulation is widely used both to evaluate enterprises and in enterprise planning [16,29]. By running a simulation based on an enterprise model under various sets of parameters, one can get insight into how an enterprise might behave in complex or future scenarios. Various managerial interventions can be analysed for the likely outcomes. Hence, decision makers (DM) putting these models into practice are often interested in finding optimal inputs with respect to an observed 'problem' [18]. A problem describes an undesired property of the system that can be tackled by taking action. For the DM there is uncertainty about what course of action is best to take [6]; simulation can provide insights.

However, finding these inputs by trying out them all through simulation can be applied with only limited success on complex simulation processes, as the number of possible inputs grows exponentially with respect to the number of input parameters [18]. On the other hand, using a pure optimization model – i.e., omitting simulation – can be incapable of capturing all complexities and dynamics of a system [18]. Hence *simulation–optimization* (SO) seeks to combine

© Springer Nature Switzerland AG 2022
D. Aveiro et al. (Eds.): EEWC 2021, LNBIP 441, pp. 58–73, 2022.
https://doi.org/10.1007/978-3-031-11520-2_5

the benefits of both by using simulation to represent the actual system and optimization to find optimal simulation inputs [28].

Misinterpretation between DM and optimization model in a SO approach can be disastrous, then, as it can result in the wrong problem being solved. As such, a valid translation from problem description to formal model is crucial [1]. This translation is non-trivial. From a modeller's perspective, existing enterprise modelling (EM) methods offer only tenuous concepts of 'problems' [6]. From a computational perspective, optimization models can be difficult for a DM to understand, especially when the model is full of formal mathematics. Indeed, Grossman [12] points out that the four common decomposition techniques used in enterprise-wide optimization all have a mathematical basis, in the sense that they aim to reduce the solution space or number of constraints. The emphasis in the literature is on model performance rather than easing the DM's process. A practical example can be found in [32], where the optimization model for a clothing line is modelled by several pages full of mathematical formulae.

This paper puts forward a novel use of Constraint Programming (CP), a declarative paradigm for defining combinatorial optimization problems. CP is seen as the closest approach to "the user states a problem, the computer solves it" [8]. It allows one to describe diverse real-world problems through constraints, i.e., statements which pose some relation among the problem's variables [25]. Notably, the expressiveness of CP means its formal models can be more human-like than, for instance, mixed integer programming models. Given a CP model, algorithms called 'solvers' assign values to variables of the CP model such that every constraint is satisfied. A constraint program thus only needs to express *what* we want to solve, not *how*.

Many leading EM frameworks are descriptive in nature [29]. Since CP is declarative, we argue CP can form an effective way to model problems in an more understandable but computer-parsable format. This requires keeping the CP model simple, which can be done by modelling complex properties of the system by a simulation model and have this incorporated into the CP model according to an automatic process.

Specifically, in this paper the simulation model is represented by a "model of a model", i.e., *meta-model* [15]. Meta-modelling techniques range from descriptive representations of ontological concepts to algorithms to make faster approximations of complex computer code [3,15]. We focus on the latter, by representing the simulation model by neural networks (NN). NN are capable of learning behaviour of complex systems and require little engineering by hand, making them applicable in many domains [4,19,28]. In this paper, a NN is trained on simulation data and *automatically embedded* into the CP model. We argue this adds additional flexibility during the problem solving process, since a change of objective can be evaluated without making additional simulation calls.

This flexibility can be desirable in various situations, for example when: 1) The DM does not know all specifications of the problem it wants to solve (for example, information by a third party is required) but does know how the system currently behaves, and would like to make preparations such that problems can be solved on-the-go without making computationally expensive simulation calls. 2) The DM has a large collection of problems that needs to be solved, making setting up a separate feedback loop for every problem infeasible. 3) The DM is not able to do simulation during the problem-solving phase.

Summarising, the contributions of this paper to the literature are: 1) Showing how an easy-to-understand CP program can be constructed which is interpretable for solver software, starting from a descriptive problem description. 2) Showing how NNs can be embedded in a CP model by means of *empirical model learning*, such that no additional simulation calls are necessary when a different problem needs to be tackled for the same enterprise. 3) Providing experiments together with supplementary code for a novel SO approach that embeds a NN into a CP model. 4) Showing how a pareto front can be approximated through soft constraints, such that a DM can get proper insight in the scope of possible actions and their impact on the system.

2 Background and Related Work

2.1 Constraint Programming

CP is an expressive yet practical approach to optimization, used in a wide variety of applications [25,30]. It solves constraint satisfaction problems (CSP), which consist of a set of variables, each with a domain of permitted values, and a set of constraints specified in a logical formalism. A solution to a CSP is an assignment of a value to every variable from its domain, such that all the constraints are satisfied. *Soft CSPs* permit the constraints to be satisfied to a degree, rather than binary satisfaction. Constraint Optimization Problems (COP) include an objective function. For both CSP and COPs, the resulting model is passed to a solving algorithm. A wide variety of such solvers, complete and incomplete, are available, such as `or-tools` from Google.

Although CP and Mathematical Programming (MP) share a similar model-and-solve paradigm – there is a set of decision variables, an objective function to maximize or minimize and a set of constraints – CP is a more expressive formalism. It can be thought of as a generalisation of mixed integer programming to non-linear and non-arithmetic constraints [30]. Table 1 provides an overview of the differences between CP and MP. Notably for the purpose of this paper, the expressive nature of CP allows for models which are closer to human-level expression of problems [9].

2.2 Closely-Related Approaches

The approach of this paper, elaborated in Sect. 3, has two main characteristics. First, we use simple CP to model the problem. Second, we represent the simulation model automatically in an optimization model by representing it as a NN.

Using CP in modelling enterprises and in business analytics is not a new concept. Several studies couple Business Process Management with CP. These

Table 1. Mathematical programming vs. constraint programming [13].

Mathematical programming	Constraint programming
Typically restricted to linear and quadratic problems	Typically discrete but also continuous problems
Proves optimality with techniques such as a lower-bound proof provided by cuts and linear relaxation	Proves optimality by showing that no better solution than the current one can be found
Algebra as theoretical basis	Logic as theoretical basis
Requires that the model falls in a well-defined mathematical category	Does not make assumptions on the mathematical properties of the solution space
Is specific to a class of problems whose formulation satisfies certain mathematical properties	Has no limitation on the arithmetic constraints that can be set on decision variables

Table 2. Black box optimization vs. empirical model learning [20].

Black box optimization	Empirical model learning
Designed for problems without a complex combinatorial structure (discrete variables and non-trivial constraints)	Tends to provide best results for problems with a complex combinatorial structure
Relies on performing simulation during the search process	Simulation time has no direct impact on the solver performance
Function that describes the system is a black box	No black box assumption, allowing exploitation of its structure during the search process

typically focus on (complex) planning and scheduling problems and require the DM to describe the flow of the system in the CP model [14,31]. In contrast, this paper studies CP model that merely describe the problem to solve and do not require the DM to describe how the system operates. Differently stated, the DM can treat the simulation model as a black-box. As a result, the DM should solely focus on describing what relation between simulation in- and outputs she would like to be satisfied and does not have to consider details of internal processes, as these are modelled by means of a simulation model. We believe this makes it applicable to a wider variety of problems in the sense that the only requirement is access to a simulation model, and easier to understand as the DM can describe its problem in a more direct fashion.

The literature on SO tend to favour evolutionary search to find optimal simulation inputs [18,28,33]. This is convenient when fast evaluation of the simulation model is possible. However, if simulation is expensive – frequently the case with simulators – advanced techniques are necessary to limit the number of simulation calls [20]. Table 2 summarizes the differences between empirical model learning and classical black box optimization.

3   Methodology

Figure 1 provides an overview of our approach. The simulation model is assumed to represent an enterprise; it can for example be derived from an enterprise model [29]. How to design a qualitative simulation model is not in the scope for this paper: the reader is refered to Kampik and Najjir [16], Laguna and Marklund [18]. This section details the two main components of our approach, namely the Neural Network and the CP model. Then, some specifications about the solving procedure are discussed.

Table 3. Concepts from the meta-model presented by Bock et al. [6] and their CP equivalents. A factual aspect describes something regarded as true, i.e., a constraint. A goal is a metric to improve upon that is expressed by other metrics, i.e., an objective function. Multiple stakeholders can be modelled by soft constraints, which provides foundation to model individual preferences [27]. An action describes something that can be undertaken, hence corresponds with a variable that can be decided upon.

Problem conceptualization meta-model	CP equivalent
Factual aspect	Constraint
Goal	Objective function
Value	Variable
Stakeholder preference	Soft-constraint
Possible action	Decision variable

3.1   The Neural Network

The first main component is a meta-model, derived from a simulation model representing the behaviour of a system. This allows the DM to consult the meta-model instead of the simulation, such that simulation calls do not have to be made during the solving procedure. Deriving such a meta-model poses a trade-off. On one hand it should reflect the simulation model properly. On the other hand it should be convenient enough to allow optimization. This dilemma corresponds with a fundamental computational reality, namely the trade-off between expressiveness and tractability. A model should be detailed enough such that it makes sense – it is expressive – but not too detailed because otherwise computations can not be made feasibly – it lacks tractability [7]. This paper proposes using NNs as meta-model for several reasons:

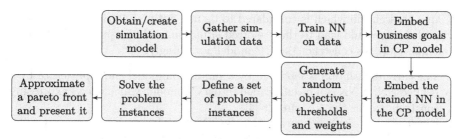

(a) Workflow: from simulation model to pareto front.

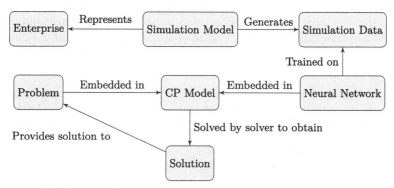

(b) Overview of the various components and how they interact.

Fig. 1. Approach summarized. A simple NN is trained on simulation data. Next, business goals and the trained NN are embedded in the CP model. By utilizing soft constraints and various weight and threshold parameters, an approximation of the pareto front for the various objectives is formed.

- NNs are able to learn behaviour of opaque or very complex systems, without requiring detailed knowledge of their components and interactions [4,19]. They are capable in dealing with both the non-linearity and uncertainty of the underlying system [28].
- NN embeddings in optimization models have shown good performance in comparison to other combinations of optimization methods with machine learning techniques [20].
- Compared to other machine learning techniques, NN are very capable in identifying what features are interesting and excel at handling high-dimensional input data. The result is that NN require very little engineering by hand and are applicable in many domains [19].

3.2 The Constraint Program

The second main component is the CP model. It intends to represent a problem to be solved. There are three main aspects to be identified in problems, namely

1) an as-is scenario which is considered to be non-optimal, 2) uncertainty about what decision would lead to the preferred situation, and 3) a preferred situation to achieve [6]. We construct the CP model accordingly:

1. The current situation is *modelled* by a simulation model and *represented* by a trained NN. A NN can be embedded into a CP model, which allows expressing constraints over the NN output [4].
2. Uncertainty is also incorporated by the NN. Training an NN creates a predictive model. In other words, the NN is used to tackle the uncertainty involved in the problem by giving insight in the correlation between variables and parameters in the decision model.
3. The preferred situation is incorporated by the objective function. In our approach, the objective function is expressed by soft-weighted constraints. The main idea is that this helps in finding an approximation of the set of dominating solutions, also referred to as the pareto front. This provides good insight into the solution space when dealing with multiple objectives.

It is reasonable to believe most – if not all – problems can be described by elements also found in CP. This is based on the theoretical conceptualization of a problem by a meta-model presented in Bock et al. [6], where the concept of a problem is decomposed. The interconnection between this decomposition and CP is shown in Table 3.

```
1   % pseudocode for the restaurant case as a CP model
2
3   % NN_4layer represents the neural network and maps the correlation between
        buyingStrategy and spoilage, success
4   include NN
5
6   % parameters of the model
7   float [] buying_constraints = [c1 ,..., cn]
8
9   % decision variables
10  var [] buyingStrategy = [b1 ,..., bn]      % strategy to propose
11  var spoilage              % spoilage percentage of resources
12  var success               % success percentage of customer orders
13
14  % buying strategy should be positive and is limited by buying_constraints
15  constraint forall (i in 1..n) (0 <= bi <= ci)
16
17  % solve two weighted soft constraints, with some (randomly) assigned weight and
        threshold
18  solve (
19  weighted-soft-constraint(spoilage <= spoilage_threshold , spoilage_weight),
20  weighted-soft-constraint(success >= success_threshold , success_weight)
21  )
22
```

Fig. 2. Pseudocode for the restaurant CP model. It closely matches a MiniZinc implementation.

As noted in Sect. 2, constraints expressed in natural language can be formalised in CP at a higher level compared to other optimization methods. The result is that constraints expressed by the DM describing what solution it aims to seek can be conveniently expressed in the CP model. For example, CP makes it convenient to state some relationship between variables should always be satisfied, such as 'machine A should never produce more than machine B' or 'department C should always have more employees than department D'; so-called *global constraints* are particularly useful [30]. Figure 2 shows an example CP model that highlights its readability.

Our approach embeds a NN into a CP model by expressing the value of a node as a function of values of nodes in a previous layer. This is based on the concept of *neuron constraints*, which allow one to encode complex networks using a limited number of basic components [4].

3.3   Soft Constrained Multi-Objective Solving

Most methods on multi-objective decision making in business analytics are *posteriori*, in the sense they obtain preference information – how much each objective is preferred over the others – from the DM *after* computing solutions [33]. These methods are useful when the DM is interested in the scope of actions she can take – particularly useful when there is no single dominating solution – as multiple solutions are provided instead of a single one. In CP, preference information *is* the input, since the CP model is asked what inputs are necessary to satisfy certain objectives. As such, the approach can be made posteriori by evaluating a set of problems covering the variety of possible preferences.

Our approach does not require preference information beforehand as it constructs a type of soft CSP called a *possibilistic CSP*, in which a Weighted Soft Constraint (WSC) is defined for each objective [27]. A WSC has a weight, indicating the importance of it being satisfied, and a threshold. For a maximization objective, the WSC is satisfied if the objective value exceeds the threshold, and for a minimization objective if it does not. Then, random weights and thresholds are generated in order to create a set of problem instances. Next, this set of problems is solved. Their dominating solutions form the output.

3.4   Computational Solving

As just explained, our approach produces a set of soft CP problem instances. These instances are solved and their solutions brought to bear upon the objectives of interest to the DM (Fig. 1). This solving is done by existing solver software.

However, a DM might encounter the solving procedure is slow depending on the complexity of the enterprise and managerial problem being studied, raising interest to speed it up. There are several ways this can be achieved. One way is to reduce the complexity of the problem by using less variables, putting more constraints on the problem to solve or discretizing continuous variables. The trade-off here is that it limits the system in what solutions it is able to present. Another method would be to reduce the complexity of the NN, by reducing the amount of nodes and layers, which has a trade-off against accuracy. Alternatively, the DM could experiment with different search strategies or solvers, and might find one that works particularly well on its problem. An analysis of the various options was out of the scope for this paper. For more details on different solvers and search strategies, we refer to Wallace [30].

4   Experimental Validation

This section assess the approach from Sect. 3 by means of two experiments. Three further experiments, one based on a simulation model derived from a DEMO model, one based on a simulation study performed by other work and one based on an agent-based simulation model, are reported in Andringa [2]. The goal of the experiments is to examine the proposed approach for applicability, generalizability, flexibility and ease of use.

In order to asses consistency, the same simple NN architecture was used for these experiments, as shown in Fig. 4. Training was performed in batches of 64 samples using the AdamW optimizer [21], with a learning rate set at 10^{-5}. The simulations were implemented in Python and NetLogo, the NN in PyTorch [24] and the CP model in MiniZinc [22], supported by MiniBrass [26] to implement soft-constraints. The JaCoP [17] WCSP solver was used. Source code is available under MIT licence at https://doi.org/10.4121/17060642.v1.

4.1   Experiment 1: Restaurant

The first experiment studies the case of a restaurant. It shows how to apply the approach to a simple problem. The simulation was programmed in Python. The NN was trained ± 2 h on ± 350000 simulation calls based on random inputs.

Problem Definition. The restaurant buys ingredients periodically according to some buying strategy and processes these into various dishes. Its buying strategy is represented by an integer per resource that indicates the quantity being bought each period. Buying strategies have limitations, for example due to seasonal ingredients. Resources can spoil if stored for too long. The restaurant has two objectives that characterize a trade-off: it should not buy too many resources in order to minimize spoilage but also should not buy to little in order to maximize the number of successful orders. The restaurant is interested in how its buying strategy affects its spoilage and success ratio.

Results. The corresponding CP model can be found in Fig. 2 and the solving times in Table 4. The results in Fig. 3 show the CP model is able to recognise how various courses of action have different impact on the objective outcomes. It also shows it was able to make accurate predictions.

4.2   Experiment 2: Supply Chain

Supply chain models describe how various manufacturing units interact with each other by passing products and materials to each other towards some resulting product. A freely-available NetLogo model, based on a supply chain was consulted for this experiment [11]. The NN was trained on ± 5 h and ± 14000 random simulation calls. The purpose of the experiment is show the approach is applicable on more complex simulation models. The experiment conducted matches the

Restaurant

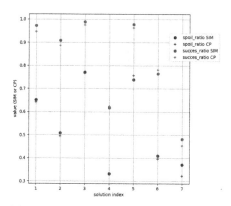

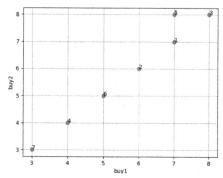

(a) Spoil and succes ratio per proposed solution.

(b) Scatter plot of the proposed actions. Number annotations correspond to the index in Figure a.

Supply Chain

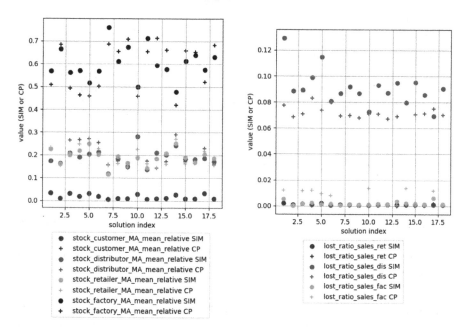

(c) Relative inventory ratio per proposed solution.

(d) Lost sales ratio per proposed solution.

Fig. 3. Experimental results. a, b and c show CP-estimations (+) and simulation estimations (•) for the objective metrics. Accuracy of the CP model can be measured by the difference between the CP and simulation estimations.

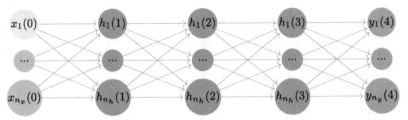

(a) General NN architecture used. Three hidden layers of width $n_h = \sqrt{n_x^2 + n_y^2} + a$, where n_x, n_y are respectively the amount of in and outputs. a is an added parameter to deal with datasets that have low n_x, n_y and was set to 4 for our experiments. Further optimization of a is out of the scope for this paper.

$$h_i(j) = \text{ReLu}\left(w_i(j)\sum_{i=0}^{n_h} w_i(j-1) + b_i(j)\right) \quad y_i(j) = \phi\left(w_i(j)\sum_{i=0}^{n_h} w_i(j-1) + b_i(j)\right)$$

$\phi(x)$	Condition
ReLu(x)	$\forall_y y \geq 0$
Tanh(x)	$\forall_y 1 \geq y \geq -1$
Sigmoid(x)	$\forall_y 1 \geq y \geq 0$
Softmax(x)	$\sum(y_i) = 1 \wedge \forall_y 1 \geq y \geq 0$
x	else

(b) Equations for hidden and output neurons. A neuron consists of a weight $w_i(j)$, a bias $b_i(j)$ parameter and an activation function. Neuron values depends on neuron values of the previous layer. The hidden layers used ReLu as activation function. The activation function applied to the output layers depended on the upper and lower bounds of the simulation output according to the table.

Fig. 4. Description of the NN architecture used for the conducted experiments.

famous Beer Game that represents a supply chain with a non-coordinated process [23]. Problems arise due to lack of information sharing, causing a bull-whip effect – an increase of variance of orders placed by each stage when we move from downstream stage to upstream stages – resulting in inefficient inventory management [10].

Problem Definition. The supply chain of a product consists of factory, distributor, retailer and client. They make individual marketing decisions based upon a strategy picked by the DM. Furthermore, the DM decides upon the total number of factories, retailers and distributors. There are two issues observed regarding the current state of the supply chain. First, too many sales are lost. Second, too many products are stored in the factories instead of the distributors and retailers. The number of clients and their demand is given. The DM is

Table 4. Mean and standard deviation runtimes for solving a single problem for both experiments. The number of NN parameters gives an indication about the complexity differences of the CP models.

Experiment	Solving duration (s)	Number of NN parameters
Supply chain	14.23 ± 0.79	1255
Restaurant	0.544 ± 0.025	116

interested in finding the optimal number of factories, retailers and distributors, as well as the optimal inventory policy and costumers strategy, such that little sales get lost and fewer products are stored in factories.

Results. The CP model used for this experiment has a similar structure as the model in Fig. 2, only with more in- and outputs. Solving runtimes are given in Table 4. The results in Fig. 3 show how the CP-estimations are clearly correlated with the simulation values but were sometimes off target.

From the proposed actions, the DM is able to make two main observations about the process. First, less factories with respect to the distributors and retailers resulted in less products being stored at the factories but also in more unsuccessful orders as demand could not be kept up. Second, random inventory and buying strategies performed best for our problem. To investigate this observation further, a variant of this experiment where random strategies were excluded was also performed. The outcome was that less complex strategies – strategies where market participants do not take too many factors in account to adjust their buying behaviour – were proposed. This shows a trend. The more a market participant aims to maximize its own profit by incorporating complex strategies, the more unpredictable its behaviour gets for other participants, making the market prone to the bullwhip effect. This is in line with how literature tends to tackle this problem – by regulation – as that limits market participants to put complex strategies into practice [10].

4.3 Discussion

The experiments indicate that the approach has some desirable properties:

- *Applicability* The approach can be applied to both simple and complex simulation models. The first experiment is considered to be simple, as the simulation model only had a few in- and outputs. The second experiment was performed on a complex agent-based simulation, which is used widely in real-world business problems and is capable to model complex systems properties, indicating the approach can be used for practical application [16].
- *Generizability* The same architecture as described in Fig. 4 was used for both experiments. This indicates the potential in using already existing designs, allowing a DM unfamiliar with deep learning to apply the approach on a

custom problem. This observation supports the claim that deep learning tends to require little extra engineering [19].

- *Flexibility* The solution evaluation process happens within reasonable time (see Table 4). For the supply chain experiment, a single simulation call took around the same time as a single CP evaluation and thus a significant speedup is put into place. Furthermore, solving time can be tweaked accordingly (see Sect. 3.4). As such, a change of problem can be quickly evaluated, making the approach flexible to a change of problem.
- *Ease of use* The experiments showed that a simple, easy-to-understand CP model (see Fig. 2) is sufficient to allow solving of it when following the presented approach. We believe this makes it doable for a DM with little technical knowledge to construct a CP model for its problem.

5 Conclusion and Future Work

This paper considered enterprise simulation–optimization and addressed how to find optimal simulation inputs more effectively. The proposed approach adopts a meta-model in the form of a NN to capture simulation behaviour, and embeds the NN automatically into a soft CP model.

The demonstrated proof of concept has multiple advantages: 1) DMs with little technical expertise are expected to be more comfortable with designing a CP model that a MP model, due to CP being more expressive. 2) DMs need not have expertise about deep learning to put this approach into practice, since already existing NN architectures can be used. 3) The approach is applicable to already-existing simulation models. 4) Complex properties are kept intact during the decision making process, as both NN and simulation models are able to model them. 5) A change of problem can be quickly evaluated since a meta-model is used to represent the simulation model. 6) It is not required for the DM to input preference information over the importance of objectives since a set of non-dominating solutions is presented instead of a single solution. 7) There is room for many extensions on this approach due to the general concept of using a machine learning based meta-model.

The paper demonstrated the potential of the approach. Although Fig. 3 shows good accuracy for the Restaurant experiment, for the Supply Chain experiment this can still be improved upon. As such, there is room for development. First, the simple NN architecture can be revisited. This paper used a generic and somewhat arbitrary architecture for generality and applicability reasons. What architecture suits best for this application is left for future work. An interesting direction for a better architecture is transfer learning [34]. Second, more advanced techniques regarding data extraction from simulations can be investigated for example by having what parameters to send to the simulation model depend upon what data is gathered so far. Third, in this paper we assumed the simulation model to be a black box. Not doing so allows the use of formal model checking and verification methods to create more accurate meta-models as deeper properties of the simulation model can be taken into account.

Furthermore, there is potential in improving the solving procedure. The thresholds and weights of the soft constraints are randomly generated. More effective strategies can be put into place such that the generated problems more evenly spread the objective space. This paper did only minor experiments with trying various solvers and search strategies. Solving time can possible be reduced by experimenting with these, as mentioned in Sect. 3.4.

Building on the approach of this paper, it can be interesting to consider constraint acquisition [5]. Here, the CP model is allowed to make simulation calls to obtain more knowledge when it considers it possesses too less. This gives up a form of flexibility, in that solving becomes dependent on the simulation runtime. However, it is expected to be more accurate than our approach as it can consult the simulation model in case of doubt. Constraint acquisition is different from black box optimization, and allows exploitation of the model structure (see Table 2). An interesting follow-up study would be a performance comparison between the proposed methodology, constraint acquisition and other multi-criteria optimization methods such as evolutionary search.

Acknowledgements. We thank the EEWC'21 reviewers for their suggestions. This research was partially supported by TAILOR, a project funded by EU Horizon 2020 research and innovation programme under grant number 952215.

References

1. Abushark, Y., Thangarajah, J., Miller, T., Winikoff, M., Harland, J.: Requirements specification in the prometheus methodology via activity diagrams. In: Proceedings of the International Conference on Autonomous Agents & Multiagent Systems (AAMAS), pp. 1247–1248. ACM (2016)
2. Andringa, S.: Applying Constraint Programming to Enterprise Modelling. Master's thesis, Delft University of Technology (2021)
3. Atkinson, C., Kuhne, T.: Model-driven development: a metamodeling foundation. IEEE Softw. **20**(5), 36–41 (2003)
4. Bartolini, A., Lombardi, M., Milano, M., Benini, L.: Neuron constraints to model complex real-world problems. In: Lee, J. (ed.) CP 2011. LNCS, vol. 6876, pp. 115–129. Springer, Heidelberg (2011). https://doi.org/10.1007/978-3-642-23786-7_11
5. Bessiere, C., Koriche, F., Lazaar, N., O'Sullivan, B.: Constraint acquisition. Artif. Intell. **244**, 315–342 (2017)
6. Bock, A., Kudryavtsev, D., Kubelskiy, M.: Towards more expressive problem structuring: A theoretical conceptualization of 'problem' in the context of enterprise modeling. In: Proceedings of the 20th Conference on Business Informatics (CBI), IEEE (2018)
7. Brachman, R.J., Levesque, H.J.: The tradeoff between expressiveness and tractability. In: Knowledge Representation and Reasoning, pp. 327–348. Elsevier (2004)
8. Brouard, C., de Givry, S., Schiex, T.: Pushing data into CP models using graphical model learning and solving. In: Simonis, H. (ed.) CP 2020. LNCS, vol. 12333, pp. 811–827. Springer, Cham (2020). https://doi.org/10.1007/978-3-030-58475-7_47
9. Buscemi, M.G., Montanari, U.: A survey of constraint-based programming paradigms. Comput. Sci. Rev. **2**(3), 137–141 (2008)

10. Chinna Pamulety, T., Madhusudanan Pillai, V.: Performance analysis of supply chains under customer demand information sharing using role play game. Int. J. Ind. Eng. Comput. **3**(3), 337–346 (2012)
11. Gil, A.: Netlogo model: Artificial supply chain (2012), École Polytechnique Montréal
12. Grossmann, I.E.: Challenges in the application of mathematical programming in the enterprise-wide optimization of process industries. Theor. Found. Chem. Eng. **48**(5), 555–573 (2014). https://doi.org/10.1134/S0040579514050182
13. IBM: Mathematical programming versus constraint programming, DOcplex v2.22 documentation (2021)
14. Jimenez-Ramirez, A., Barba, I., Del Valle, C., Weber, B.: Generating multi-objective optimized configurable business process models. In: 6th International Conference on Research Challenges in Information Science (RCIS), IEEE (2012)
15. Jin, R., Chen, W., Simpson, T.: Comparative studies of metamodelling techniques under multiple modelling criteria. Struct. Multi. Optim. **23**(1), 1–13 (2001)
16. Kampik, T., Najjar, A.: Integrating multi-agent simulations into enterprise application landscapes. In: De La Prieta, F., et al. (eds.) PAAMS 2019. CCIS, vol. 1047, pp. 100–111. Springer, Cham (2019). https://doi.org/10.1007/978-3-030-24299-2_9
17. Kuchcinski, K., Szymanek, R.: JaCoP - java constraint programming solver. In: Abstract from CP Solvers: Modeling, Applications, Integration, and Standardization, co-located with the 19th International Conference on Principles and Practice of Constraint Programming. Uppsala, Sweden (2013)
18. Laguna, M., Marklund, J.: Optimizing business process performance. In: Business Process Modeling, Simulation and Design, 2nd Edn, pp. 439–472. Chapman and Hall CRC (2013)
19. LeCun, Y., Bengio, Y., Hinton, G.: Deep learning. Nature **521**(7553), 436–444 (2015)
20. Lombardi, M., Milano, M., Bartolini, A.: Empirical decision model learning. Artif. Intell. **244**, 343–367 (2017)
21. Loshchilov, I., Hutter, F.: Decoupled weight decay regularization. In: Proceedings of 7th International Conference on Learning Representations (ICLR). OpenReview.net (2019)
22. Nethercote, N., Stuckey, P.J., Becket, R., Brand, S., Duck, G.J., Tack, G.: MiniZinc: towards a standard CP modelling language. In: Bessière, C. (ed.) CP 2007. LNCS, vol. 4741, pp. 529–543. Springer, Heidelberg (2007). https://doi.org/10.1007/978-3-540-74970-7_38
23. O'donnell, T., Maguire, L., McIvor, R., Humphreys, P.: Minimizing the bullwhip effect in a supply chain using genetic algorithms. Int. J. Prod. Res. **44**(8), 1523–1543 (2006)
24. Paszke, A.e.: PyTorch: an imperative style, high-performance deep learning library. In: Proceedings of the 33th Conference on Neural Information Processing Systems (NeurIPS), vol. 32, pp. 8024–8035 (2019)
25. Rossi, F.: Constraint (Logic) programming: a survey on research and applications. In: Apt, K.R., Monfroy, E., Kakas, A.C., Rossi, F. (eds.) WC 1999. LNCS (LNAI), vol. 1865, pp. 40–74. Springer, Heidelberg (2000). https://doi.org/10.1007/3-540-44654-0_3
26. Schiendorfer, A., Knapp, A., Anders, G., Reif, W.: MiniBrass: soft constraints for MiniZinc. Constraints **23**(4), 403–450 (2018). https://doi.org/10.1007/s10601-018-9289-2

27. Schiex, T.: Possibilistic constraint satisfaction problems or "how to handle soft constraints?". In: Uncertainty in Artificial Intelligence, pp. 268–275. Elsevier (1992)
28. Teerasoponpong, S., Sopadang, A.: A simulation-optimization approach for adaptive manufacturing capacity planning in small and medium-sized enterprises. Exp. Syst. Appl. **168**, 114451 (2021)
29. Vernadat, F.: Enterprise modelling: research review and outlook. Comput. Ind. **122**, 103265 (2020)
30. Wallace, M.: Building Decision Support Systems. Springer, Cham (2020). https://doi.org/10.1007/978-3-030-41732-1
31. Wiśniewski, P., Kluza, K., Jemioło, P., Ligęza, A., Suchenia, A.: Business process recomposition as a way to redesign workflows effectively. In: Proceedings of the 16th Conference on Computer Science and Intelligence Systems, IEEE (2021)
32. Yaghin, R., Sarlak, P., Ghareaghaji, A.: Robust master planning of a socially responsible supply chain under fuzzy-stochastic uncertainty (a case study of clothing industry). Eng. Appl. Artif. Intell. **94**, 103715 (2020)
33. Yalcin, A., Kilic, H., Delen, D.: The use of multi-criteria decision-making methods in business analytics: a comprehensive literature review. Technol. Forecast. Soc. Change **174**, 121193 (2022)
34. Zhuang, F., et al.: A comprehensive survey on transfer learning. Proc. IEEE **109**(1), 43–76 (2021)

Adapting and Evaluating
the Story-Card-Method

Marné De Vries(⊠) (iD)

Department of Industrial and Systems Engineering, University of Pretoria, Pretoria, South Africa
Marne.DeVries@up.ac.za

Abstract. Domain modelling languages (DMLs) grow and change over time. These languages are artefacts that are developed within communities via multiple participants. Methods, associated with the emerging DMLs, also need to be supported and need adaptation, informed by practice. This study refers to a DML called DEMO (Design and Engineering Methodology for Organizations), of which the language specification evolved from the DEMO Specification Language (DEMOSL) version 3 to version 4. We adapt a method, called the story-card-method (SCM), to accommodate DEMOSL 4. Also, the previous DEMOSL 3-based SCM implied physical interaction between participants, using sticky notes to create a shared understanding, whereas the adapted SCM has to facilitate a digital way-of-collaboration due to COVID-19 restrictions. We re-visit participant feedback from the initial version of the SCM and demonstrate how we applied design science research to design an adapted SCM as the main contribution of this article. In addition, we evaluate whether the adapted SCM is useful in providing ample guidance in compiling a Coordination Structure Diagram (CSD) in a collaborative way, and we evaluate the quality of the CSDs. Finally, we demonstrate how the CSD can be used within a low-code-development ecosystem to structure user stories.

Keywords: Domain modelling · Method engineering · Enterprise engineering · Requirements elicitation · DEMO · Agile methodologies

1 Introduction

Enterprises need to continuously adapt their existing business models, innovating on new products and services that are well-supported by information systems. The COVID-19 pandemic emphasized the need for rapid adaption, driving process automation and technology adoption. A survey performed by Mckinsey & Company [1] in 2020, involving 899 C-level executives and senior managers across regions, industries, company sizes and functional specialties, indicates that the COVID-19 crisis has accelerated the digitization of customer interactions by several years. Some of the largest shifts during the crisis are also among the most likely to stick through the recovery, e.g. increase in remote working and/or collaboration [1]. According to CEO Satya Nadella of Microsoft,

© Springer Nature Switzerland AG 2022
D. Aveiro et al. (Eds.): EEWC 2021, LNBIP 441, pp. 74–94, 2022.
https://doi.org/10.1007/978-3-031-11520-2_6

"We've seen two years' worth of digital transformation in two months" [2]. For software development, the challenge is to increase the development speed and agility of the software development teams when enterprise operations need to be digitized.

Agile methodologies are effective when applied to small teams, i.e. between five and nine team members [3]. Due to success on a small scale, large-scale agile methods receive increased attention, both in academia and in industry [4, 5]. However, when used in scaled contexts, many software development efforts fail, mainly due to lacking requirements engineering practices [6, 7]. Additional requirements elicitation practices are needed to supplement agile software development methodologies [8].

Agile teams, especially within scaled contexts, need to have shared mental models of software development goals [9], as well as a shared understanding of requirements [10]. Agile methodologies primarily use individual *user stories* i.e. a "general-purpose agile substitute for what traditionally has been referred to as *software requirements*" [11, p 37]. Although *user stories* are short user-oriented descriptions of software requirements, useful to package and release development work, scaled agile projects need to create additional structure in allocating *user stories* to domains and subdomains [12]. The purpose is to assign all user stories of all teams to the subdomain they belong to, minimizing the overlap between the domains and subdomains, reducing dependencies across teams [12]. Uludag et al. [12, p 239] emphasize that domain models and the allocation of user stories should be performed during *Domain-Driven Design (DDD) event storming workshops*, "bringing domain experts and developers together in a room to build a model collaboratively". The question is: How should the design-domains and sub-domains be demarcated?

Forward & Lethbridge [13] present a taxonomy with the aim of assisting researchers to apply their research systematically to a particular type of software. The root level of their taxonomy divides software into four main categories, based on the *dominance of a particular facet*: (A) Data-dominant software, (B) System-services software, (C) Control-dominant software, and (D) Computation-dominant software. The data-dominant software (root category A) has four categories, based on the target audience: (i) Consumer-oriented software, (ii) Business-oriented software, (iii) Design and engineering software, and (iv) Information display and transaction entry.

This study primarily focuses on the development of *business-oriented software*, i.e. software to support the daily *enterprise operations and their management*. Human beings need to interact regarding work activities that need to be performed. They need to share information on new production facts that come into existence, as well as the statuses of coordinating their activities. Within this operating context, information systems could semi-automate the coordination activities and facilitate information sharing.

The Design and Engineering Methodology for Organizations (DEMO) aspect models are appropriate in specifying the *operating domain*. The operating domain could be further decomposed in *operating sub-domains*, each sub-domain requiring different domain expertise. As an example, the nature of operations within the manufacturing sub-domain is vastly different to operations related to the financing sub-domain.

The operating domain of an enterprise provides a starting point for structuring *user stories* that relate to this domain [14]. DEMO aspect models incorporate a concept called an elementary transaction kind. Every elementary transaction kind synthesizes a unique production act and multiple associated coordination acts in a consistent way with no overlap between the elementary transaction kinds. Even though DEMO aspect models can be useful in structuring user stories in a consistent way, these models are not as easy to understand and use when compared to other languages that also represent the operating domain, such as BPMN [15].

An additional Story Card Method (SCM) was suggested as a means to incorporate one of the DEMO diagrams, called the Organisation Construction Diagram (OCD) into scaled-agile methodologies [14]. Adopting the principles of the Agile Manifesto [14] the SCM had to address three requirements elicitation criteria: (1) should *encourage collaboration*, (2) should be *easy to understand* and (3) have the ability to relate back to a *concrete world* [14]. The SCM was constructed to link *user stories* to a *big picture* representation of the operating domain, as represented by the DEMO's OCD. Feedback from participants that applied the SCM were positive. Also, the SCM was applied to a real-world project [14].

DEMO, like many other domain modelling languages, evolve over time. The SCM was based on the DEMO Specification Language (DEMOSL) version 3, which has changed to version 4 in 2020. The SCM was associated with the DEMOSL 3's Organization Construction Diagram (OCD), whereas the OCD was replaced by a Coordination Structure Diagram (CSD) in DEMOSL 4. The CSD includes new concepts (e.g. the interimpediment structure), changing the graphical representation of some constructs to a tree-like structure. Also, the previous DEMOSL 3-based SCM implied physical interaction between participants, using sticky notes to create a shared understanding, whereas the adapted SCM has to facilitate a digital way-of-working due to COVID-19 restrictions. We re-visit participant feedback from the initial version of the SCM and demonstrate how we applied design science research (DSR) to design an adapted SCM as the main contribution of this article. In addition, we evaluate whether the adapted SCM is useful in providing ample guidance in compiling a CSD in a collaborative way; and we evaluate the quality of the SCM diagrams.

Next, we briefly introduce the remaining sections of the article. Section 2 introduces the DEMOSL 4's CSD. Section 3 introduces design science research (DSR) as an appropriate research methodology to evolve the existing artefact, the SCM. We present the adaptations that are required, as well as the adapted SCM in Sect. 4 and discuss evaluation results of the adapted SCM in Sect. 5. Since we argue that the CSD will be useful as a taxonomy in structuring emerging software requirements, Sect. 5.4 also provides a demonstration of how the CSD, resulting from the SCM, can be used to structure emerging requirements for a software application that needs to support the operations of a fictitious pet-sitting enterprise. Finally, we summarize the results and limitations in Sect. 6 and suggest opportunities for future research.

2 Background and Related Work

Similar to Leffingwell [11], Dietz and Mulder [16] acknowledge that a user's *needs* for information system support starts with an understanding of their *day-to-day operations*. They present four ontological aspect models that are coherent, comprehensive, consistent, and concise and that are useful to represent the essence of enterprise operation [16]. The Cooperation Model (CM) is the most essential model and consists of two representations, the Coordination Structure Diagram (CSD) and the Transactor Product Table (TPT) [16].

The CSD provides a graphical representation of actor roles (implemented by human beings) that perform a number of coordination acts (e.g. requests and promises) with regards to production acts. The production acts may be either immaterial (e.g. devising, deciding or judging) or material (e.g. manufacturing or transporting) [16]. Furthermore, production acts may be classified as original (e.g. devising, deciding or judging), informational (e.g. sharing, remembering or calculating), or documental (e.g. saving, transforming or providing) [16]. Yet, original production acts are supported by informational production acts, which are in turn supported by documental production acts. Many business-oriented software are developed as technologies to semi-automate or implement some of the coordination acts and the production acts [16].

Dietz and Mulder [16] argue that software development stakeholders need to have a common understanding of the original production acts, since other acts (informational and documental) and implementation technologies (software applications) merely support the original production acts. Focusing on the original production acts, it is possible to compile a concise representation or *big picture* of the operational context.

In discussing the main constructs of a CSD, Fig. 1 provides a graphical representation of a CSD that consists of eight original transaction kinds, each of the seven elementary transaction kinds resembles a complete transaction pattern where actor roles collaborate via coordination acts with the main objective of executing an original production act.

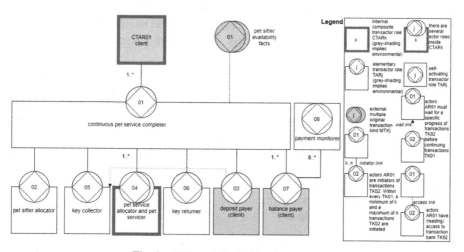

Fig. 1. CSD modelled with Diagrams.net

The CSD presented in Fig. 1, is a concise representation of a fictitious enterprise that offers continuous pet sitting services. As an example, Client A receives a continuous pet service from the pet siting enterprise when Client A's dog receives services for a continuous period, such as 3 weeks of pet-care during the school holidays. As part of the *continuous pet service*, Client A's dog may also receive multiple *pet services*. Thus, as part of the 3 weeks continuous pet-care service, pre-selected services are included, such as pet food supply (twice a day) and dog walking (once a day).

The analyst (and software development team) has to decide on a scope of interest (SoI), i.e. some enterprise operations that need to be supported by software. For our fictitious case, we selected *some pet-sitting operations* of the fictitious pet-sitting enterprise. Based on the selected SoI, all white quadrilaterals indicate human actor roles that are considered to be *inside* the selected SoI, whereas grey-shaded quadrilaterals indicate human beings that are within the *environment*, i.e. grey-shaded quadrilaterals are outside the SoI, but directly interacting with humans that are inside the SoI [16].

The CSD highlights three different kinds of coordination structures: (1) interaction structure, (2) interstriction structure, and (3) interimpediment structure [16]. Partially explaining Fig. 1 as a representation of *some pet-sitting operations*, demonstrating the three coordination structures, we use *italics* style when we refer to a construct in Fig. 1. The legend for constructs included in Fig. 1, is shown on the right-hand side, in accordance with [16]. At this stage, we do not discuss the CSD (shown in Fig. 1) in too much detail, since the adapted SCM, presented in Sect. 4.2, needs to bridge the gap, training the non-DEMO-experienced participant with flow-chart knowledge to gradually grasp DEMO-based concepts.

Interaction Structure. The first type of link displayed in Fig. 1 is the initiator link, represented by a solid line between constructs. As an example, a *client* initiates interaction with a *continuous pet service completer* who will only be able to perform continuous pet service completion effectively when multiple other interactions are initiated with the *pet sitter allocator*, the *key collector*, the composite transactor role *pet service allocator and pet servicer*, the *key returner*, the *deposit payer* and the *balance payer*. The *payment monitorer* is self-activating, i.e. time alone actives payment monitoring and no external initiator is involved in the initiation process. The *payment monitorer* also initiates the *balance payer* for balance payment.

Some of the initiation links in Fig. 1 also include annotations that indicate the minimum and maximum number of initiations that could be created. For instance, the initiation link between *client* and *continuous pet service completer* indicates "1..*" as the annotation. The implication is that a *client* can initiate a minimum of 1 and a maximum of many instances of continuous pet servicing. As a second example, the initiation link between *payment monitorer* and *balance payer* indicates "0..*". The implication is that a payment monitorer may initiate a minimum of 0 and a maximum of many instances of balance payment, i.e. for a particular month, i.e. one instance of payment monitoring, there will be no (zero) initiation of balance payment instances, since all clients already paid in full with no balance due.

Interstriction Structure. A second type of link exists in Fig. 1, namely the access link, represented by a dotted line. The access link implies access to certain facts. The dotted line between the *continuous pet service completer* and *pet sitter availability facts* indicate that the *continuous pet service completer* needs to have access to facts that have been created already, since these facts restrict the operating behavior of the *continuous pet service completer*.

Interimpediment Structure. A third type of link exists in Fig. 1, namely the wait link, represented by a dotted line with arrow-head. The wait link indicates that the progress of a particular transactor role for an instance of the associated transaction kind, may be impeded by the progress of other transaction kind instances. The single wait link with default cardinality 1..1 in Fig. 1, indicates that progress regarding one instance of deposit payment impedes the *key collector*'s progress with one instance of key collection.

As indicated in Sect. 1, *user stories* are concise descriptions of software requirements, useful to package and release development work for agile software development projects. Yet, scaled agile projects need to create additional structure in allocating *user stories* to domains and sub-domains [12]. The *Design and Engineering Methodology for Organizations* (DEMO) *aspect models* are appropriate in specifying the *operating domain* of an enterprise and provide a starting point for structuring *user stories* that relate to the operating domain [14]. Yet, DEMO as a domain modelling language, is not as easy to understand and use when compared to other languages, such as BPMN, in representing the operating domain [15]. A DEMOSL 3-based Story Card Method (SCM) was suggested in 2018 as a means to incorporate one of the DEMO diagrams into scaled-agile methodologies [14]. The SCM was constructed to link *user stories* to a *big picture* representation of the operating context, consisting of ten steps. Feedback from participants that applied the SCM were positive [14] and the SCM was applied to a real-world project [17].

3 Research Methodology

Using the classification genres identified by Peffers et al. [18], our study falls within the Design Science Research Methodology (DSRM) genre promulgated by [19], since the focus of the study is the development of a practically useful artefact. A DSRM research effort may start in many different ways, "even with an already designed version of an artefact" [18, p 131]. The study applies the DSRM genre, developing a new version of an artefact, namely an adapted *story-card method*, addressing the *five steps* of the DSR cycle (presented in [19]) in the following way:

Identify a Problem: Three inter-linked problems initiated this study: (1) Initial feedback from practitioners that were involved during the development of the original SCM was not incorporated yet in an updated SCM; (2)The SCM was based on the DEMO Specification Language (DEMOSL) version 3, which has changed to version 4 in 2021 and therefor the SCM should be adapted; and (3) The previous DEMOSL 3-based SCM implied physical interaction between participants, using sticky notes to create a shared understanding, whereas COVID-19 restrictions impose digital collaboration.

Define Objectives of the Solution: The main objectives of the adapted SCM are consolidated into a list of requirements (presented in Sect. 4.1) related to the three inter-linked problems: (1) Initial feedback from practitioners need to be converted into requirements for an adapted SCM; (2) The SCM has to be adapted, replacing DEMOSL 3's Organization Construction Diagram (OCD), with a Coordination Structure Diagram (CSD) in accordance with DEMOSL 4; and (3) A digital collaborative platform has to be incorporated as part of the SCM, replacing the use of physical sticky-notes.

Design and Development: In accordance with the solution objectives, an adapted SCM was designed to introduce CSD concepts to *participants* from different backgrounds.

Demonstration: The SCM was demonstrated to industry participants during an interactive online session. During the demonstration, participants had the opportunity to criticize the *method*. The feedback was also used to refine the adapted SCM so that participants could apply the SCM that is also presented in this article.

Evaluation: The industry participants evaluated the adapted SCM in practice by involving a colleague. A survey, consisting of 22 questions/probes, was used to evaluate whether the adapted SCM is useful in providing guidance in compiling a CSD in a collaborative way, addressing the solution objectives. In addition, we evaluated the quality of the SCM diagrams.

4   The Story Card Method Adaptation Requirements

In this section we first discuss required adaptations, based on the feedback from evaluating the SCM that was based on DEMOSL 3. In addition, we also list new requirements that have emerged since the SCM's publication in 2018.

4.1 Adaptations Required

The adapted SCM has to address the following requirements, as motivated:

Requirement 1: Conceptualization of the initial process in the form of a flow chart has to include responsibility swim lanes. *Motivation:* A participant indicated that s/he preferred a swim-lane diagram to assign actor roles to process steps.

Requirement 2: The SCM should enable better distinction between original versus informational/documental activities: *Motivation:* Participants indicate difficulty in deciding whether an activity is an original production activity.

Requirement 3: The SCM should provide more guidance in re-phrasing tasks that represent *original* production acts, keeping the verb + noun format, but using "execute" as a standard verb. *Motivation:* Participants indicated difficulties in changing the sticky note descriptions from verb + noun to adjective + noun for transaction kinds.

Requirement 4: The SCM should provide more guidance in explaining the production fact. *Motivation:* A participant had difficulty in explaining the purpose of the red diamond to his/her colleague.

Requirement 5: The SCM should provide more guidance on explaining the final diagram during validation. *Motivation:* A participant indicated that it is difficult to validate and confirm the OCD (DEMOSL 3 terminology) with the colleague.

Requirement 6: The SCM should provide better guidance for conveying theoretical concepts that underlie the cooperation model, requesting that the colleague also participate in the modelling exercise. *Motivation:* A participant indicated difficulty in obtaining participation from Step 4 onwards, since non-technical staff "zoned out" when new concepts were introduced.

Requirement 7: The new CSD of DEMOSL 4 should be incorporated as part of the SCM, replacing the previous OCD of DEMOSL 3. *Motivation:* DEMOSL 3 has been replaced by DEMOSL 4.

Requirement 8: The SCM should suggest a modelling tool that: (1) allows collaboration of multiple modelers to co-compose a flow-charting diagram as well as the CSD; (2) is free to use; and (3) is easy to use. *Motivation:* A new digital collaboration working practice emerged due to COVID-19, where physical meetings, using physical sticky notes, are not always possible. Also, participants that applied the DEMOSL 3-based SCM indicated that they would prefer to use a software modelling tool, rather than sticky notes, since it would enable changes and increase diagram readability. Also, the sticky notes did not always stick.

4.2 The Adapted Story Card Method

The *story-card method* specifies 3 *inputs* and 12 *method steps*.

Inputs: (1) IT hardware, e.g. laptop/computer and internet connection for co-modelers, (2) freeware, such as Diagrams.net (see template in Fig. 2) that allows collaboration of multiple modelers to co-compose a flow-charting diagram as well as a CSD, and (3) an analyst that received appropriate DEMO training and a colleague that is knowledgeable about some existing operations at a real-world enterprise.

Fig. 2. DEMOSL4 template availed to participants that experimented with the adapted SCM

Method Steps:

Step 1: Ask a colleague to explain a short process (about 10 to 15 tasks) that s/he is involved with. Ensure that the process incorporates the use of information technology (e.g. the process followed from requesting vacation leave up to receiving notification about the approval of the request). Explain to your colleague that s/he needs to formulate the tasks (*verb + noun*) using rectangular shapes for tasks, mapping out the *tasks* in sequence of occurrence, left to right. A decision-making *gateway* may be used to represent different paths, based on the gateway's decision-outcomes. Use *swim lanes* to represent task-responsibilities associated with *existing actor roles* (these are often composite actor roles) at the enterprise. A standard flow-charting language may be used.

Step 2: Explain Dietz's red-green-blue *production triangle* (i.e. a means to classify production tasks).

Step 3: Explain the *complete transaction pattern* for actor-collaboration regarding production acts. Identify an *original* production act from the process flow chart to explain the collaborative interaction around the *original* production act.

Step 4: Collaborate to classify some process *tasks* as *original* production facts using red-color-coding. Also identify some of the associated *coordination* facts associated with the original production acts, using light-red-color-coding.

Step 5: Edit each *task* that was classified as an *original* production act, adding an alternative description to highlight the transaction kind, i.e. "execute + <transaction kind>". Take turns in formulating alternative descriptions for *tasks* that were classified as *original* production acts.

Step 6: Check the remaining flow-chart *tasks* and use green color-coding for those tasks that are informational acts, i.e. sharing/remembering/calculating acts. Take turns in analyzing the remaining tasks. Not all tasks need to be color-coded, since some may imply business rules or documental acts and these will not be shown on the CSD.

Step 7: Copy the tasks that were identified as *original* production act to the bottom of the drawing space. For each of the original production acts, create an internal elementary transactor role (or environmental elementary transactor role if the executing actor role is outside the scope-of-interest). It is also possible that a transactor role is *self-activating* when *time alone* initiates the transaction kind.

Step 8: Complete the *interaction structure* adding *initiation links* where every transactor role should be initiated at least by one transactor role (for transactor roles that have been mapped out). *No initiation links* are shown for self-activating transactor roles. It is also possible that composite environmental transactor roles should be added as initiators. These transactor roles help to demarcate the scope-of-interest.

Step 9: Explain *parent-part-structures*, i.e. how one transaction kind becomes *a part of* one or more *parent* transaction kinds via initiation. Also indicate *cardinality* when a *parent* instance initiates *part* instances if the cardinality deviates from the default of 1..1.

Step 10: Copy the tasks that were identified as *informational* production acts to the bottom of the drawing space. Use the informational production acts to guide you in completing the *interstriction structure* adding *access links* when transactor roles need access production facts from *original* transaction kinds, *multiple original* transaction kinds and *external multiple original* transaction kinds.

Step 11: Complete the *interimpediment structure*, adding *impediment links*, indicating that progress of an instance of one transaction kind may impede the progress of another transaction kind's instance(s).

Step 12: Validate your CSD with your colleague, enquiring whether the leaves of the upside-down tree are truly elementary. If some of the leaves should be further expanded, by adding parts, replace the elementary transactor role with an appropriate composite (internal or environmental) transactor role. Using the pet-sitting case as an example, the bubble in Fig. 5 with text *perform multiple pet services, such as dog walking and feeding* may indicate the existence of a composite transactor role (CTAR), named *pet service allocator and pet servicer*. The double-disk labelled 04, indicates that several actor roles are included, e.g. (1) pet service allocator, and (2) pet servicer.

The method steps were demonstrated to the participants. Figure 3 represents the result for performing *Steps 1 to 3*. Figure 4 resulted from performing *Steps 4 to 6* and Fig. 5 resulted from performing Steps 7 to 12.

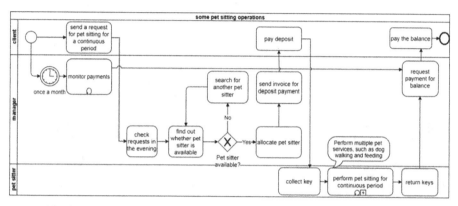

Fig. 3. Example of a pet sitting process to demonstrate Step 1 to 3 of the SCM

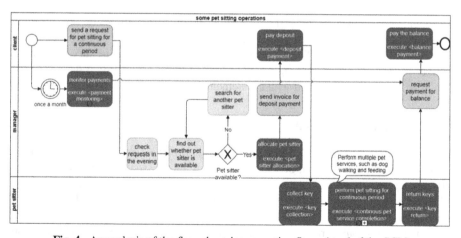

Fig. 4. An analysis of the *flow-chart,* incorporating Steps 4 to 6 of the SCM

The CSD is shown in Fig. 5 is similar to Fig. 1, except for the color-coded flow-chart-task-constructs that were added in Fig. 5.

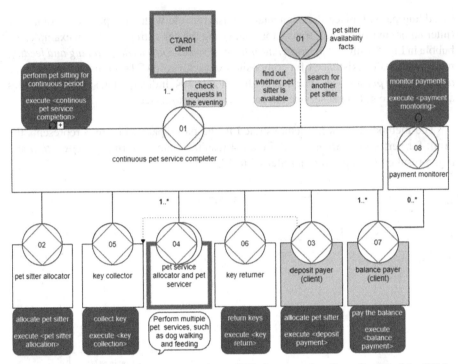

Fig. 5. Converting flow-chart constructs into a CSD, incorporating Steps 7 to 12 of the SCM

5 Results

Although 34 participants applied the adapted SCM, only 21 participants completed the voluntary survey that consisted of 22 questions. Also, some of the participants did not answer all of the questions. The following sub-sections synthesize the survey results. A number of questions were probing questions, requesting a motivation if the participant disagreed or strongly disagreed with a statement.

5.1 Participant Background

Responding to the question *"Indicate your existing role at the enterprise"*, 36.8% of the responding participants (7 out of 19 responses) are business/systems/process analysts, whereas the remaining participants represented various roles as managers, engineers, full-time students and educators. Multiple sectors were covered, ranging from the mining sector (7 out of 19), education sector (7 out of 19), retail, logistics, automotive, construction and transportation. Industrial Engineering is strongly represented (8 out of 19, i.e. 6 BEng and 2 BTech Industrial Engineering participants), whereas other engineers (Mining, Metallurgical, Chemical, Civil and Electrical) and a BSc (Mining) participant were also involved. Participants could indicate their experience in modelling tools by selecting more than one response from a list of pre-defined tools, or specifying other tools. The responses indicate that participants mostly have experience in drawing tools, such as Microsoft Visio, Diagrams.net, Open Modelling and Lucidchart (13 out of 24). Only 4 responses indicated repository-based enterprise modelling tools, including ARIS, Enterprise Architect and Symbio, whereas 7 (out of 24 responses) indicated no experience of enterprise modelling tools.

5.2 Feedback on the Story-Card Method

Participants had to count the number of tasks that were included in the process flow-chart that had to be compiled in Step 1 of the SCM. A median number of 15 tasks were included, with a minimum of 8 and a maximum of 18. Participants also had to indicate the time duration for completing the 12 steps of the SCM. The average time to complete was 5.1 h with a large standard deviation of 3.7 h.

As indicated in Sect. 4.1, the SCM had to address some of the deficiencies that were identified when experimenting with the DEMOSL 3-based SCM. Also, the SCM had to incorporate the DEMOSL 4-based CSD that replaced the DEMOSL 3-based OCD, whilst complying with the initial requirements that were identified in [14]. Therefore, participants had to evaluate whether the adapted SCM was still *useful* in relating to a concrete world when explaining abstract concepts of the CSD to a colleague. Feedback was positive. Participants (20 out of 21) that answered the question of whether *the SCM helped to relate process steps to OCD constructs,* either agreed (13 out of 20) or strongly agreed (7 out of 20). In addition, participants either strongly agreed (7 out of 20), agreed (12 out of 20) or were neutral (1 out of 20) when they responded to the question on whether *the SCM encouraged discussion with my colleague to classify appropriate activities as original activities versus informational or documental activities.*

Participants were also positive to use the SCM in future to explain CSD concepts, i.e. they either agreed (15 out of 19) or strongly agreed (4 out of 19) that *if I had to explain CSD concepts to another colleague in future, I would use the SCM, rather than my own/another way of explanation.*

The SCM presented had to replace the sticky notes that were used in [14] with a software modelling tool that would allow for collaboration of multiple modelers to co-compose a flow-charting diagram as well as the CSD, is free to use and is easy to use. Participants were positive about the collaborative software tool, Diagrams.net, when they indicated that *the software tool Diagrams.net facilitated the process of transforming a process flow "story" into a CSD.* They either agreed (12 out of 20) or strongly agreed (8 out of 20).

Referring to Sect. 4.1 (i.e. the method steps of the SCM) participants had to indicate whether they *experienced any difficulties in using the SCM.* Only 3 responses were submitted:

- Step 4: "With the classification of the different tasks it was a bit challenging because some tasks didn't necessarily fall into the 3 levels."
- Steps 11 and 12: "The last part I did not understand. Limitation to asking questions during class."
- Steps 7 to 12: "I have found steps 7–12 challenging, because it consumed more time."

Evaluating whether participants *consider using the CSD within their own working environment*, rendered mostly positive results, since participants strongly agreed (4 out of 20), agreed (13 out of 20) or remained neutral (3 out of 20).

The *story-card method* had to ensure *ease-of-understanding*, relating *abstract concepts* of the CSD to a *concrete world*. In accordance, we evaluated whether the colleagues *would be confident to use the SCM to model another process by him/herself to construct a CSD*. The *colleagues* agreed (14 out of 20), strongly agreed (3 out of 20), whereas few were neutral (3 out of 20).

Finally, participants had to present a CSD (i.e. Figures 18.9–18.11 from [16]) to the collaborating colleague to enquire whether *a similar kind of diagram would be useful to represent a blue print of their enterprise operations*. The intension was to evaluate whether the CSD could be adopted as a means for representing a *big picture* for *essential enterprise operations*. The responses were overall positive, ranging from strongly agreeing (1 out of 20), agreeing (13 out of 20) and being neutral (6 out of 21).

5.3 Evaluating the Quality of the Story-Card Method

The 34 participants that applied the SCM, had to submit three diagrams (section A, B and C) as evidence for implementing the 12 method steps. The evaluation criteria and descriptive statistics for evaluation results are summarized in Table 1.

Table 1. Evaluation criteria and descriptive statistics for evaluation results

SCM diagram	Evaluation criteria		Evaluation results	
	Limited understanding (Score: 2.5)	Full understanding (Score: 5)	Average	Standard deviation
A: Diagram similar to Fig. 3 (Steps 1 to 3)	Followed some instructions for SCM Step 1	Followed all instructions for SCM Step 1	4.26 (85.2%)	1.31
B: Diagram similar to Fig. 4 (Steps 4 to 6)	Followed some instructions for SCM Steps 4–6	Followed all instructions for SCM Steps 4–6	3.16 (63.2%)	1.12
C: Diagram similar Fig. 5 (Steps 7 to 12)	Followed some instructions for SCM Steps 7–12; AND/OR CSD errors (see training notes); AND/OR Incomplete mapping	Followed all instructions for SCM Steps 7–12 to generate a valid CSD according to the DEMOSL 4 standard	2.87 (57.4%)	1.09

The results indicate that participants scored an average 85.2% for completing section A, i.e. following the flow-chart-related steps of the SCM. The lower average scores for section B (63.2%) and section C (57.4%) corroborates the qualitative feedback from participants regarding the difficulty of performing steps 7 to 12. During evaluation, the primary researcher also identified a pattern in the submissions, namely that participants largely tried to mimic a three-level hierarchy, as depicted in the demonstration case (see Fig. 1), even though a more comprehensive demonstration case was also presented as part of their DEMO training.

5.4 Using the CM's Transactor Roles as a Taxonomy for Enterprise Operations

Once the CSD has been validated, the identified transactor roles can be used to structure requirements that emerge as user stories for business-oriented software. According to Leffingwell [11], user stories need to be documented, using a fixed format, addressing 3 main concerns: (1) A particular operating *role* that provides context for an end user's need; (2) The *need* to perform an activity that requires semi-automation; and (3) The *business value* that will be obtained from the software application that will be developed. Table 2 provides the user story template on the left-hand side and an example of applying the template on the right-hand side.

Table 2. Demonstrating the user story template with an example

Template	Example of applying the template
As a <role>,	**As a** continuous pet service completer,
I <need to perform an activity>,	**I** need to maintain facts regarding continuous pet service,
so that <business value is obtained>	**so that** I improve efficiency

Limited guidance exits on interpreting or defining a role that is used in the user story template. Therefore, members of an Agile team may refer to an enterprise-specific role, associating the role with a particular individual that may be responsible for executing multiple transaction kinds. For the pet sitting enterprise, the manager of the enterprise may be assigned to multiple executor roles in practise, especially for a small-scale enterprise. When an agile software team defines software requirements with user stories in an ad hoc way due to a lack of knowledge on cooperation modelling, they may be using composite executor roles for which the responsibility areas regarding production acts and coordination acts are unclear or overlapping, introducing duplication, ambiguity and an incomplete set of requirements. We suggest that the agile team members need to use elementary transactor roles in their user story descriptions. Most of the user stories that communicate functional requirements to support the operating context of the enterprise, should start with an elementary transactor role that is modelled as an elementary transactor role on the CSD.

Although the adapted SCM created a bridge for converting flow-chart logic into a first draft of a CSD, further *refinement* and *validation* of the CSD is necessary, before we use the CSD as a taxonomy for structuring emerging software requirements.

Refinement of the CSD is necessary to ensure that the CSD only includes elementary transactor roles. The CSD, presented in Fig. 1, includes a composite transactor role, CTAR04 named *pet service allocator and pet servicer*, which indicates that multiple elementary transactor roles are included in CTAR04. Since we would like to use elementary transactor roles as a taxonomy for structuring some emerging functional requirements, the CSD needs further refinement, converting the composite transactor role (CTAR04) into elementary transactor roles. Figure 6 presents the refined CSD where CTAR04 has been converted into two elementary transactor roles, namely TAR041 (pet service allocator) and TAR042 (pet servicer).

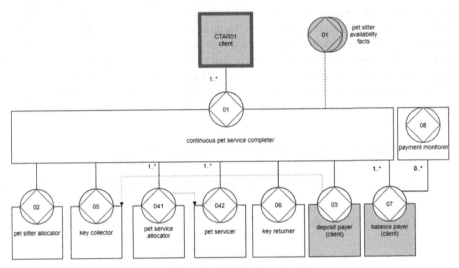

Fig. 6. Refining the CSD for the pet sitting case

The interaction structure (initiation links) also needed adaptation, indicating that TAR01 (continuous pet service completer) initiates both TAR041 (pet service allocator) and TAR042 (pet servicer). Also, the interimpediment structure changed, indicating that an instance of TK041 (pet service allocation) impedes TAR042 when the pet servicer must be allocated prior to starting TK042 (pet servicing). Thus, an instance of pet servicing can only commence once a pet servicer has been allocated.

Validation of the CSD, using the transactor product table (TPT), further ensures that the modelled transactor roles are original, i.e. no informational and documental transactor roles are included in the CSD. Table 3 validates the CSD depicted in Fig. 6, where each elementary transactor role in Fig. 6, is indicated as a *transactor role* in the second column of Table 3. Each *transactor role* is associated with a unique *transaction kind* and *product kind* in Table 3. An interpretation of the first row (beneath the heading) of Table 3 is that the **transactor role** *continuous pet service completer* is responsible for executing the **transaction kind** *continuous pet service completion* to produce a new production fact of **product kind** *[continuous pet service] is completed*.

Table 3. The transactor product table (TPT) of the pet sitting case

TAR ID	Transactor role	TK ID	Transaction kind	PK ID	Product kind
TAR01	Continuous pet service completer	TK01	Continuous pet service completion	PK01	[continuous pet service] is completed
TAR02	Pet sitter allocator	TK02	Pet sitter allocation	PK02	the pet sitter of [continuous pet service] is allocated
TAR03	Deposit payer	TK03	Deposit payment	PK03	the deposit of [continuous pet service] is paid
TAR041	Pet service allocator	TK041	Pet service allocation	PK041	[pet service allocation] is done
TAR042	Pet servicer	TK042	Pet servicing	PK042	[pet service] is done
TAR05	Key collector	TK05	Key collection	PK05	[continuous pet service] is key-collected
TAR06	Key returner	TK06	Key return	PK06	[continuous pet service] is key-returned
TAR07	Balance payer	TK07	Balance payment	PK07	the balance of [continuous pet service] is paid
TAR08	Payment monitorer	TK08	Payment monitoring	PK08	payment monitoring for [month] is done

We used a low-code-development tool, called Mendix (see Mendix.com) to demonstrate how we used the content of Table 3 to structure emerging functional requirements for a software application system that supports some pet sitting operations. The Mendix ecosystem facilitates collaboration between agile team members, based on the Scrum way-of-working. Scrum incorporates structured user stories to define software requirements that are scheduled for development within a development sprint [3].

Using the *transactor roles* in Table 3 as our taxonomy for structuring user stories, we created matching *labels* on the Developer Portal of Mendix for a software application project. The *labels* are indicated as coloured rectangles (with rounded edges) in Fig. 7. Unfortunately, Mendix limits the number of characters for labels and therefor we had to use the abbreviation *cont* for *continuous*, when creating the label *cont pet service completion*.

Since we assume that our new software application system needs to semi-automate all of the 9 elementary transaction kinds indicated in Table 3, the new software application system has to enable maintenance of production facts that are associated with the 9 elementary transaction kinds. Mendix provides the functionality of importing user stories

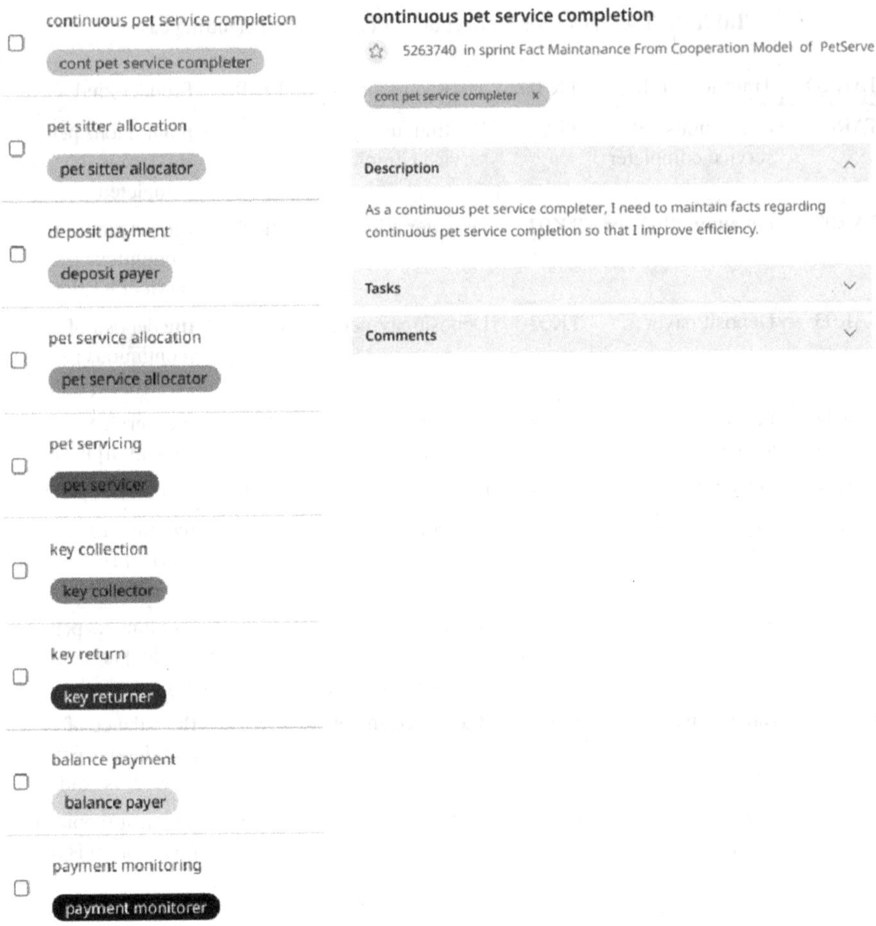

Fig. 7. Using the CSD as a taxonomy to structure user stories on the Mendix platform

when the user stories are structured according to a template in a.csv format. For each of the transaction kinds in Table 3, we formulated 9 corresponding user stories, using the *transaction kind* as the user story's title. In addition, we used the TEXTJOIN function of MS Excel to formulate user stories from the *transactor role* and *transaction kind* descriptions in Table 3. Figure 7 presents the results of the Mendix-import, indicating 9 user stories. For each user story, we had to manually link the appropriate label. Thus, for user story *continuous pet service completion*, we linked the label *cont pet service completer*. When a Mendix user clicks on the title of a user story, e.g. clicking on *continuous pet service completion*, the detailed description of the user story is displayed, indicated on the right-hand side of Fig. 7, i.e. *As a continuous pet service completer, I need to maintain facts regarding continuous pet service completion so that I improve efficiency.* When new user stories emerge, agile team members need to use the 9 existing labels to classify emerging user stories. Within Mendix, it is possible to search and display stories that are linked to one particular label, e.g. viewing all user stories that are associated with a particular *transactor role*. The search results then provide a summary of requirements associated with the particular transactor role.

We acknowledge that the taxonomy is useful to structure functional requirements that relate to the operating context of the enterprise and is not a comprehensive taxonomy for all emerging requirements. As an example, a non-functional requirement, such as *ease-of-use*, cannot be associated with a single elementary transactor role. Furthermore, our demonstration indicated that we only created labels for elementary transactor roles and not for any composite transactor roles. Referring to Fig. 6, emerging requirements for CTAR01 (client) as end-user of the software application under development, need to be accommodated. Hence, we suggest that an additional label should also be added for each composite transactor role that is modelled as *initiator-only* on the CSD.

6 Discussion, Limitations and Future Research

This study was initiated when the domain modelling language, DEMO changed significantly from version 3 to version 4. A previous method, the SCM, associated with one of DEMO's aspect models, also required adaptation. The SCM was initially developed as a means to facilitate requirements elicitation in agile-at-scale software development [14]. Yet, since some of the DEMO-related concepts are very abstract, whilst software developers and end users need to relate to a concrete world, the SCM bridged this gap, opening the opportunity for end users and the software development team to develop a shared understanding of the operating domain of an enterprise, before software development starts.

Participants of the 2018 SCM-evaluation indicated some difficulties when they applied the SCM, which had to be addressed. In addition, the adapted SCM had to replace the sticky notes that formed part of the DEMOSL 3-based SCM with a digital way-of-collaboration, mainly due to COVID-19 restrictions.

The adapted SCM was applied by 34 research participants of which 21 participants completed the voluntary survey. The background of survey participants indicated a prominent representation of business/systems/process analysts (36.8%), also including managers, engineers, full-time students and educators. Multiple sectors were covered, but the mining sector and education sectors were prominent. A large portion of the participants had a tertiary qualification in engineering, whereas only one participant studied BSc (Mining). Although most participants had some experience with software modelling tools, 31.2% did not have such experience, which may also explain the large variance in duration when applying the SCM, i.e. participants indicated an average of 5.1 h for applying the SCM with a large standard deviation of 3.7 h.

Replicating most of the questions from the 2018 survey, feedback from the 21 research participants were positive, indicating that the adapted SCM still facilitated collaboration and translation of concrete concepts into more abstract (and concise) concepts of the CSD.

Participants were also positive about the collaborative software tool, Diagrams.net. One of the negative aspects of the tool becomes evident when we evaluated the quality of the CSDs, since the tool did not have any built-in validation functions that are available in other DEMOSL 3-based tools, such as [20]. The primary researcher also experimented with the tool, interactively engaging with the participants during DEMO training. The latency of Diagrams.net is a problem, since there is a considerable delay in updating the diagram, which hampers interactive co-modelling. One of the limitations of the survey that was used as part of the research methodology, is that no evidence was extracted to confirm that a participant applied interactive modelling with the selected colleague, as required by the SCM. Informal feedback from some participants indicated that the latency problems of the tool discouraged interactive modelling. Future evaluation of the SCM should also measure the level of participation during interactive modelling.

On evaluating the quality of the CSDs when 34 participants used the SCM in composing a CSD, an average of 57.4% corroborates the qualitative feedback from participants regarding the difficulty of performing steps 7 to 12 of the SCM. During evaluation, the primary researcher also identified a pattern in the CSDs, namely that participants largely tried to imitate a three-level hierarchy, as depicted in the demonstration case. Even though the DEMO training provided guidance on when to use a flat hierarchy versus a deep hierarchy, the SCM does not provide this guidance. For the next design cycle, we are planning to present a case that demonstrates both a flat and deep structure. It is also worthwhile to experiment whether an extension of the SCM, adding a transactor product table (TPT), increases the quality of the CSD. Another possible extension for increasing the quality of the CSD, is to convert the CSD back into flow-chart logic for further validation. Previous work [21] already suggested a tool to facilitate semi-automatic transformation of CSD-logic into BPMN collaboration diagrams.

For future work, the adapted SCM could be further refined to provide additional guidance for steps 7 to 12, e.g. adding explanations in terms of the pet-sitting case. Yet, we still believe that analysts, that use the SCM to introduce the CSD to their enterprise and/or software development teams, should receive adequate training on DEMO, currently presented at many institutes and universities, as indicated in [16]. We also believe that the SCM has to be applied in a real-world agile software development project where multiple team members are involved.

Once team members have a common understanding of a validated CSD, some of the emerging user stories can be linked to the elementary transactor roles that form part of the CSD, as demonstrated for the pet sitting case in Sect. 5.4. Since the CSD only provides context for the operating domain, an additional classification schema is needed to also classify user stories that relate to general software features and non-functional requirements. We acknowledge an initial investment is required, providing adequate training on DEMO-related theory, focusing on the CSD, to reap the benefits of structuring emerging requirements within an agile software development project according to an unambiguous taxonomy.

Acknowledgements. We are grateful towards the research participants for their valuable feedback.

References

1. McKinsey and Company: How COVID-19 has pushed companies over the technology tipping point - and transformed business forever: Survey. https://www.mckinsey.com/business-functions/strategy-and-corporate-finance/our-insights/how-covid-19-has-pushed-companies-over-the-technology-tipping-point-and-transformed-business-forever. Accessed 13 May 2021

2. Spataro, J.: Two years of digital transformation in two months. https://www.microsoft.com/en-us/microsoft-365/blog/2020/04/30/2-years-digital-transformation-2-months/. Accessed 13 Nov 2021

3. Lacey, M.: The Scrum Field Guide: Agile Advice for Your First Year and Beyond, 2nd edn. Addison-Wesley, Boston (2017)

4. Uludag, Ö., Pascal, P., Putta, A., Paasivaara, M., Lassenius, C., Matthes, F.: Revealing the state-of-the-art in large-scale agile development: a systematic mapping study. https://arxiv.org/abs/2007.05578. Accessed 10 May 2021

5. Dingsøyr, T., Moe, N.B.: Towards principles of large-scale agile development. In: Dingsøyr, T., Moe, N.B., Tonelli, R., Counsell, S., Gencel, C., Petersen, K. (eds.) XP 2014. LNBIP, vol. 199, pp. 1–8. Springer, Cham (2014). https://doi.org/10.1007/978-3-319-14358-3_1

6. Bhat, J.M., Gupta, M., Murthy, S.N.: Requirements engineering challenges: lessons from offshore outsourcing. IEEE Softw. **23**(5), 36–44 (2006)

7. Dikert, K., Paasivaara, M., Lassenius, C.: Challenges and success factors for large-scale agile transformations: a systematic literature review. J. Syst. Softw. **119**, 87–108 (2016)

8. Paasivaara, M., Lassenius, C.: Scaling scrum in a large globally distributed organisation: a case study. In: IEEE 11th International Conference on Global Software Engineering. IEEE Computer Society (2016). https://doi.org/10.1109/ICGSE.2016.34

9. Salas, E., Sims, D.E., Burke, C.S.: Is there a "big five" in teamwork? Small Group Res. **36**(5), 555–599 (2005)

10. Buchan, J.: An empirical cognitive model of the development of shared understanding of requirements. Requirements Eng. **432**, 165–179 (2014)

11. Leffingwell, D.: Agile Software Requirements: Lean Requirements Practices for Teams, Programs, and the Enterprise. Addison-Wesley, New Jersey (2011)

12. Uludağ, Ö., Hauder, M., Kleehaus, M., Schimpfle, C., Matthes, F.: Supporting large-scale agile development with domain-driven design. In: Garbajosa, J., Wang, X., Aguiar, A. (eds.) XP 2018. LNBIP, vol. 314, pp. 232–247. Springer, Cham (2018). https://doi.org/10.1007/978-3-319-91602-6_16

13. Forward, A., Lethbridge, T.: A taxonomy of software types to facilitate search and evidence-based software engineering. In: CASCON 2008, pp. 179–191. (2008). https://doi.org/10.1145/1463788.1463807

14. Vries, M.: DEMO and the story-card method: requirements elicitation for agile software development at scale. In: Buchmann, R.A., Karagiannis, D., Kirikova, M. (eds.) PoEM 2018. LNBIP, vol. 335, pp. 138–153. Springer, Cham (2018). https://doi.org/10.1007/978-3-030-02302-7_9

15. De Vries, M., Bork, D.: Identifying scenarios to guide transformations from DEMO to BPMN. In: Aveiro, D., Guizzardi, G., Pergl, R., Proper, H.A. (eds.) EEWC 2020. LNBIP, vol. 411, pp. 92–110. Springer, Cham (2021). https://doi.org/10.1007/978-3-030-74196-9_6

16. Dietz, J.L.G., Mulder, H.B.F.: Enterprise Ontology: A Human-Centric Approach to Understanding the Essence of Organisation. Springer, Cham (2020). https://doi.org/10.1007/978-3-030-38854-6

17. Djan, E., de Vries, M.: Business process re-engineering and agile software development: applying the story-card method. In: Hattingh, M., Matthee, M., Smuts, H., Pappas, I., Dwivedi, Y.K., Mäntymäki, M. (eds.) I3E 2020. LNCS, vol. 12066, pp. 370–382. Springer, Cham (2020). https://doi.org/10.1007/978-3-030-44999-5_31

18. Peffers, K., Tuunanen, T., Niehaves, B.: Design science research genres: introduction to the special issue on exemplars and criteria for applicable design science research. Eur. J. Inf. Syst. **27**(2), 129–139 (2018). https://doi.org/10.1080/0960085X.2018.1458066

19. Peffers, K., Tuunanen, T., Rothenberger, M., Chatterjee, S.: A design science research methodology for information systems research. J. MIS **24**(3), 45–77 (2007). https://doi.org/10.2753/MIS0742-1222240302

20. Gray, T., De Vries, M.: Empirical evaluation of a new DEMO modelling tool that facilitates model transformations. In: Grossmann, G., Ram, S. (eds.) Advances in Conceptual Modeling. ER 2020. Lecture Notes in Computer Science, vol. 12584, pp. 189–199. Springer, Cham (2020). https://doi.org/10.1007/978-3-030-65847-2_17

21. Gray, T., Bork, D., De Vries, M.: A new DEMO modelling tool that facilitates model transformations. In: Nurcan, S., Reinhartz-Berger, I., Soffer, P., Zdravkovic, J. (eds.) BPMDS/EMMSAD -2020. LNBIP, vol. 387, pp. 359–374. Springer, Cham (2020). https://doi.org/10.1007/978-3-030-49418-6_25

Business Driven Microservice Design
An Enterprise Ontology Based Approach to API Specifications

Marien R. Krouwel[1,2](✉) and Martin Op 't Land[1,3]

[1] Capgemini Netherlands, PO Box 2575, 3500 GN Utrecht, The Netherlands
{Marien.Krouwel,Martin.OptLand}@capgemini.com
[2] Radboud Universiteit, Comeniuslaan 4, 6525 HP Nijmegen, The Netherlands
[3] Antwerp Management School, Boogkeers 5, 2000 Antwerp, Belgium

Abstract. As technology is evolving rapidly and market demand is changing quicker than ever, many are trying to implement service orientation and adopt market standards to improve adaptivity. A microservice architecture makes applications easier to scale and faster to develop, enabling innovation and accelerating time-to-market for new features. The question then arises how to design a manageable and stable set of microservices that is sufficient for the business. In this paper we systematically deduce an algorithm to derive a set of microservices, expressed according to the OpenAPI standard, from the ontological model of an enterprise, that is stable by nature, sufficient for the business, and based on units of clear size. This algorithm has the DEMO operating cycle at its heart and has been evaluated with the real-life Social Housing case at ICTU by creating a SwaggerHub implementation. Further research should clarify the role of implementation choices in the algorithm.

Keywords: Enterprise Engineering · DEMO · Microservices · API

1 Introduction

As technology is evolving rapidly and market demand is changing quicker than ever, many enterprises are trying to implement service orientation and adopt market standards to improve adaptivity [3,23]. The microservice architecture is rapidly becoming a popular market standard, providing mechanisms to decouple IT and allowing organizations to (a) easier scale applications, (b) faster develop or change applications independently, while maintaining their interoperability, (c) enable innovation, and (d) accelerate time-to-market for new or changed products [21,23]. However, when applying microservices at an industrial scale, the manageability of its underlying IT service portfolio can become a problem [9]. Indeed, a large portfolio of "small" services enables high adaptivity – just as sand is much more flexible in the construction world than stones or prefab walls – but its governance can be a nightmare, lowering its business value. This research aims to find a method to design a manageable, complete and stable set

© Springer Nature Switzerland AG 2022
D. Aveiro et al. (Eds.): EEWC 2021, LNBIP 441, pp. 95–113, 2022.
https://doi.org/10.1007/978-3-031-11520-2_7

of microservices that is sufficient for the business, while being adaptable in its (IT) implementation.

Microservices are an architectural and organizational approach to software development where software is composed of small, independent (micro)services [13]. Microservices are independently deployable, operable and scalable and may be implemented with different technologies [14]. In practice these services are owned by small, self-contained teams, and typically built around business capabilities [14]. Literature however is limited on specifying the "right" size of a microservice, or is sometimes even in contradiction:

- Steghuis' research for optimal service granularity [30] found mainly functional considerations such as business process flexibility, a maintainable and low-cost landscape, and performance. She recommends to split services in logical parts with different stability characteristics – leaving open how to discern "logical units of work" and degrees and drivers of stability.
- Compared to "traditional" Service Oriented Architecture (SOA), microservices are (more) fine-grained and protocols of the involved Application Programming Interfaces (APIs) are (more) lightweight [9,10,35].
- The largest sizes reported follow Amazon's notion of the Two Pizza Team – i.e. the whole team can be fed by two pizzas –, meaning no more than a dozen people. On the smaller size scale we've seen setups where a team of half-a-dozen would support half-a-dozen services [14].
- A microservice should not be as small as possible, but as small as needed to make it understandable [11].
- Moreover, the size of a microservice might depend on the business and organizational context [36] and it is considered bad practice to make the service too small, as the runtime overhead and the operational complexity can overwhelm the benefits of the approach [34].
- Others mention that a microservice should be focused on one specific task [13], one single business capability [9], or one atomic business activity [32], similar to applying the well known principle of 'Separation of Concerns' [8] as adopted by Normalized Systems theory [24]. It still however does not provide a clear measure of size for the microservice.

In this research, we aim to find a clear size for the microservice, that is sufficient for the business and independently changeable from an IT perspective.

In order for a (micro)service to be able to be used, it will need to expose an API [2]; a clearly defined method and protocol for communication that define how other services can access the service's functions and data, making it possible to use the service without knowing its internal construction or technology behind it [19]. This also implies that APIs should be stable in definition, while typically their implementation (in microservices) can change. Henning mentions that poorly defined APIs – or microservices – lead to increased development costs and often miss important use cases entirely [16], while O'Reilly, in a survey with 1502 respondents, finds the decomposition of (business) functions into microservices on of the biggest challenges in adopting microservices. In this research, we aim to find a set of microservices that is stable and complete from a business perspective, thus with a traceable mapping from business to microservices – as soon as an enterprise changes its Line of Business, e.g., from pigsty to restaurant, its portfolio of (business) products and services will change anyhow, including its supporting microservices.

Summarizing, we aim to find an algorithm to define a set of microservice definitions that

C1 is **stable** from a business perspective with respect to a set of (business) products and services;

C2 is **complete** – i.e. sufficient and not more than strictly necessary – from a business perspective;

C3 is **changeable** in its internal (IT) implementation, while the external behavior remains unchanged;

C4 contains services of a **well defined size** – i.e. with a clear scope.

As the ontological model of an enterprise provides a complete and implementation independent business perspective that is stable with respect to a set of (business) products and services [6], we will use these kind of models as input for our algorithm, thereby supporting all types of Enterprise Information Systems (EISs) [7] and already meeting criteria C1 and C2. By defining microservices in terms of APIs, we meet criterion C3. Our algorithm explicitly defines the (traceable) mapping from an ontological model to APIs, making sure no use cases are left out and resulting in a clear scope, focused on a single task, and thus with a well defined size, meeting criterion C4. The algorithm has been evaluated on the Social Housing case from the ICTU organization.

The Research Design (Sect. 2) introduces the Way of Working. The Way of Thinking (Sect. 3) introduces concepts regarding ontological modeling for enterprises and ontological model based service design, resulting in a deduction of the algorithm (Sect. 4) that is being evaluated on the real life case 'Social Housing' (Sect. 5). The paper ends with conclusions and future research directions (Sect. 6).

2 Research Design

The goal of this research is to create an algorithm to define microservice APIs from ontological business models. As this algorithm is an artifact that needs to be designed, we adopt the Design Science methodology [29] as main methodology. Where behavioral science seeks to develop and justify theories that explain or predict phenomena related to the identified business need, design science seeks to construct and evaluate artifacts designed to meet the identified business need [25]. However, as Hevner states, these methodologies cannot be separated and should be used complementary [1]. Because design is inherently an iterative and incremental activity, Hevner suggests three cycles for Design Science Research [17] which can be applied in as many iterations as needed (Fig. 1).

– the *relevance cycle* provides the requirements for the research and determines whether the resulting artifact improves the environment;

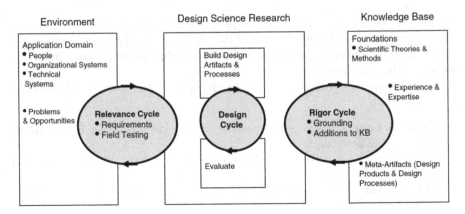

Fig. 1. Design science research cycles [17]

- the *rigor cycle* provides past knowledge to the project and ensures new contributions are added to the knowledge base;
- the *design cycle* is where the artifact is constructed and evaluated.

The main focus of this article will be on the design cycle: constructing the algorithm by means of deduction (Sect. 4). The algorithm is evaluated iteratively by applying it to the chosen real life case (Sect. 5). The requirements for the relevance cycle are covered in the introduction (Sect. 1). The grounding in the rigor cycle is outlined in the Way of Thinking (Sect. 3), while the additions to the existing knowledge base will be discussed in the conclusions (Sect. 6).

3   Foundations on Enterprise Ontology and Service Design

Ontological models for enterprises are by definition [7] *coherent* – i.e. the aspect models constitute a logical and integral whole –, *comprehensive* – i.e. all relevant issues are covered and the whole is complete –, *consistent* – i.e. the aspect models are free from contradictions or irregularities –, and *concise* – i.e. no redundant matters are contained in it. Earlier attempts have been made to define (micro)services from these models, because they are (a) are stable with respect to a set of (business) products and services, (b) are complete with regards to all real-world business actions, and (c) use the transaction notion, which decouples actors in a way very similar to SOA. Because of these properties we will use the ontological model of an enterprise as input for our algorithm, thereby already addressing criteria C1, C2 and C3. In this section we will further introduce relevant concepts of Enterprise Ontology and outline earlier research on defining (micro)services from ontological models.

3.1   Enterprise Ontology

Enterprise ontology concerns the highest level white-box model of the construction and operation of the organization of an enterprise [7]. Since it only depends on an enterprise's products and services, it is fully independent from the way in which it is realized and implemented [4]. Ontological models are therefore considered more stable than implementation dependent models [6]. The Design and Engineering Methodology for Organizations (DEMO) is the leading methodology in Enterprise Engineering and Enterprise Ontology. From DEMO we primarily use (a) the Complete Transaction Pattern (CTP), (b) the operating cycle, and (c) the ontological aspect models.

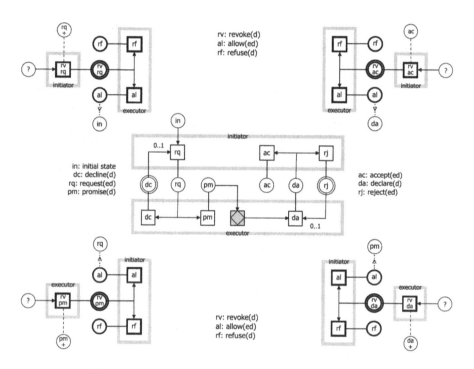

Fig. 2. Complete transaction pattern, adapted from [7]

Complete Transaction Pattern. DEMO sees an enterprise – any goal-oriented cooperative – as a network of actors that enter into and comply with commitments [7]. Each commitment is raised in a coordination act (C-act) and results in a corresponding coordination fact (C-fact); the coming into existence of a C-fact is called a coordination event (C-event). Coordination acts/facts – the atomic building blocks of organizational processes – about the same product (or production fact (P-fact)), such as "pizza pepperoni #125 is baked", occur in particular patterns of interaction, called transactions – the molecular building block of organizations. This *Complete Transaction Pattern*, which is considered to be the universal pattern in all organizations, comprises the "basic pattern" (request, promise, [execute,] declare, accept), but also its "discussion and discourse layers" (decline, reject, and revocations) – 18 C-act kinds and 1 production act in total (see Fig. 2). Every transaction (instance) is of a particular transaction kind – e.g., "pizza baking". A transaction kind concerns one specific product kind – e.g., "[pizza] is baked" – has one specific actor role – e.g., "pizza baker" – as its executor role, and can have multiple actor roles as its initiator role. An actor (human being) can fulfill more than one actor role – e.g., Mario may fulfill both the actor roles "pizza baker" and "stock controller".

The Actors Operating Cycle. Every actor is considered to loop constantly through its operating cycle (see Fig. 3), at a pace that is sufficiently frequent to deal with her/his agenda on time [7]. Each item in such an agenda is a C-event, the coming into existence of a C-fact with which the actor has to deal. The cycle starts with an actor selecting an agendum to be settled – at this stage it is irrelevant how such an agendum is chosen, typically based on internal or external defined priorities. Then, the actor fetches the applicable action rule(s) (from the Action Model, see below). After having assessed the conditions in the action rule – for which the actor usually needs to fetch information saved earlier or by someone else –, the actor decides how to respond to the selected C-event. Then, the actor performs the act(s) that follow from the decision. Action rules are guidelines, because actors are autonomous in deciding how to act. However, as actors are responsible and possibly also accountable for their acts, sometimes they will have to act not in line with the action rules, implying they need to be able to explain why they acted that way.

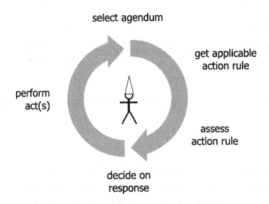

Fig. 3. The operating cycle of actors [7]

Ontological Aspect Models. The ontological model of an organization consists of an integrated whole of four aspect models [7]:

Cooperation Model (CM) models the *construction* of the enterprise; it consists of transaction kinds, associated (initiating and executing) actor roles, fact banks, the access links between actor roles and fact banks, and wait links between transaction kinds and actor roles. The CM is expressed in one or more Coordination Structure Diagrams (CSDs) and a Transactor Product Table (TPT);

Process Model (PM) models the *processes* that take place as the effect of acts by actors, by detailing the coordination between actor roles – specifying the state and transition space of the *coordination world* by making explicit the causal and wait links between C-(f)acts from the CTP. The PM is expressed in one or more Process Structure Diagrams (PSDs) and one or more Transaction Pattern Diagrams (TPDs);

Fact Model (FM) is the semantic model of *products* of the enterprise – specifying the state and transition space of its *production world* in terms of fact types (entity types with their related product kinds, property types, attribute types and value types), existence laws and occurrence laws. The FM is expressed in an Object Fact Diagram (OFD) and zero or more Derived Fact Specifications (DFSs);

Action Model (AM) is a model of the *operation* of the enterprise, guiding actors in performing P-acts (through Work Instruction Specifications (WISs)) and C-acts (through Action Rule Specifications (ARSs)) – specifying for every C-event with which the enterprise has to deal (agendum kind) one or more ARSs. Each ARS contains an *event part* – stating the agendum kind –, an *assess part* – to check for certain conditions – and a *response part* – stating how to respond –, thereby fully supporting the operating cycle of actors.

3.2   Earlier Research on EO Based Service Design

Several attempts have been made to design (micro)services from ontological models. Some define a (business) service as synonymous with a DEMO transaction [15,31,33], supporting the decoupling between consumer and provider as defined by SOA [32]. However, as a transaction consists of one P-act and many C-acts, involving acts performed by the initiator and executor of the transaction in an alternating way (see CTP in Subsect. 3.1), this is too coarse-grained for a microservice, which should focus on a single business activity or responsibility – a condition that is fulfilled by the unit of a single (P- or C-) act.

Another example shows one transaction for remembering more than one C-act [7], which also does not conform to the principle of focusing on a single business activity. De Jong [18] suggests a more granular approach where there can be many services to support a single business responsibility, by defining different types of supporting services for sharing, recalling, remembering and archiving P-facts. However, no services are defined to share or remember C-facts, which implies this approach does not comply to criterion C2. Earlier approaches ignore the operating cycle to define a set of (micro)services, whereas our algorithm will mostly be build around this concept.

4 Devising the Algorithm

The input of the algorithm is an ontological model of the enterprise – expressed in DEMO Specification Language (DEMO-SL) [5] –, where the output will be a set of API specifications for microservices. As ontological models are stable with respect to the products and services, the resulting API specifications are stable by nature, meeting criterion C1 for the algorithm. By defining microservices in terms of API specifications, which only contain a stable method and protocol for communication while the technological implementation behind it remains unknown for the consumer of the API and thus can change, we also meet criterion C3. For the API specifications, we will use the OpenAPI Specification (OAS), a technology independent and widely adopted industry standard for describing HTTP APIs, based on YAML [22]. Tools supporting this standard can (often) easily generate mock APIs or stubs from API definitions and generate API documentation and tests from code.

4.1 Deducing the Algorithm from the Operating Cycle

By starting from the actors operating cycle, we can claim completeness from a process perspective: in the operation of an organization, actors typically select an agendum from a list of agenda and process the selected agendum by retrieving the applicable action rule, assessing the action rule, deciding on the response and performing new acts (see Fig. 3). As DEMO itself claims comprehensiveness and conciseness on the content, together this makes sure we meet criterion C2.

By taking apart the different steps in the operating cycle, we come to different kind of microservices: *agenda services* providing the possible agenda for an actor in an actor role to select an agendum from, *assess services* providing the information on how to proceed, resulting in one or more *read services*, and *response services* providing a single service for performing one or more acts, resulting in one or more *write services*. These services will be explained in more detail below. For the operating cycle steps 'get applicable action rule' and 'decide on response' no microservices are defined; the first one is not needed as it is guaranteed by the definition of the other services, while the decision remains for the actor and thus needs no IT implementation, thereby conforming to the autonomy of actors.

Write Services: Following the CTP, for every C-act type (18 per transaction kind) and the P-act a write service must be defined that deals with performing the C-act. For the definition it is irrelevant who performs the C-act – that will be a matter of authorization.

Read Services: As information needs to be available for the actors, for every fact type in the DEMO FM (both OFD and all DFSs) a read service must be created. The assess service for every action rule is also considered to be a read service (using or aggregating other read services), but will be detailed below.

Assess Services: For every action rule, an assess service must be defined that performs the assess part of the action rule. In the assessment, it will evaluate some business rules which are basically comparisons, therefore using read services to retrieve the necessary information.

Response Services: One response service is needed for each action rule, to easily perform one or the other branch of the response part of the action rule, thereby using write services.

Agenda Services: For every actor role, an agenda service is needed in order for the actor to gain insight in the agenda he or she can select from. It might be useful or necessary to create more detailed services to only retrieve the open agenda with a certain state (e.g., being promised), in order to be able to deal with delegations.

4.2   Complete Algorithm

We will only show how to generate a set of services, defined by name, operation type[1] and summary, taking a DEMO model as starting point (see also Fig. 4). For simplicity, we leave out the parameters (input and/or for filtering or sorting) and response (output) that are required by OAS, while the name is shown by example and the summary is in the description.

Input: Ontological model of the enterprise, covering all aspect models, expressed in DEMO-SL;
Output: Set of microservice API definitions, expressed in OAS;
Steps:
1. For each transaction kind in the CM: generate 19 write (POST) services (one for every C-act kind and one additional for the P-act) for performing the event, e.g. TK01request;
2. For each (non-derived) entity type and value type in the OFD: generate 1 read (GET) service for retrieving the related data, e.g. registration;
3. For each DFS (derived fact types): generate 1 read (GET) service for calculating the derived fact, e.g. calculateAge. This service will use other read services;
4. For each ARS in the AM: generate 1 assess (GET) service and 1 response (POST) service, possibly introducing additional services for several sub parts, e.g. assessARS01 and responseARS01. The assess service will use other read services while the response service will use write services;

---

[1] While typical HTTP operation types or methods include GET, PUT, POST, DELETE, PATCH, OPTIONS, HEAD, TRACE and CONNECT [12,28], we only consider the first five methods relevant for the information level, while the others are more on an infrastructural level.

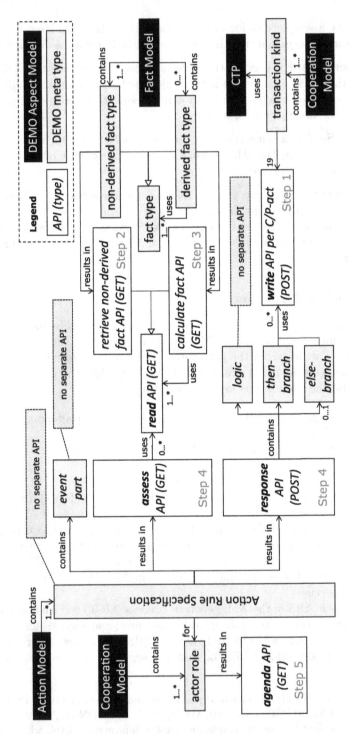

Fig. 4. Visualization of the mapping of DEMO metamodel to APIs

5. For each (elementary and composite) actor role in the CM: generate 1 agenda (GET) service, e.g. agendaForAR01.

The algorithm includes no POST services on the entity and value types: instances of internal types are only created as part of a C-act while instances of external types are created outside the focus of the enterprise – i.e. there might be such a service, but it is not relevant for the current focus. The algorithm also does not specify PATCH, PUT or DELETE services, as from an ontological perspective information and data are never changed or deleted.

5 Evaluation of the Algorithm

First of all a suitable business domain had to be chosen. We selected Social Housing because of its representativity for ICTU and because of the availability of documentation, building upon previous work on this case [27]. ICTU wants to invest in methods, ICT solutions and platforms that take continuous change in organization and technology as a starting point – a context that is quite typical for the Social Housing domain. In Social Housing two main areas can be discerned: (1) the registration of a home seeker as a member, and (2) assigning a house to the member; the focus is on the first.

5.1 Input: Ontological Model of the Social Housing Domain

The Cooperation Model (Fig. 5 and Table 1) reveals the starting, periodic renewal and ending of a registration. Starting the registration is initiated by the (aspirant) member and executed after at least paying the registration fee. Every year the registration is renewed against payment of a renewal fee. Ending a registration can be initiated by the member (e.g., when moving to another area) or by the Social Housing organization (e.g., in case of non payment of the renewal fee). The model shows that actors in this domain need access to facts about costs & terms, and about person & living – intentionally abstracting from how this access should be provided.

Table 1. TPT for Social Housing

Transaction kind	Product kind	Executor role
TK01 registration starting	PK01 [registration] is started	AR01 registration starter
TK02 registration paying	PK02 the fee for [registration] in [year] is paid	AR02 registration payer
TK03 registration ending	PK03 [registration] is ended	AR03 registration ender
TK04 registration management	PK04 registration management for [year] is done	AR04 registration manager

The Object Fact Diagram (Fig. 6) constitutes the semantics, expressing REGISTRATION as core entity type, and the starting and ending of a registration as event types. Next to that the (grey-colored, because determined outside the

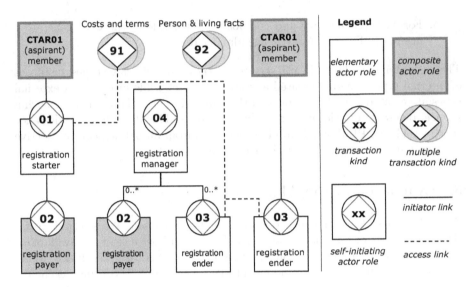

Fig. 5. CSD for Social Housing

focus) entity type PERSON appears, including the property type that a person may be the member and/or payer of a registration. The value type {YEAR} is included, to express (a) the event type of annual registration payment, (b) the definition of the (aggregated) entity type REGISTRATION × {YEAR} for the payment event type, and (c) several decisions taken yearly – modeled as attribute type of the entity type {YEAR} –, such as the standard registration fee. In deciding upon starting a registration, the existence of active registrations for and the age of a person are needed; Table 2 shows the algorithms for calculating those.

Actor rules guide actors in their decisions; Table 3 shows the action rule for AR01 to settle the agendum kind *registration starting is requested* (T01/rq). This rule assesses that the participants are authorized to play their (performer and addressee) role in this request, that the (aspirant) member is at least 18 years old and Dutch, and that (s)he doesn't have an active registration already at this moment. In that case, normally the registration starter can proceed to request the (aspirant) member to pay the registration and also to promise that his/her registration will be started; otherwise the registration starter normally should decline to do so. The action rule is not deterministic; the registration starter remains free to responsibly deviate from this rule. For Social Housing, 11 ARSs were defined.

5.2   Output: List of API Specifications

Because of lack of space, we only show the names of the generated APIs and not all details in Table 4. All $(76 + 4 + 2 + 22 + 6 = 110)$ services have been put into SwaggerHub, a tool for API design and documentation based on OAS, to confirm that the output of the algorithm conforms to OAS. Additionally, the

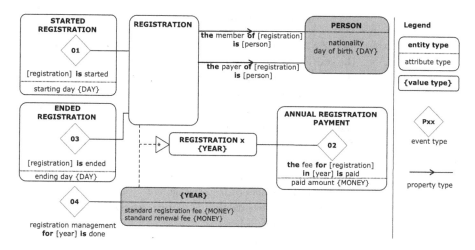

Fig. 6. OFD for Social Housing

complete definitions for two services (Fig. 7) are provided as example. During the test and development of the algorithm reusable (definition) components for e.g. *CFact* were created to simplify some of the definitions, that can be used for other cases as well.

Table 2. DFSs for Social Housing

the age **of** [person] **on** [day] $\equiv$ [day] **minus the** day of birth **of** [person];
[person] has active registrations **on** [day] $\equiv$ **there exists a** [registration]
for which the member of [registration] **equals** [person]
and [registration] is started
and starting day **of** [registration] **is smaller than or equal to** [day]
and (**NOT** [registration] is ended
or ending day **of** [registration] **is greater than** [day])

5.3 Reflection on Case Level

As criteria C1, C2 and C3 follow from the definition of the algorithm, it is not possible to reflect on them empirically. Considering C4 we claim that all microservices are well defined and focus on one (business) responsibility, possibly using other services, and therefore have a clear size.

During the application of the algorithm we had to choose data types for the value types in the OFD. Although this mapping seems quite clear, it is not (yet) made specific in the algorithm. In a next iteration, this should be made clear for defining the parameters and responses.

Table 3. ARS01 for AR01

event	**when** registration starting **for** [registration] **is** <u>requested</u>			(TK01/rq)
		with	the starting day **of** [registration] **is some** day	
			the member **of** [registration] **is some** person	
			the payer **of** [registration] **is some** person	
assess	**if**	*rightness:*	the <u>performer</u> **of the** <u>request</u> **is the** member **of** [registration]	
			the <u>addressee</u> **of the** <u>request</u> **is a** registration starter	
		sincerity:	* *no specific condition* *	
		truth:	the age **of** member **of** [registration]	
			on starting day **of** [registration] **is greater than or equal to** 18;	
			nationality **of** member **of** [registration] **is** Dutch;	
			NOT member **of** [registration] has active registrations	
			on starting day **of** [registration]	
response	**if**	*performing the action after* **then** *is considered justifiable*		
	then <u>promise</u>	registration starting **for** [registration]		[TK01/pm]
		to the <u>performer</u> **of the** request		
	else <u>decline</u>	registration starting **for** [registration]		[TK01/dc]
		to the <u>performer</u> **of the** <u>request</u>		
		with * *reason for declining* *		

A very specific choice we made for this case is that person details are not completely delivered by the initiator, but only referred to by a key (e.g. Social Security Number) completed with the explicit consent from the initiator that the executor can use this key to retrieve the person details required. These concern only details in the parameters of the services.

Table 4. Full list of APIs generated by the algorithm for Social Housing

Step 1:	TK01request, TK01promise, TK01decline, . . . (4 * 19 = 76 in total; all POST)
Step 2:	Registration, person, year, annualRegistrationPayment (all GET)
Step 3:	CalculateAge, calculatePersonHasActiveRegistrations (all GET)
Step 4:	assessARS01, responseARS01, assessARS02, . . . (2 * 11 = 22 in total; all POST)
Step 5:	agendaForAR01, agendaForAR02, agendaForAR03, agendaForAR04, agendaForCTAR01, agendaForCTAR02 (all GET)

6   Conclusions and Future Research

6.1   Conclusions and Reflection

We will evaluate the algorithm for defining microservice APIs to the criteria as defined in Sect. 1. As the set is generated from an ontological model of the enterprise, it's by definition stable with respect to a set of products and services,

```
/TK01request:                                    /agendaForAR01:
  post:                                            get:
    summary: create a new TK01 request               summary: show list of C-acts to be dealt
     (registration starting)                          with by AR01 (registration starter)
    requestBody:                                     responses:
      required: true                                  '200':
      content:                                          content:
       application/json:                                 application/json:
        schema:                                           schema:
          ref: '#/components/schemas/TK01request'          type: array
    responses:                                             items:
      '201':                                                 type: object
        description: C-fact created                          properties:
        content:                                             id:
         application/json:                                     type: integer
          schema:                                           cfact:
            type: integer                                    ref: '#components/schemas/CFact'
```

Fig. 7. Definition of TK01request and agendaForAR01 in OAS format

meeting criterion C1. As new products or services are identified, the algorithm can easily generate the additional microservices. As ontological models are said to be comprehensive and concise, and we use the operating cycle as a basis for our algorithm, the resulting set is complete, meeting criterion C2. Organization implementation [20], such as delegations, might require additional services or additional parameters in existing services. As the set only specifies APIs for the microservice, their (IT) implementation is undecided yet and thus changeable, meeting criterion C3. All services in the generated set are well-defined, focused on one task – therein possible using other services – and thereby clear in size, meeting criterion C4. Although we have not provided an externally measurable size for the microservice, we believe we have made progress in defining the 'right' size for a microservice. We also believe that this level makes it easier to maintain the (large amount) services, also by multiple and distributed teams.

Our algorithm mostly produces read/GET services on the 'raw' data (such as registration) and only provides write/POST services on the process level, leaving out POST services on the entity types and completely leaving out services of another operation type, such as PUT, PATCH and DELETE. This is in contrast to current practices that define services of (almost) all HTTP types on the data level and usually leaves out services on the process level. Taking the C-act as unit of work – embedding one independent and several dependent facts – provides integrity from a process perspective, ensuring that only a consistent set of data can come into existence. As a result, our algorithm creates services that are business demand driven, where current practice typically seems to define microservices from a supplier perspective on top of existing data sources. Again, organization implementation [20] might require additional services, possibly including DELETE services to delete data from the system. There might be some HTTP methods currently defined, that are not needed when implementing from an ontological perspective.

Our algorithm does not use the concept of informational and documental transactions as proposed by Dietz [7] and de Jong [18]. We don't think they are needed in a world of automation, as the implementation typically is in IT; instead we propose to directly define the microservices from the original transactions. Moreover, tables 11.1-3 in [7] show a remember transaction (or POST service), even for dealing with the request. From an ontological perspective we think this is wrong: the request was already there – since this is the action rule for dealing with it –, so a share transaction (or GET service) would be better. Possibly the choice for a remember transaction is the result from an implicit design decision where the executor of the transaction still needs to save the information in its own data storage.

6.2   Limitations and Future Research Directions

Some of the definitions in the algorithm are or can be influenced by (organization and/or IT) implementation choices, such as regulations regarding archiving or security, delegation of work from one actor to another, the mapping from value types to technical (primary) data types, as well as *how* external information is provided – e.g. completely given by the initiator or referenced by with a key, including the permission for the executor to use the key to retrieve the required information. The role of such implementation choices should be made more explicit in a next version of the algorithm, along with more details on the definition of the parameters and response of the APIs.

While HTTP is one of the more popular internet protocols, others exist, such as SMTP, (S)FTP, MQTT, AMQP and XMPP. A next iteration of the algorithm can include extension or abstraction to other protocols, especially where there are relevant standards available, similar to OAS for HTTP.

Currently we left out the decision part – the first and default sentence of the response part – of an action rule in the design of APIs. One could however argue that this can also be seen as a microservice, though often – or at least: preferably – executed by a human actor. Adding such a decision API would also create the opportunity to add an action rule API, covering the complete execution of a single action rule (steps 2–5 of the actor cycle), thereby making it possible to completely outsource its implementation – as part of further research on the mutual dependence of organization splitting with IT splitting [26].

In the algorithm read services are defined on the entity and value type level. However, one could consider to further detail this into different microservices on the level of attribute type, property type and event type, supporting an even more distributed data storage model and possibly a better performance as only the strictly required data is retrieved. The downside however can be that splitting this up into several services introduces an overhead in computing and network latency with a lower performance as result. Further research should investigate whether splitting up to an even lower level is useful.

During the evaluation of the algorithm, we found that we wanted to validate the meaningfulness for the business end users. As it wasn't part of the design cycle, we left it out for now. In a further evaluation it would imply to do additional field testing with end users.

Finally, additional research is needed to define a method to measure the size of a microservice, as well as to define the 'right' size for a microservice, possibly depending on many variables.

Acknowledgments. For this inspiring collaboration of industry with academia, we want to thank ICTU, and especially its Senior Advisor Steven Gort, for their sponsorship in evaluating the algorithm.

References

1. Bichler, M.: Design science in information systems research. WIRTSCHAFTSIN-FORMATIK **48**(2), 133–135 (2006). https://doi.org/10.1007/s11576-006-0028-8
2. Bush, T.: What is the difference between APIs and microservices? January 2019. https://nordicapis.com/what-is-the-difference-between-apis-and-microservices/. Accessed 18 Nov 2021
3. Desai, V., Koladia, Y., Pansambal, S.: Microservices: architecture and technologies. Int. J. Res. Appl. Sci. Eng. Technol. (IJRASET) **8**(X) (2020). https://doi.org/10.22214/ijraset.2020.31979
4. Dietz, J.L.G.: Enterprise Ontology – Theory and methodology. Springer, Berlin (2006). https://doi.org/10.1007/3-540-33149-2_2
5. Dietz, J.L.G.: The DEMO Specification Language v4.5. Technical Report, Enterprise Engineering institute, July 2020. https://demo.nl/mdocs-posts/2020-07-31-demo-specification-language-4-5/
6. Dietz, J.L.G., Hoogervorst, J.A.P.: Enterprise ontology and enterprise architecture - how to let them evolve into effective complementary notions. GEAO J. Enter. Archit. **2007**, 1 (2007)
7. Dietz, J.L.G., Mulder, J.B.F.: Enterprise Ontology – A Human-Centric Approach to Understanding the Essence of Organisation. The Enterprise Engineering Series, Springer, Cham (2020). https://doi.org/10.1007/978-3-030-38854-6
8. Dijkstra, Edsger W: On the role of scientific thought. In: Selected writings on Computing: A Personal Perspective. Texts and Monographs in Computer Science. Springer, New York, pp. 60–66 (1982). https://doi.org/10.1007/978-1-4612-5695-3_12
9. Dragoni, N., et al.: Microservices: yesterday, today, and tomorrow. CoRR, June 2016. http://arxiv.org/abs/1606.04036
10. Farinelli, D., McAllister, D.: API vs. Microservices: a microservice is more than just an API, October 2019. https://dzone.com/articles/api-vs-microservices-a-microservice-is-more-than-j. Accessed 11 Nov 2021
11. Farley, D.: The problem with microservices, October 2020. https://www.youtube.com/watch?v=zzMLg3Ys5vI. Accessed 18 Nov 2021
12. Fielding, R., et al.: RFC 2616, Hypertext Transfer Protocol - HTTP/1.1, June 1999. http://www.rfc.net/rfc2616.html. Accessed 04 Jan 2022
13. Folwer, M., Lewis, J.: Microservices: Nur ein weiteres Konzeptin der Softwarearchitektur oder mehr? Online Themenspecial Innovation in und durch Architekturen 2015 (2015)
14. Fowler, M.: Microservices, March 2014. http://martinfowler.com/articles/microservices.html. Accessed 05 Nov 2021
15. Hardjosumarto, G.: An Enterprise Ontology basedApproach to Service Specification. Master's thesis, Delft University of Technology (2008)

16. Henning, M.: API design matters. Commun. ACM **52**(5), 46–56 (2009). https://doi.org/10.1145/1506409.1506424
17. Hevner, A.R.: A three cycle view of design science research. Scandinavian J. Inf. Syst. **19**(2), 87–92 (2007)
18. de Jong, J.: A Method for Enterprise Ontology based Design of for Enterprise Information Systems. Ph.D. thesis, TU Delft (2013)
19. Juviler, J.: Microservices vs. APIs: what's the difference? November 2020. https://blog.hubspot.com/website/microservices-vs-api. Accessed 18 Nov 2021
20. Krouwel, M.R., Op 't Land, M., Offerman, T.: Formalizing organization implementation. In: Advances in Enterprise Engineering X, pp. 3–18. EEWC 2016, Funchal, Madeira Island, Portugal (2016). https://doi.org/10.1007/978-3-319-39567-8_1
21. Kwan, A., Jacobsen, H.A., Chan, A., Samoojh, S.: Microservices in the modern software world. In: Proceedings of the 26th Annual International Conference on Computer Science and Software Engineering, pp. 297–299. CASCON 2016, IBM Corp., USA (2016)
22. Linux Foundation: OpenAPI Specification v3.1.0, February 2021. https://spec.openapis.org/oas/v3.1.0. Accessed 21 Nov 2021
23. Loukides, M., Swoyer, S.: Microservices Adoption in 2020. Technical Report, O'Reilly, July 2020. https://www.oreilly.com/radar/microservices-adoption-in-2020/. Accessed 06 Jan 2022
24. Mannaert, H., Verelst, J.: Normalized systems: re-creating information technology based on laws for software evolvability. Koppa, Kermt, Belgium (2009)
25. March, S.T., Smith, G.F.: Design and natural science research on information technology. Decis. Support Syst. **15**(4), 251–266 (1995). https://doi.org/10.1016/0167-9236(94)00041-2
26. Op 't Land, M.: Applying Architecture and Ontology to the Splitting and Allying of Enterprises. Ph.D. thesis, Delft University of Technology, June 2008. http://resolver.tudelft.nl/uuid:0edd0472-39df-4296-b692-e9916e79fb1e
27. Op 't Land, M., Krouwel, M.R., Gort, S.: Testing the concept of the *RUN-Time Adaptive* enterprise. In: Aveiro, D., Guizzardi, G., Pergl, R., Proper, H.A. (eds.) EEWC 2020. LNBIP, vol. 411, pp. 228–242. Springer, Cham (2021). https://doi.org/10.1007/978-3-030-74196-9_13
28. Sandoval, K.: Ultimate Guide To 9 Common HTTP Methods, January 2020. https://nordicapis.com/ultimate-guide-to-all-9-standard-http-methods/. Accessed 04 Jan 2022
29. Simon, H.A.: The Sciences of the Artificial, 3rd edn. MIT Press, Cambridge (1996)
30. Steghuis, C.: Service granularity in SOA-projects : a trade-off analysis. Master's thesis, University of Twente, June 2006. http://essay.utwente.nl/57339/
31. Terlouw, L.I., Albani, A.: An enterprise ontology-based approach to service specification. IEEE Trans. Serv. Comput. **6**(1), 89–101 (2013). https://doi.org/10.1109/TSC.2011.38
32. The Open Group (TOG): Microservices Architecture (2016). http://www.opengroup.org/soa/source-book/msawp/. Accessed 21 Nov 2021
33. Wiersma, R., Ravesteyn, P.: A method for defining optimum service granularity. In: 21st Annual International Information Management Association (IIMA), Utrecht, The Netherlands (2010)
34. Wikipedia: Microservices. https://en.wikipedia.org/wiki/Microservices. Accessed 11 Nov 2021
35. Zimmermann, O.: Microservices tenets. Comput. Sc. Res. Dev. **32**(3), 301–310 (2016). https://doi.org/10.1007/s00450-016-0337-0

36. Zimmermann, O.: domain specific service decomposition with microservice API patterns, February 2019. https://www.conf-micro.services/2019/slides//keynotes/Zimmerman.pdf. Accessed 11 Nov 2021

Evaluation of the Perceived Quality and Functionality of Fact Model Diagrams in DEMO

Dulce Pacheco[1,2,3(✉)] ⬚, David Aveiro[1,3,4] ⬚, Bernardo Gouveia[1,3,4] ⬚, and Duarte Pinto[1,3] ⬚

[1] ARDITI - Regional Agency for the Development of Research, Technology and Innovation, 9020-105 Funchal, Portugal
{dulce.pacheco,bernardo.gouveia,duarte.nuno}@arditi.pt
[2] School of Technology and Management, University of Madeira, Caminho da Penteada, 9020-105 Funchal, Portugal
[3] NOVA-LINCS, Universidade NOVA de Lisboa, Campus da Caparica, 2829-516 Caparica, Portugal
[4] Faculty of Exact Sciences and Engineering, University of Madeira, Caminho da Penteada, 9020-105 Funchal, Portugal
daveiro@uma.pt

Abstract. DEMO's Way of Modeling comprises a set of models and diagrams to represent an organization. They are interconnected, representing the organizational reality in a coherent and platform-independent way; however, it has been argued that the syntax and semantics of DEMO's Fact Model are too complex and cluttered, being difficult to interpret by laypeople. It has been claimed that a novel version of the Fact Model and its synthesizing and expressive powers allow it to overcome the complexity and intricacies of processes. And also to create representations that are more easily understood and productively discussed by the full range of stakeholders, regardless of their technical prowess or background. A pilot study was undertaken where test subjects assessed and compared both versions of the Fact Model regarding their perceived Empirical Quality, Social Pragmatic Quality, and Functionality. This study, here reported, withstands previous claims, arguing that when comparing these representations of the Fact Model, the novel version of the diagrams was evaluated as having a higher perceived Quality and Functionality. Also, it was the preferred version of the majority of the subjects in the pilot study.

Keywords: Enterprise engineering · DEMO · Fact model · Fact diagram · Cognitive effectiveness · Perceived quality · Perceived functionality

1 Introduction

Modeling is performed to achieve business or organizational goals. For everything apart from elementary and highly intersubjectively agreed-upon domains, total validity, completeness, comprehension, and agreement cannot be achieved, as it would lead to unlimited use of time and money in the modeling activity [1]. For the goals in these areas to

© Springer Nature Switzerland AG 2022
D. Aveiro et al. (Eds.): EEWC 2021, LNBIP 441, pp. 114–128, 2022.
https://doi.org/10.1007/978-3-031-11520-2_8

be realistic, they must be somewhat relaxed by introducing the idea of feasibility. The DEMO (Design and Engineering Methodology for Organizations) Way of Modeling comprises a set of models and diagrams to represent an organization. They are interconnected, representing organizational reality coherently and platform-independently [1]. It has been argued that the syntax and semantics of DEMO's Fact Model are too complex and cluttered, being difficult to interpret by laypeople, and an alternative representation was proposed in [2].

This paper evaluates the perceived Quality and Functionality of the Fact Model's diagrams. As such, and hereafter, the version proposed in [2] will be designated as Version C, and the DEMO version [3] as Version D. A set of seven hypotheses was raised and tested in our study (see Table 1).

Table 1. Hypotheses formulated

Hypothesis	Description
H_1	Version C is perceived as having higher overall perceived Quality and Functionality
H_2	Version C is evaluated as having a higher overall perceived Quality and Functionality by the subjects with higher self-reported knowledge of the modeled processes ($>= 4.5$)
H_3	Version D is evaluated as having a higher overall perceived Quality and Functionality by the subjects with higher self-reported knowledge of the modeling language ($>= 4.5$)
H_4	Version C is perceived as having higher perceived Functionality
H_5	Version C is perceived as having a higher perceived Empirical Quality
H_6	Version C is perceived as having a higher perceived Social Pragmatic Quality
H_7	Version C is picked by the majority of the subjects, rather than Version D or legislation, when prompted to decide where to look to clarify their questions about a specific task

The paper is structured as follows: Section 2 presents our literature review regarding the evaluation of diagrammatic representations. Section 3 describes the context of our study along with both versions of the Fact Model that were evaluated. In Sect. 4, the evaluation method is described. The paper closes with the results and discussion section, followed by the study's conclusions.

2 Literature Review

To evaluate the diagrammatical models (referred to as diagrams from now on), which are based on DEMO's MU theory [3], it is necessary to take into account that previous research in diagrammatical reasoning has shown that representations have the potential to at least be as cognitively effective, if not more, than content [4]. Different frameworks that support process modeling have emerged based on research, e.g., GoM - Guidelines of Modeling [5], 7PMG - Seven Process Modeling Guidelines [4], SEQUAL - Semiotic Quality Framework [7], and the Physics of Notations theory [8]. Even though criteria and guidelines to design process models exist, metrics and clear criteria to evaluate some of the principles are uneven [9]. When available, the metrics and criteria are mostly focused on a technical evaluation of the diagram by the modelers [9]. Authors [10] have identified user satisfaction as one of the four measures of their process modeling success model. However, its evaluation method and criteria were not defined [10].

This section will briefly focus on the two most popular frameworks to design and evaluate process models: Physics of Notations theory and SEQUAL.

2.1 Physics of Notations Theory

A framework specifically developed for visual notations is provided by the Physics of Notations theory [8]. It defines nine evidence-based principles to evaluate and improve the visual notation of modeling languages: Cognitive Fit, Semiotic Clarity, Perceptual Discriminability, Visual Expressiveness, Complexity Management, Cognitive Integration, Semantic Transparency, Graphic Economy, and Dual Coding. These principles may be used to generate empirically testable predictions [6].

The elementary characteristics that form the visual alphabet of diagrammatic notations (i.e., the values of visual variables) contribute to evaluating notations against the nine principles [9]. Once the set of symbols and the set of semantic constructs are defined, the Physics of Notations does provide the most accomplished theory to analyze and improve the cognitive effectiveness of visual modeling languages [9].

2.2 SEQUAL

The Semiotic Model Quality (SEQUAL) is a framework that proposes a list of general qualities for modeling languages [11]: Physical, Empirical, Syntactic, Semantic, Pragmatic, Social, and Deontic.

SEQUAL has a constructivist view of modeling activities, where dialogue occurs between the stakeholders involved in modeling. Therefore, the knowledge of the modeling domain changes as modeling occurs in a socially driven manner [12].

This framework differentiates between Empirical Quality and Social Pragmatic Quality, each respectively related to comprehensibility and actual human comprehension. This differentiation is motivated by empirical investigation of the framework's applicability and the utility of distinguishing between technical and social aspects [12].

2.3 Perceived Quality and Functionality in Diagrams

Quality is a difficult notion to grasp and, within the field of information systems, many approaches to quality have been proposed [12]. Process models may be difficult to comprehend due to the modeling language's formality, the complexity or size of the model, or the effort needed to deduce its important properties [11].

Our study hypothesized that subjects would evaluate Version C as having higher overall perceived Quality and Functionality (H_1) and would also perceive the diagrams of Version C as more functional (H_4).

Previous research mentions that familiarity with the processes and the language used helps to better understand the representations [11]. Therefore, we anticipated that participants with higher self-reported knowledge of the modeled processes ($>= 4.5$) would evaluate Version C as having a higher perceived Quality and Functionality (H_2). On the other hand, subjects with higher self-reported knowledge of the modeling language ($>= 4.5$) would evaluate Version D as having a higher perceived Quality and Functionality (H_3).

Empirical Quality (EQ). EQ entails eight different variables: planar variables (horizontal and vertical position) and retinal variables (shape, size, color, brightness, orientation, and texture) [11]. Other uses of emphasis can also be considered when evaluating the EQ of a model [11]. Visual emphasis can also factor in: solidity, differences in patterns; foreground/background differences; change (movement); position, and connectivity [11]. A color code that defines the usage in diagrams must be defined. Although some authors have reported the need to avoid using colors as a part of the notation for conveying meaning, color has been reported as an important differentiator in visual representations [12].

Previous studies have identified guidelines for graph aesthetics [1], which are, in turn, part of the EQ. This enables the definition of metrics to technically assess and improve the representation [11]. Because aesthetics are a subjective matter, familiarity with a diagram often positively influences the evaluation of its EQ [11]. Furthermore, considering that Version C has more attractive aesthetics and introduces color in the representation, we hypothesized that participants would evaluate Version C as having a higher EQ (H_5).

Social Pragmatic Quality (SPQ). The correspondence between the available part of the diagram and the actor's interpretation is its Pragmatic Quality [12]. These actors can be either human stakeholders or technical actors [11]. The perceived SPQ, i.e., the extent to which people understand the model, is distinguished from the Technical Pragmatic Quality, as the latter refers to the extent to which tools can be developed with the capability to interpret the model [12]. While evaluating these variables, we assess whether the diagram has been understood and who has understood (the relevant parts of) it [11].

Pragmatic Quality encompasses four dimensions [11]: Language Perception, Content Relevance, Structured Analysis, and Behavior Experience. Considering that familiarity with formal languages can influence the perception of Pragmatic Quality, a formal model could be more intelligible for one person but, still, other individuals will find a mix of formal and informal statements to be more understandable, even if the set of statements in the complete model is redundant [11].

We hypothesized that participants would evaluate the novel representation in Version C as having a higher perceived SPQ (H_6). Moreover, when prompted to decide between Version C, Version D, or legislation (to clarify their questions about the process), the majority would pick Version C (H_7).

3   Study Context

3.1   MU Theory and the DEMO Methodology

The Design and Engineering Methodology for Organizations (DEMO) consists of a method and language standard based on the theories of Enterprise Ontology, to capture the essence of an enterprise or scope of interest. One of its core theories, the Model Universe (MU) theory, as explained in [3], addresses how concrete, conceptual and symbolic complexes can be viewed as models of each other.

As a fully-developed methodology, DEMO encompasses not only a Way of Thinking consisting of its theories (including the MU theory) [3], but also a Way of Modeling comprising a set of four aspect models in which the essence of an enterprise is expressed [3]: the Cooperation Model (CM), the Action Model (AM), the Process Model (PM), and the Fact Model (FM) [13].

The FM of an enterprise is a model of its products [13]. Similar to the PM, but in the production world, the FM of an organization connects its CM and AM, whereas its state space contains the relevant entity types, value types, property types, and attribute types. Applicable event types and occurrence laws are considered in the transition space of the production (or p-)world of an organization.

To formally convey the rationale of the conceptual schema into symbols and constructs, the General Ontology Specification Language (GOSL) was created. It is a language for the specification of the state space and the transition space of a p-world whose logical constructs are transformable to first-order logic.

We argue in [2], that the GOSL notation for the FM, as it stands, is not an ideal choice to produce representations that are easily understood and productively discussed by the full range of stakeholders regardless of their technical prowess, experience, or background.

We identified a need for different representations of the GOSL-based FM concerning DEMO's theories and concepts. These are essentially composed of two artifacts: (1) the Fact Diagram (FD) and (2) the Fact Description Table (FDT). Both will be summarily presented in the following subsections.

3.2   Fact Model Representations

The Fact Diagram of Version C is mainly composed of the Concepts and Relationships Diagram (CRD) and its "expansion", the Concept Attribute Diagram (CAD) [2]. We adopted a change in nomenclature in [2], where DEMO's *entities* and *properties* are replaced, only in name, by *concepts* and *attributes*, respectively. For clarity, we will respect this nomenclature with the assurance that both refer to traditional DEMO *facts*.

The CRD is a generic, global, and synthetic view of an entire domain's concepts while abstracting from their attributes. The bottom part of Fig. 1 presents the CRD of a conceptual domain scope related to the Urban Appraisal knowledge domain.

Moreover, and besides the importance of identifying the main concepts and relationships in the CRD's representation, the ability to inspect which attributes each concept possesses was regarded as being highly useful [2]. For this purpose, we also proposed the Concept Attribute Diagram as part of the Fact Model. It can be considered a variation or "expansion" of the CRD presented previously. In the CAD, a concept is represented by a collapsible box whose expansion discloses its attributes, one per line (*Application Deliverable* in Fig. 1). The value type of an attribute is specified to the left of the line, whilst to the right, the name of the attribute and eventually a list of possible values, usually for categorical value types (e.g., the *State of the application deliverable* in Fig. 1).

The Fact Description Table (FDT) presents details of relevant information not shown in the diagrams (see Fig. 2). Every concept in the diagrams is mirrored in this table, along with every attribute description. Traceability is the primary motivation for this artifact because not only the source that supports the existence of the attribute is referenced (e.g., a legal source), but there are also multiple references to the transactions that are responsible for updating the values of the attribute at hand.

In the reported project experience [2], layering the representations in the CRD with the CAD along with the FDT allows for greater synthesization in the CRD and leaves more detail towards the FDT. This tradeoff promotes inclusion and facilitates the interpretation and discussion of the underlying organization among stakeholders.

Because the changes to the FM's representations were motivated by a project for a particular knowledge domain, five practical requirements directed the refinements: 1) provide insight and overview of the massive complexity of the legislation in a way that could be easily understandable/intelligible by all stakeholders; 2) provide traceability in all modeled artifacts regarding their composing elements; 3) make the rationale for each fact explicit; 4) clear reference to applicable legal rules; 5) provide a diagram with the simplicity of elements capturing the relevant concepts and their attributes.

Looking at the top diagram of Fig. 1, regarding Application Deliverable Management in the context of Urban Planning, it is evident that the current format of the OFD in GOSL has several different elements, symbols, and text, which makes it very difficult to be interpreted by officers without experience in DEMO. It is of the utmost importance to know which steps of a transaction are responsible for creating values for a particular attribute, as shown in the last columns of the FDT of Fig. 2. DEMO's current OFD shows only the p-fact associated with each class, while any transaction step may create original facts, that is, values that are instances of attributes. The solution presented in [2] solves two problems: it respectively reduces the complexity of the diagrams and presents further detail in the CRD and CAD, while allowing the specification, not only of the transaction responsible for originating the fact but also of its respective step, and of possibly other transactions/steps that might create or update it in the FDT.

Visual notations are considered to convey information more effectively than text [8]. Our approach is to have a minimal set of symbols to represent the main and more common restrictions in the CRD. We argue that cardinalities are better represented with arrows pointing to relationships' "one side". We also claim that dependency laws are better represented in the ORM way and not within a cardinality's numbers, as in the current GOSL way.

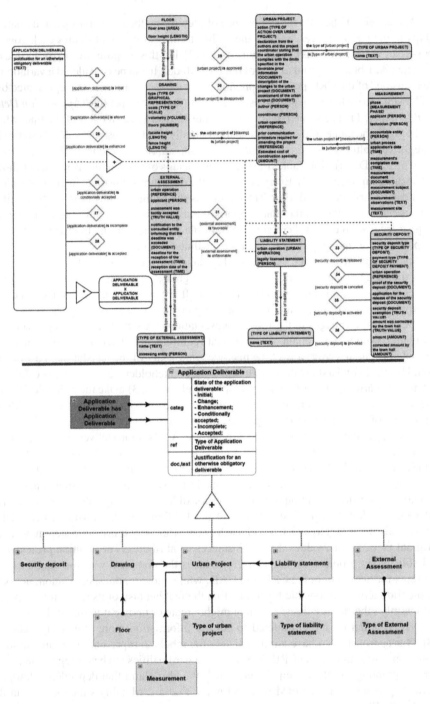

Fig. 1. Object fact diagram (Version D - top) and concept and relationships diagram (Version C - bottom)

Concept	Attribute name	Value Type	Referenced Concept / Category values	Description	Source · task 1	Step	Task 1 (creates or updates the attribute)
Concepts of Application Deliverable Management							
Application Deliverable	Application Deliverable			The "Deliverable" concept specifies the instances that are handed over to the Municipality's services as part of the management of deliverables procedure. Supports the preliminary analysis task by making it possible to discriminate which deliverables were effectively delivered.	RJUE - Art. 11	Ex	T197CP5 Preliminary analysis of urban building process (preliminary assessment)
Application Deliverable	State of the application deliverable	category	Change	This attribute holds the the state of deliverables (e.g. if it is the initial handing over of the element, if it is an enhacement or if this element has already been accepted): Possible options for the state of the deliverable are presented as follows: - Initial: the initial delivery; - Change: a change (potentially unsolicited) of a given deliverable; - Improvement: a new iteration of a deliverable following an enhacement request; - Conditionally Accepted: the deliverable was accepted minus some impending changes which are yet to be delivered; - Accept: an accepted deliverable; - Incomplete: the deliverable has flaws in its components;	RJUE - Art. 11	Ex	T197CP5 Preliminary analysis of urban planning / building process (preliminary assessment)
Application Deliverable	Justification for an otherwise obligatory deliverable	document		According to the Decree No. 113/2015 of April 22nd there may be deliverables which are exceptionally considered unnecessary to hand over for a particular urban operation.	RJUE - Art. 11	Ex	T197CP5 Preliminary analysis of urban planning / building process (preliminary assessment)
Application Deliverable	Type of deliverable	reference	Type of Application Deliverable	From the analysis of Decree No. 113/2015 of April 22nd, a survey of types of deliverables was promoted. Given that upon delivery, there is a need to maintain which types of deliverables were actually handed over, the correspondence between what was delivered and the type of deliverable is implemented in this attribute.	RJUE - Art. 11	Ex	T197CP5 Preliminary analysis of urban planning / building process (preliminary assessment)

Fig. 2. Fact description table

GOSL's domain-specific value types, such as the type of graphical representation or the measurement phase in Fig. 1 (top), were represented inline in their respective entity class and not separately because it would needlessly expand the diagram's size. In fact, claims of clutter, mainly regarding text, and the need for a cleaner representation with simplified semantics were reported by the officers of the urban appraisal division. These claims reinforce the need for a simpler notation, one where the essence of a property is not semantically or visually impaired by the notions of value type, sort, base type, measuring unit, or dimension.

4 Method

4.1 Participants

As shown in Table 2, we recruited a group of professionals with knowledge of the processes modeled (Sample A: $N = 8$, six female and two male, $M_{age} = 45$, age range: 33–54 years) and a group of students experienced in the modeling language, DEMO (Sample B: $N = 14$, five female and nine male, $M_{age} = 24$, age range: 20–43 years).

The participants evaluated the perceived Quality and Functionality of the diagrams. The overall sample (N = 22) had gender equality (50% females and 50% males) and a mean age of 32 years (age range: 20–54 years). The participants had heterogeneous education.

Table 2. Characterization of the sample

	Background				Scholar level		
	Architecture	Human/Social Sciences	Law	Other	High school	Bachelor	Master
Sample A	4	0	3	1	0	5	3
Sample B	0	3	0	11	2	11	1
N	4	3	3	12	2	16	4

4.2 Materials and Procedure

The informed consent was collected after a briefing where the project's goals were explained to the potential participants. All subjects voluntarily agreed to participate in the study. The briefing was conducted by a DEMO certified teacher who recapped the main DEMO concepts: distinction axiom, transaction axiom; what are assigned roles, the responsibilities and the possibility to delegate; what are transactions (called tasks in [14]), and that they imply the creation of facts (being them ontological, infological, or datalogical); how a chain of transactions was called a scope of interest and the flow is regulated by rules and restrictions (temporal, causal, conditional, etc.); and, finally, that concepts aggregate a collection of attributes relevant to a domain and a fact is an instance of concept that aggregates concrete values.

After this introduction, DEMO's Object Fact Diagram was presented as Version D (see Fig. 1 - top) and the Concept and Relationships Diagram, Concept Attribute Diagram, and Fact Description Table as Version C [2] (see Fig. 2 and Fig. 1 - bottom). At the end of the session, the participants filled out a questionnaire to assess the perceived Quality and Functionality of the diagrams. Just before this evaluation, the same group of subjects participated in a study to evaluate the Quality and Functionality of the Process Model. The data regarding the Process Model evaluation is reported separately [15].

Considering the SEQUAL dimensions of Empirical Quality and Social Pragmatic Quality [12], we designed a questionnaire to evaluate the Quality and Functionality of diagram representations. We selected five dimensions from Krogstie's work to measure Empirical Quality and another five to measure Social Pragmatic Quality [12]. We also had three other questions to assess better the perceived Quality and Functionality of the diagrams [4, 8]. The complete questionnaire can be found in Appendix A[1].

An 11-items instrument, on a six-point scale ranging from 1 = *strongly disagree* to 6 = *strongly agree*, was designed. Two questions were negatively phrased and reversed before the statistical analyses. The questionnaire included questions related to both the scale Empirical Quality (e.g., "is it aesthetically attractive?"), Social Pragmatic Quality (e.g., "is it easy to read?") and Functionality (e.g., "is it functional?"). The scale Empirical Quality revealed good internal consistency (5-items, $N = 22$, $\alpha = .77$), as well as the scale Social Pragmatic Quality (5-items, $N = 22$, $\alpha = .8$).

In the first section of the questionnaire, participants were instructed to assess versions C and D of the Fact Model's diagrams for the same items.

---

[1] Available in https://bit.ly/QuestQualFunc.

In a second section of the questionnaire, participants were asked to compare both versions of the diagrams and pick which one was perceived as: (a) the easiest to understand the sequence of facts; (b) the easiest to visualize and understand the facts related to their professional activity; and (c) the most suitable for the execution of their daily tasks.

In the third section, the questionnaire included a question asking participants to suppose that, when executing their daily tasks, they had a doubt about which information should be included in the scope of a task and, in that case, where would they prefer to look up that information: in the Version C of the diagram + Fact Description Table, the Version D, or the legislation? Subjects assessed their preference on a six-point scale ranging from $1 = definitely$ not to $6 = definitely$ yes.

Finally, besides the demographic questions (age, gender, scholar level, and background), the participants were asked to self-report, on a six-point scale ranging from $1 = null$ to $6 = very good$, their knowledge level of: urban appraisal procedures, instruction of urban appraisal processes procedure, and DEMO. To guarantee that the comments were not associated with the answers in the survey, a separate page was attached with an open question, "Comments and suggestions for improvement".

Statistical analysis of the data was performed using computer software (IBM SPSS Statistics, version 27 for macOS X).

5   Results and Discussion

Overall results show that the CRD, CAD and FDT (Version C) were perceived as having a higher level of Quality and Functionality ($Mdn = 4.73$, $SD = .63$), when compared to the current DEMO representation ($Mdn = 3.32$, $SD = .84$), $z = -3.84$, $p = .000$, having a large [16] effect size ($r = -.82$). These results confirm our initial predictions (H_1). This might be explained by the aesthetics of the novel representation (Version C), as the collapsible boxes permit a more pleasant view of the information and allow to hide details that are not needed in a macro-view of the OFD (see Fig. 1) [2]. The FM representations of Version C seem to have overcome a limitation of the current format of the OFD in GOSL, which has several different elements, symbols, and text, making it very difficult to be interpreted by laypeople without experience in DEMO. Furthermore, we found that, in an overall analysis, even the participants of Sample B who don't have any self-reported knowledge of the modeling language DEMO, have perceived Version C's representations as having higher quality and functionality (Sample A: $Mdn_{VersionC} = 4.54$, $SD = .67$; $Mdn_{VersionD} = 2.77$, $SD = .51$; Sample B: $Mdn_{VersionC} = 4.77$, $SD = .61$; $Mdn_{VersionD} = 3.86$, $SD = .84$) assessed the Version C at a higher level, $z_{VersionC} = -2.524$, $p = .012$, $r = -.89$ and $z_{VersionD} = -2.972$, $p = .003$, $r = -.79$, respectively.

We hypothesized (H_2) that participants with higher self-reported knowledge of the modeled processes ($>= 4.5$) would evaluate as having a higher Quality and Functionality level, the Version C ($Mdn = 4.59$, $SD = .73$), when comparing with Version D ($Mdn = 2.86$, $SD = .83$), $z = -2.023$, $p = .043$, $r = -.83$. Results have confirmed this claim (H_2). It might be explained by the fact that Version C seems to be more cognitively effective, as it has less cluttered information, making it more pleasant to observe and with fewer elements to grasp [2]. This fact might have allowed the subject experts (Sample A) to understand the represented facts easily and, consequently, perceive this diagram as having a higher level of Quality and Functionality.

We explored our data to find out which version would have a higher perceived Quality and Functionality when assessed by participants with higher self-reported knowledge of the modeling language (knowledge of $>= 4.5$) (H$_3$). Results showed that these subjects also preferred Version C ($Mdn = 4.73, SD = .61$) over Version D ($Mdn = 3.91, SD = .77$), $z = -2.383, p = .017$, with a large [16] effect size ($r = -.79$), not confirming our initial hypothesis (H$_3$). Data shows us that even the modeling language knowledgeable subjects perceived the Version C as having more quality and being more functional. Literature shows that familiarity with a diagram often positively influences the evaluation of its EQ [11], but this was not true in our sample. We will further explore the data with a detailed analysis per variable.

We predicted that Version C would be assessed as having a higher level of Functionality (H$_4$) and data support this claim, in Sample B ($Mdn_{VersionC} = 5, SD = .77$; $Mdn_{VersionD} = 4, SD = 1.03, z = -2.565, p = .010, r = -.69$). Sample A also perceived the Functionality of Version C as having a higher level, but the results did not reach statistical significance. This confirms that participants perceive Version C as more functional than Version D.

Comparing the two versions of the diagrams, participants clearly preferred Version C. The large majority of the subjects selected the new representation as: the easiest to understand the facts and their relations; the easiest to visualize and understand the facts related to their professional activity; and the most suitable for executing their daily tasks (see Fig. 3). Literature mentions that some subjects prefer to acquire new information through formal models, while others prefer to get a mix of formal and informal statements to be more comprehensive [11]. Our data revealed that, when needed to clarify a question, the majority of the participants preferred to look up Version C, which attests to its perceived quality, functionality, and attractiveness.

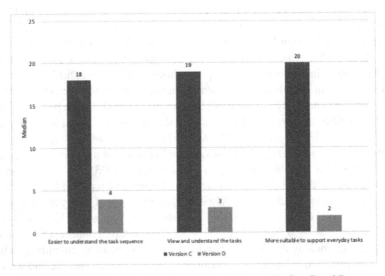

Fig. 3. Participants' preferences of the diagrams Version C and D.

5.1   Empirical Quality and Social Pragmatic Quality

To explore whether there was a statistically significant difference between the evaluation of both diagrams, we conducted a Wilcoxon matched-pairs signed-ranks test. We found that the level of scale EQ was higher in the Version C (Version C: $Mdn = 4.6$, $SD = .67$; Version D: $Mdn = 3.2$, $SD = .89$; $z = -3.876$, $p = .000$), with a large [11] effect size ($r = -.83$), which confirms hypothesis H_5. The items related to scale EQ (Color, Solidity, Aesthetics, Shape, Orientation) were better evaluated by our participants in Version C (see Table 3). When running an analysis per sample, the Empirical Quality (Color, Solidity, Aesthetics) of Version C has obtained a higher level, also with a large [16] effect size, on both Samples A and B (see Table 3). Version C emphasizes the represented information with retinal variables (like shape, size, and color), which may contribute to the perception of higher EQ on this representation, confirming previous studies [11]. While Version D is static, Version C is more dynamic, allowing to hide/show some details on the representation and even rearranging the boxes in the diagram without

Table 3. Comparison of the global assessment of Version C and D.

Items	Global means		Sample A (modeled process knowledgeable)		Sample B (modeling language knowledgeable)	
	z ($N = 22$)	r	z ($N = 8$)	r	z ($N = 14$)	r
EQ - Color	−3.165 (.002)	Large (−.68)	−1.997 (.046)	Large (−.71)	−2.401 (.016)	Large (.64)
EQ - Solidity	−3.064 (.002)	Large (−.65)	−2.226 (.026)	Large (−.79)	−2.090 (.037)	Large (−.56)
EQ - Aesthetics	−3.800 (.000)	Large (−.81)	−2.410 (.016)	Large (−.85)	−2.956 (.003)	Large (−.79)
EQ - Shape	−3.151 (.002)	Large (−.67)	NS*	–	−3.002 (.003)	Large (−.8)
EQ - Orientation	−2.728 (.006)	Large (−.58)	−2.271 (.023)	Large (−.8)	NS*	–
SPQ - Language Perception-Intelligibility	−3.297 (.001)	Large (−.7)	−2.116 (.034)	Large (−.75)	−2.508 (.012)	Large (−.67)
SPQ - Language Perception-Readiness	−3.516 (.001)	Large (−.75)	−2.539 (.011)	Large (−.9)	−2.442 (.015)	Large (−.65)
SPQ - Language Perception-Comprehension	−2.883 (.003)	Large (−.62)	−2.263 (.024)	Large (−.8)	NS*	–
SPQ - Content Relevance	−3.226 (.001)	Large (−.69)	−2.070 (.038)	Large (−.73)	−2.495 (.013)	Large (−.67)
SPQ - Structured Analysis	NS*	–	NS*	–	NS*	–

* Non-significant.

losing their connections. Participants may have viewed these features as a sign of a higher EQ of Version C and scored accordingly.

Results of the SPQ showed that our hypothesis H_6 was true, as the representations of Version C were evaluated as having a higher SPQ (Version C: $Mdn = 4.7, SD = .69$; Version D: $Mdn = 3.6, SD = .85; z = -3.652, p = .000$), with a large [11] effect size ($r = -.78$) (see Table 3). These results show that participants seem to have a better understanding of the Fact Model representation in Version C. Analyzing the results of SPQ on both samples separately, we found that the items Language Perception-Intelligibility, Language Perception-Readiness, and Content Relevance were better assessed in Version C, when compared to Version D (see Table 3).

Literature suggests that individuals knowledgeable of formal languages would prefer a formal model. In contrast, laypeople will find a mix of formal and informal statements to be more understandable, even if the set of statements in the complete model is redundant [11]. In our study, the participants who have self-reported knowledge of formal languages (Sample B) and the laypeople group (Sample A), preferred Version C, where we can find a mix of formal and informal elements. This might be explained by the fact that the sample of individuals with knowledge of formal languages was composed of students who might not be experienced enough and, therefore, would still prefer a mix of formal and informal statements [11]. Future research is needed to understand if the familiarity with formal languages mediates the option that participants find more intelligible: (a) formal model (Version D), or (b) model including a mix of formal and informal statements (Version C).

In the question "Imagine that in the course of your duties, you had a doubt about which information should be included in the scope of a task, we presented three options: I would consult the... a....diagram version C – conference + Fact Description Table; b....diagram version D - DEMO; c....the legislation". Subjects revealed that they clearly preferred to look up the information on Version C (Version C: $Mdn = 5, SD = .62$; Version D: $Mdn = 3, SD = 1.42; z = -3.496, p = .000, r = -.76$; and Version C: $Mdn = 5, SD = .62$; Legislation: $Mdn = 3, SD = 1.83; z = -2.982, p = .003, r = -.65$). The results in this question show that, when looking for information to clarify questions about the scope of their tasks, the majority of the participants would prefer Version C, over Version D and over the legislation itself. It confirms our hypothesis H_7 and reveals the huge potential that participants find in this new representation.

6   Conclusions

In this paper, we present the results of the evaluation of the Fact Model diagrams proposed in [2], namely the Concepts and Relationships Diagram, the Concept Attribute Diagram, and the Fact Description Table (Version C). Furthermore, we compared them to the previous version of the Fact Model representation in [13] (Version D). We found that the new representations are evaluated as cognitively more effective than DEMO's Fact Model representations. Our data revealed that, when needing to clarify a question, the majority of the participants say they would prefer to look up the novel representations, which certifies their perceived quality, functionality, and attractiveness.

As discussed at the conference, it is relevant to stress that these representations of the Fact Model (Version C and D) are not strictly equivalent in their syntax and semantics.

Consequently, and motivated by practical experience with stakeholders willing to make use of the models in their daily procedures, the standard DEMO representations (Version D) were altered (Version C): (a) in its representation by excluding event types; (b) by simplifying the value types, sort, base types, measuring units and dimensions from FM's meta-model; (c) by including cross-representations from adjacent aspect-models (e.g., CM's transactions and transaction steps responsible for creating or updating an attribute's value); and (d) expanding the meta-model with new elements (e.g., attribute's description and source). Hence, version C is not semantically equivalent to Version D, and we consider it an evolution offering much more information to the stakeholders mainly due to the TDT and the new diagrams, which are easily modifiable to meet their needs. As such, this comparison should not be seen as a way to determine what are the best (semantically equivalent) representations for a specific aspect model (FM) but, instead, to determine what are the best and most functional representations to present in a layered way all the relevant information in the FM.

Nonetheless, this study is not without its shortcomings. Reaching a wider public, than the public officials and the university-level students that constituted our data source, can provide valuable insights that were not statistically captured with the limited resources at our disposal.

We invite the research community to extend this study to organizations operating in different areas and with distinct stakeholders. Only then would it be possible to mitigate the inherent risk of overgeneralizing results based on a limited sample size. We recommend controlling the subjects' backgrounds to detect variations in the perceived Quality and Functionality of the models. Different speakers should perform the initial briefings to avoid prejudice when presenting the diagrams. The new representations should be evaluated by experts, relying on the metrics of the SEQUAL framework, to uncover areas of improvement and assess the cognitive effectiveness of the diagrams.

The first main contribution of this paper is increased awareness of how users perceived the Fact Model representations in terms of their Quality and Functionality. Second, the knowledge derived from this study is an important stepping stone towards making DEMO, and the Fact Model in particular, more accessible and inclusive to the full range of stakeholders who play a role in an organization's daily operation. Third, the questionnaire in Appendix A can be reused in other studies regarding DEMO representations. We believe that applied research over the users' experience will spark a reflection on the reasoning behind the choice of representations. At the very least, there is practical evidence that the current boundaries defined by DEMO's aspect models should not be written in stone and that representations should be, to a varying degree, dependent on the intended stakeholders or client organization's needs.

Acknowledgments. Special thanks to the participants in the study that contributed with their fruitful insights and feedback. This work was supported by the Regional Development European Fund (INTERREG MAC), projects Dynamic eGov MAC2/5.11a/359 (MAC-2014-2020), and FiiHUB MAC2/2.3d/335 (MAC-2014-2020).

References

1. Dietz, J.L.G.: Enterprise Ontology: Theory and Methodology. Springer, Heidelberg (2006). https://doi.org/10.1007/3-540-33149-2
2. Gouveia, B., Aveiro, D., Pacheco, D., Pinto, D., Gouveia, D.: Fact model in DEMO - urban law case and proposal of representation improvements. In: Aveiro, D., Guizzardi, G., Pergl, R., Proper, H.A. (eds.) EEWC 2020. LNBIP, vol. 411, pp. 173–190. Springer, Cham (2021). https://doi.org/10.1007/978-3-030-74196-9_10
3. Dietz, J.L.G., Mulder, H.B.F.: The enterprise engineering theories. In: Dietz, J.L.G., Mulder, H.B.F. (eds.) Enterprise Ontology: A Human-Centric Approach to Understanding the Essence of Organisation, pp. 23–48. Springer, Cham (2020). https://doi.org/10.1007/978-3-030-388 54-6_4
4. Larkin, J.H., Simon, H.A.: Why a diagram is (Sometimes) worth ten thousand words. Cogn. Sci. **11**, 65–100 (1987). https://doi.org/10.1016/S0364-0213(87)80026-5
5. Bertin, J.: Sémiologie graphique. Les diagrammes, les réseaux, les cartes. Éditions de l'École des hautes études en sciences sociales (1973)
6. Mendling, J., Reijers, H.A., van der Aalst, W.M.P.: Seven process modeling guidelines (7PMG). Inf. Softw. Technol. **52**, 127–136 (2010). https://doi.org/10.1016/j.infsof.2009. 08.004
7. Krogstie, J., Sindre, G., Jørgensen, H.: Process models representing knowledge for action: a revised quality framework. Eur. J. Inf. Syst. **15**, 91–102 (2006). https://doi.org/10.1057/pal grave.ejis.3000598
8. Moody, D.: The "Physics" of notations: toward a scientific basis for constructing visual notations in software engineering. IEEE Trans. Softw. Eng. **35**, 756–779 (2009). https://doi. org/10.1109/TSE.2009.67
9. Genon, N., Heymans, P., Amyot, D.: Analysing the cognitive effectiveness of the BPMN 2.0 visual notation. In: Malloy, B., Staab, S., van den Brand, M. (eds.) SLE 2010. LNCS, vol. 6563, pp. 377–396. Springer, Heidelberg (2011). https://doi.org/10. 1007/978-3-642-19440-5_25
10. Sedera, W., Rosemann, M., Doebeli, G.: A process modelling success model: insights from a case study. In: Proceedings 11th European Conference on Information Systems, Naples, Italy (2003)
11. Krogstie, J.: SEQUAL specialized for business process models. In: Krogstie, J. (ed.) Quality in Business Process Modeling, pp. 103–138. Springer, Cham (2016). https://doi.org/10.1007/ 978-3-319-42512-2_3
12. Krogstie, J.: Quality of business process models. In: Krogstie, J. (ed.) Quality in Business Process Modeling, pp. 53–102. Springer, Cham (2016). https://doi.org/10.1007/978-3-319-42512-2_2
13. Dietz, J.L.G., Mulder, H.B.F.: The DEMO methodology. In: Dietz, J.L.G., Mulder, H.B.F. (eds.) Enterprise Ontology: A Human-Centric Approach to Understanding the Essence of Organisation, pp. 261–299. Springer, Cham (2020). https://doi.org/10.1007/978-3-030-38854-6_12
14. Pinto, D., Aveiro, D., Pacheco, D., Gouveia, B., Gouveia, D.: Validation of DEMO's concise-ness quality and proposal of improvements to the process model. In: Aveiro, D., Guizzardi, G., Pergl, R., Proper, H.A. (eds.) Advances in Enterprise Engineering XIV, pp. 133–152. Springer, Cham (2021). https://doi.org/10.1007/978-3-030-74196-9_8
15. Pacheco, D., Aveiro, D., Pinto, D., Gouveia, B.: Towards the X-theory: an evaluation of the perceived quality and functionality of DEMO's process model. In: Aveiro, D., et al. (eds.) EEWC 2021, LNBIP 441, pp. 129–148. Springer, Heidelberg (2022)
16. Field, A.P.: Discovering Statistics Using IBM SPSS Statistics: and sex and Drugs and Rock 'n' Roll. Sage, Los Angeles (2013)

Towards the X-Theory: An Evaluation of the Perceived Quality and Functionality of DEMO's Process Model

Dulce Pacheco[1,2,3](✉) ⓘ, David Aveiro[1,3,4] ⓘ, Duarte Pinto[1,3] ⓘ,
and Bernardo Gouveia[1,3,4] ⓘ

[1] ARDITI - Regional Agency for the Development of Research, Technology and Innovation,
9020-105 Funchal, Portugal
{dulce.pacheco,duarte.nuno,bernardo.gouveia}@arditi.pt
[2] School of Technology and Management, University of Madeira, Caminho da Penteada,
9020-105 Funchal, Portugal
[3] NOVA-LINCS, Universidade NOVA de Lisboa, Campus da Caparica,
2829-516 Caparica, Portugal
[4] Faculty of Exact Sciences and Engineering, University of Madeira, Caminho da Penteada,
9020-105 Funchal, Portugal
daveiro@uma.pt

Abstract. The Design and Engineering Methodology for Organizations (DEMO) comprises a set of models and diagrams to represent an organization. A proposal for a new Process Diagram and a Transaction Description Table fuses part of the contents of DEMO's Process, Cooperation, and Action models. It claims to have achieved a more agile and comprehensive solution to depict the essence of organizational reality. We designed and conducted a pilot study to evaluate the perceived Quality and Functionality of the traditional and alternative representations. Our study was designed to collect feedback both from a group of professionals experienced in the modeled processes ($N = 8$) and a group experienced in the modeling language DEMO ($N = 14$). Subjects attended a presentation about the traditional and the new diagrams and filled out a questionnaire. Our data withstands the claims that the new way to represent the Process Model is more accessible and easier to grasp by the professionals working with those processes and by students with knowledge of DEMO. These findings set the ground and first steps of the *X-theory*, which aims to set the principles of more effective representations of DEMO models based on a sound theoretical and empirical ground.

Keywords: Enterprise engineering · DEMO · Cognitive effectiveness ·
Perceived quality · Empirical Quality · Social Pragmatic Quality · Functionality ·
X-theory

1 Introduction

Representations of business processes are commonly used to support systems implementation (e.g., information systems, quality control). The perceived quality and functionality of these representations influence the system's quality. If the representations are

© Springer Nature Switzerland AG 2022
D. Aveiro et al. (Eds.): EEWC 2021, LNBIP 441, pp. 129–148, 2022.
https://doi.org/10.1007/978-3-031-11520-2_9

inaccurate, the processes are ill-represented or ambiguous, the system will most probably incorporate these inaccuracies, compromising business and workers' efficiency. Therefore, the quality, functionality, and cognitive effectiveness of diagrams representing business processes are vital for effective systems implementation.

The Design and Engineering Methodology for Organizations (DEMO) consists of a method and language standard based on the theories of Enterprise Ontology [1]. DEMO's Way of modeling comprises a set of correlated models and diagrams to represent an organization in a coherent and platform-independent way [2]. The DEMO's Cooperation Model and Process Model represent similar information (process dependencies regarding the structure and flow control), which can be a burden to keep up to date with every change, especially when modeling complex processes or in a collaborative setting. This traditional way of modeling, from here on, will be referred to as Version B.

Previous work [3] has proposed new semantically enriched representations of the Process Model (called Version A onwards), claiming to be more accessible and easier to grasp, either by professionals working with the represented processes, or professionals with knowledge of DEMO [3]. This paper presents a formal validation of these claims based on a pilot study to evaluate diagrams' perceived Quality and Functionality. We collected data from two samples: one comprising professionals experienced in the represented processes; and another composed of students experienced in the DEMO modeling language.

In this study, we defined and tested the following hypotheses:

H_i Version A is perceived as having higher overall Quality and Functionality.
H_{ii} Version A is perceived as having higher Functionality.
H_{iii} Version A is perceived as having higher Empirical Quality.
H_{iv} Version A is perceived as having higher Social Pragmatic Quality.
H_v Subjects with higher self-reported knowledge of the modeled processes ($> = 4.5$) perceive Version A as having higher overall Quality and Functionality.
H_{vi} subjects with higher self-reported knowledge of the modeling language ($> = 4.5$) perceive Version B as having higher overall Quality and Functionality.
H_{vii} The majority of subjects pick Version A rather than Version B or legislation when prompted to decide where to look to clarify their questions about a specific task.

This paper is organized into six sections. After this introduction, we present the state-of-the-art, followed by the study context, method, results, and discussion of its implications. Finally, we finish with a summary of the contributions and limitations.

2   Literature Review

Research in diagrammatical reasoning shows that representations have an equal, if not greater, influence on cognitive effectiveness (speed, ease, and accuracy) as content [4].

2.1   Process Modeling Evaluation Frameworks

Previous research has depicted different frameworks to support process modeling, e.g., GoM - Guidelines of modeling [5], 7PMG - Seven Process modeling Guidelines [6]

SEQUAL - Semiotic Quality Framework [7], and the Physics of Notations Theory [8]. Even though criteria and guidelines to design process models are available, metrics and clear criteria to evaluate some principles are uneven [9]. When available, the metrics and criteria are mostly focused on a technical evaluation of the diagram by the modelers [9]. Previous researchers [10] have identified user satisfaction as one of the four measures of their process modeling success model, but its evaluation method and criteria are not clearly defined.

This section will briefly focus on two popular frameworks to design and evaluate process modeling [11]: Physics of Notations theory and SEQUAL framework.

2.2 Physics of Notations Theory

The Physics of Notations theory [8] provides a framework developed explicitly for visual notations. It defines a set of 9 evidence-based principles to evaluate and improve the visual notation of modeling languages. In addition, these principles may be used to generate empirically testable predictions. The nine principles are [8]:

1. Semiotic Clarity: there should be a one-to-one correspondence between semantic constructs and graphical symbols.
2. Perceptual Discriminability: symbols should be undoubtedly distinguishable.
3. Semantic Transparency: use symbols whose appearance is evocative.
4. Complexity Management: includes mechanisms for handling complexity.
5. Cognitive Integration: includes explicit mechanisms to support integrating information from different diagrams.
6. Visual Expressiveness: use the full range and capacities of visual variables.
7. Dual Coding: enrich diagrams with textual descriptions.
8. Graphic Economy: keep the number of different graphical symbols cognitively manageable.
9. Cognitive Fit: use different visual dialects for different tasks and audiences.

Evaluations of notations against these principles often rely on values of visual variables, i.e., the elementary characteristics forming the visual alphabet of diagrammatic notations [9]. However, even once the set of symbols and semantic constructs are defined, the Physics of Notations does not provide a comprehensive theory to analyze, evaluate, and improve the cognitive effectiveness of visual modeling languages [9]. Furthermore, these principles are more focused on a technical evaluation of the representation, not an assessment by the users of the diagram's perceived quality and functionality.

2.3 SEQUAL

SEQUAL framework sees modeling activities as socially situated (constructivist perspective). It recognizes that significant models are typically created as part of a dialogue between the stakeholders involved in modeling and whose knowledge of the modeling domain changes as modeling occurs [12].

The Semiotic Model Quality (SEQUAL) proposes a list of general qualities for modeling languages [12]:

1. Physical: the persistence, currency, and availability of the process model.
2. Empirical: the relationship between the process model and another process model that contains the same statements, which are somehow regarded as better through a different arrangement or layout.
3. Syntactic: the relationship between the process model and the process modeling language.
4. Semantic: the relationship between the process model and the modeling domain. Perceived semantic quality is the parallel relationship between the participants' knowledge and their interpretation of the process model.
5. Pragmatic: the relationship between the process model and the stakeholder's interpretation of the model.
6. Social: the relationship between different process model interpretations.
7. Deontic: the fit between the process models and the modeling goals.

The main concepts and their relationships to the SEQUAL framework are depicted in Fig. 1.

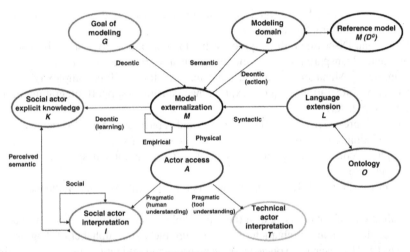

Fig. 1. SEQUAL framework [12]

This framework differentiates between Empirical Quality (on comprehensibility) and Social Pragmatic Quality (on actual human comprehension). The differentiation is based on the empirical investigation of the framework's applicability and the utility of distinguishing the dichotomy of technical and social aspects [11].

2.4 Perceived Quality and Functionality in Diagrams

Within the field of information systems, many approaches to quality have been proposed [11], but it is still a problematic notion. Process models may be difficult to comprehend due to the (un)formality of the modeling language, the complexity or size of the model, or the effort needed to infer its important properties [12].

Within the software quality models, functional suitability is described as the degree to which a system provides functions that meet stated and implied needs [13]. Functional suitability is divided into (a) functional completeness (the degree to which the set of functions covers all the specified tasks and user objectives), (b) functional correctness (the degree to which a product or system provides the correct results with the needed degree of precision), and (c) functional appropriateness (the degree to which the functions facilitate the accomplishment of specified tasks and objectives) [13]. Users tend to select artifacts that provide the needed information to perform their tasks, which they consider more functional. Our study hypothesized that subjects would evaluate Version A as having higher overall perceived Quality and Functionality (H_i) and would also perceive the diagrams on Version A as more functional (H_{ii}).

Literature mentions that familiarity with the processes and the language used helps better understand the representations [12]. Therefore, we anticipated that participants with higher perceived knowledge of the modeled processes ($> = 4.5$) would evaluate Version A as having a higher perceived Quality and Functionality (H_v). In comparison, subjects with higher perceived knowledge of the modeling language ($> = 4.5$) would evaluate Version B (current DEMO representation) as having a higher perceived Quality and Functionality (H_{vi}).

Empirical Quality (EQ). EQ entails eight different variables: planar variables (horizontal and vertical position) and retinal variables (shape, size, color, brightness, orientation, and texture) [12]. Other uses of emphasis can also be considered when evaluating the EQ of a model [12]. Factors that have been shown to have a meaningful impact on visual emphasis are as follows: solidity, differences in patterns, foreground/background differences, change (movement), position, and connectivity [12].

Rules for color usage in the diagrams must be defined. Some authors have mentioned the need to avoid using colors as a part of the notation for conveying meaning. Still, color has been reported as an essential differentiator in visual representations [11].

The aesthetics of the diagrams is part of its EQ. Previous studies have identified guidelines for graph aesthetics [12], which enables the definition of metrics to assess and improve the representation technically [12]. Aesthetics is a subjective matter, where the familiarity with a diagram often positively influences the evaluation of its EQ [12], which we tested in our hypothesis H_{iii}.

Considering that Version A has a more attractive aesthetics and presents color as a differentiator, we hypothesized that participants would evaluate Version A as having a higher EQ (H_{iii}).

Social Pragmatic Quality (SPQ). Pragmatic Quality is the correspondence between the available part of the diagram and the actor's interpretation [11]. The actors may be human stakeholders or technical actors [12]. The SPQ (to what extent people understand the model) is distinguished from the Technical Pragmatic Quality (to what extent tools can be made that can interpret the model) [11]. When evaluating these variables, we assess if the diagram has been understood and who has understood (the relevant parts of) it [12].

Pragmatic Quality encloses four dimensions [12]: Language Perception, Content Relevance, Structured Analysis, and Behavior Experience. While some individuals are familiar with formal languages and, consequently, a formal model guarantees their under-standing, others find a mix of formal and informal statements more intelligible [12]. This is true even if the set of statements in the complete model is redundant [12].

We hypothesized that participants would evaluate Version A as having a higher SPQ (H_{iv}). Furthermore, when prompted to choose just one option (between Version A, Version B, or legislation) to clarify their questions about the process, most would pick Version A (H_{vii}).

3   Study Context

3.1   DEMO Methodology

The DEMO methodology Way of modeling, based on the PSI theory [1], consists of a method and language standard based on the theories of Enterprise Ontology. DEMO comprises a set of models and diagrams set by conventions to represent an organization, namely the Cooperation Model (CM), the Action Model (AM), the Process Model (PM), and the Fact Model (FM) [14]. They are correlated with each other, representing coherent information in a platform-independent way [2]. In this article, we will focus on the CM and PM.

The CM specifies the organization's construction and transaction types and is the most concise one. It also states the identified transactor roles (the elements) and the coordination structures (the influencing relationships) between them [14].

The PM of an organization is a model of the (business) processes that take place as the effect of acts by actors [14]. The PM of an organization connects its CM and AM, as far as coordination is concerned. It contains, for all internal and border transaction kinds, the process step kinds, as well as the applicable existence laws. For all transaction kinds, the PM reveals the process step kinds and the applicable occurrence laws, including the cardinalities of the occurrences [14].

3.2   Version a of the Process Model Representations

In [3], a new way to represent the PM was proposed (Version A), which fuses some contents of the standard DEMO PM with some elements of both the CM and AM, thus extending the traditional notation (Version B) presented in [1]. These representations were created out of the need for a more agile and comprehensive solution to compile and present the essence of organizational reality. It shows all information deemed visually necessary to comprehend the process concisely, while still easy (enough) to understand by modelers and stakeholders. To fill the gaps of all the process information that would overburden the model, a Transaction Description Table (TDT) was also proposed, where the more text-intensive relevant data can be added, namely: descriptions of transactions, conditions for them to take place, associated rules, time constraints, among other ele-ments. In Fig. 2, we present the meaning of each symbol used in Version A. A partial example of a process diagram is pictured at the bottom of Fig. 3. This figure also com-pares the traditional notation in [1] (Version B), representing the exact extent of that

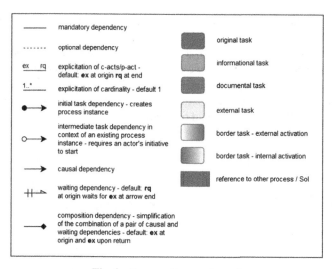

Fig. 2. Process diagram legend

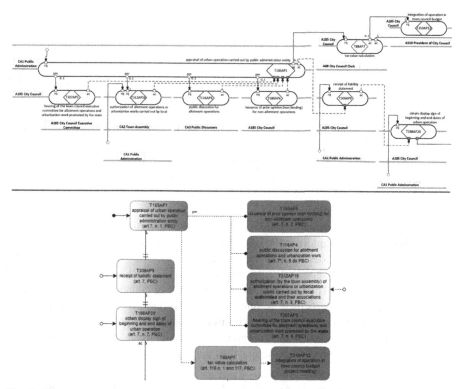

Fig. 3. Process structure diagram (version B) on the top, and process diagram (version A) on the bottom.

process. We use the terms transaction and task as synonyms due to usability concerns, as reported in [3].

In the TDT (example in Fig. 4), a detailed description of each task is provided in a structured way. For each task, we can find its scope of interest (process), name, description (often copy of the legislation), where it was originated, tasks on-hold (if needed), tasks created from it, the conditions or rules that need to be verified before the execution of the following task(s), and time constraints.

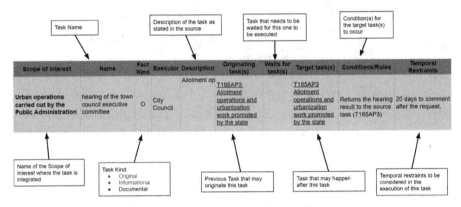

Fig. 4. Transaction description table

Version A representation [3] solved several issues regarding current DEMO CM and PM representations. The Coordination Structure Diagram and Process Structure Diagram of the latest DEMO version [14] were considered, by both stakeholders and modelers alike, to be complicated to grasp and with extensive line clutter. The way we depicted the PM (Fig. 3) is semantically richer by: (a) presenting task names, much closer to day-to-day operations; (b) it clearly separates the concerns of process composition, task causation, and task waiting; (c) the connectors represent the composition perspective with diamonds, the causal by connectors with arrows, and the waiting by the connectors with double-crossed lines.

A simpler notation was also proposed for border transactions with color gradients which could easily and rapidly make us understand which tasks are initiated by internal actors and executed by external actors and vice versa.

Regarding links between tasks, the notation was that dashed meant optional and non-dashed mandatory. The use of numbers at the end of connectors to represent that essential concept is harder/slower to interpret than the line expressing the concept, so their use was limited to reflect cardinalities higher than 1. The proposed notation in [3] offered a new layer of depth in the comprehension of the modeled process, improving the readability of the limits of the scope with the use of specific symbols to represent other related processes.

In [3], diagram complexity was significantly diminished for the same modeled artifacts. This decrease was due to: the better use of space of the task/process symbols as opposed to the traditional PSDs transaction symbol; the reduction of the represented connectors; and the removal of the explicit representation of actor roles. It was also found necessary to differentiate border transactions, thus the new special symbols with color gradients, to clearly depict external activation (external initiating actor) or internal activation (external executing actor). The TDT was found as a much better place to represent the concrete actor roles and organizational functions.

The TDT in [3] ends up being a thorough Action Model by specifying both Action Rules Specification (columns "Originating task(s)", "Target task(s)", "Waits for task(s)" and "Conditions/Rules"), as well as, some work instructions often included in the task descriptions. The TDT aims to replace the standard representation of the AM, and overcome its limitedness, rigidity, formality, and disconnection from the operational reality and needs.

4   Method

4.1   Participants

To evaluate the perceived Quality and Functionality of the newly proposed representations for DEMOs PM, two samples were recruited: a group of professionals with knowledge of the modeled processes (Sample A: $N = 8$, six female and two male, $M_{age} = 45$, age range: 33–54 years), and a group of students with knowledge of the modeling language (Sample B: $N = 14$, five female and nine male, $M_{age} = 24$, age range: 20–43 years). The overall sample ($N = 22$) had gender equality (50% females and 50% males) and a mean age of 32 years (age range: 20–54 years). The participants had diverse backgrounds and scholar levels (see Table 1).

Table 1. Characterization of the sample

	Background				Scholar level		
	Architecture	Human/Social sciences	Law	Other	High school	Bachelor	Master
Sample A	4	0	3	1	0	5	3
Sample B	0	3	0	11	2	11	1
N	4	3	3	12	2	16	4

4.2   Materials and Procedure

The experiment started with a briefing to explain the study to the participants and collect their informed consent. All subjects voluntarily agreed to participate in the study. The briefing was conducted by a DEMO certified teacher who recapped the main DEMO concepts, namely the distinction axiom, the transaction axiom, roles, responsibilities and delegations, transactions (called tasks in [3]), and their implications. It was presented to the participants the traditional Process Model representation [14] (Version B on top of Fig. 3) and the newly proposed way of representing [3] (Version A on the bottom of Fig. 3), namely the Process Diagram and Transaction Description Table (Fig. 4). At the end of the session, the participants filled out a questionnaire to assess the perceived Quality and Functionality of the diagrams (see Appendix A[1]). After that, the same group of subjects participated in another briefing about the new Fact Model diagrams and evaluated them. The data regarding the Fact Model evaluation is reported in [15].

Due to the study's goal and limited time/resources of both the research team and participants, we designed a short questionnaire to evaluate the perceived Quality and Functionality of the diagrams, based on previous work on the quality of representations and Functionality evaluations [11].

Considering the study's goal, we included: four questions to evaluate the Functionality of the diagrams; one question ("is it functional?") using a six-point scale ranging from 1 = *strongly disagree* to 6 = *strongly agree*; and three questions where subjects were forced to pick which version (A or B) they consider as more functional (e.g., which version is "more suitable to support the execution of their tasks").

Besides the questions about Functionality, we selected two dimensions from the SEQUAL framework [11] related to the perceived quality of the diagrams, namely EQ and SPQ, from which we generate predictions empirically testable. We included five questions to assess EQ (e.g., "is it aesthetically attractive?") and another five to assess SPQ (e.g., "is it easy to read?"). The questionnaire was a 10-items instrument on a six-point scale ranging from 1 = *strongly disagree* to 6 = *strongly agree*. Two questions were negatively phrased and reversed before the statistical analyses. The scale EQ revealed good internal consistency (5-items, $N = 22$, $\alpha = .72$). The scale SPQ also reached a good internal consistency (5-items, $N = 22$, $\alpha = .83$). Participants were instructed to assess, in the exact same 10-items, the Version A of the Process Model diagrams and the Version B.

The questionnaire also asked participants to imagine that they were unsure whom (person and/or department) they should forward a specific process while executing their daily tasks. Hence, they had to pick where they would prefer to look up that information: in the diagram Version A and the Transaction Description Table, the diagram Version B, or look directly into the legislation. Subjects assessed this probability on a six-point scale ranging from 1 = *definitely not* to 6 = *definitely yes*.

Finally, besides the demographic questions (age, gender, scholar level, and background), the participants were asked to self-report their knowledge of: urban appraisal procedures, instruction on urban appraisal processes procedures, and DEMO, on a six-point scale ranging from 1 = *null* to 6 = *very good*. The open question "Comments and suggestions for improvement" was attached on a separate page to ensure that the participants' comments were not associated with their survey. The complete questionnaire can be found in Appendix A[1].

Statistical analyses of the data were performed using computer software (IBM SPSS Statistics, version 27 for MacOS X).

---

[1] Available in https://bit.ly/QuestQualFunc

5   Results and Discussion

Wilcoxon tests were conducted to compare the perceived Quality and Functionality of the diagrams. Overall results showed that the Version A of the Process Diagram and Transaction Description Table was perceived as having a higher level ($Mdn = 4.68$, $SD = .5$), over Version B ($Mdn = 3.36$, $SD = 1.07$), $z = -3.31$, $p = .001$, with a large [16] effect size ($r = -.71$). These results confirmed our hypothesis H_i, that is, Version A is perceived as having higher Quality and Functionality.

Exploring the results independently per sample, we found that both the Sample A (Version A: $Mdn = 4.45$, $SD = .6$; Version B: $Mdn = 2.59$, $SD = .98$) and the Sample B (Version A: $Mdn = 5$, $SD = .80$; Version B: $Mdn = 3.5$, $SD = 1.09$) assessed the Version A in a higher level of perceived Quality and Functionality, $z = -2.103$, $p = .035$, $r = -.74$ and $z = -2.633$, $p = .008$, $r = -.7$, respectively.

Hypothesis H_{ii} predicted that Version A would be assessed as having a higher level of Functionality. Results confirmed our hypothesis, being Version A the better evaluated (Version A: $Mdn = 5$, $SD = .71$; Version B: $Mdn = 4.5$, $SD = 1.56$; $z = -2.371$, $p = .018$, $r = -.51$) (see Fig. 5). When comparing the functionality of Version A and B, data revealed that subjects perceived Version A as easier to understand task sequence, view/understand the tasks, and as more suitable to support the execution of their daily tasks (see Fig. 6). Literature mentions that some subjects preferred to acquire new information through formal models, while others believed that getting a mix of formal and informal statements to be more comprehensive [11]. Our data revealed that, when needing to clarify a question, the majority of the participants preferred to look up Version A, which attests to its perceived quality, functionality, and attractiveness.

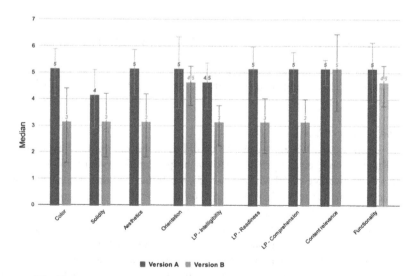

Fig. 5. Comparison of the global assessment of version A and B, per item.

We hypothesized (H_v) that participants with higher self-reported knowledge of urban appraisal processes (the modeled processes) ($> = 4.5$) would evaluate as having a higher perceived Quality and Functionality, the Version A. However, the results for this analysis did not reach statistical significance ($N = 6$; Version A: $Mdn = 4.68$, $SD = .58$; Version B: $Mdn = 2.86$, $SD = 1.35$) (see Fig. 7). This might be due to the small sample size ($N = 6$). A further study with a larger sample should be conducted to investigate this connection deeply.

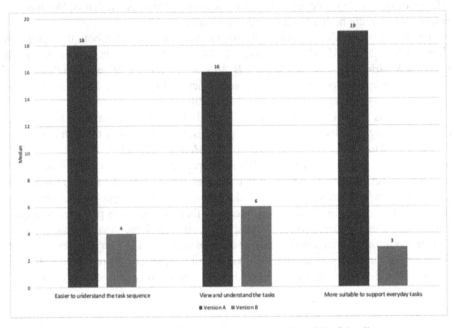

Fig. 6. Comparison of the functionality of version A and B of the diagrams.

Finally, we predicted that those with higher self-reported knowledge of DEMO ($> = 4.5$) would classify as having higher perceived Quality and Functionality, the Version B [H_{vi}]; however, data showed that even these participants conferred higher punctuation to Version A ($N = 9$; Version A: $Mdn = 4.64$, $SD = .42$; Version B: $Mdn = 3.91$, $SD = .96$), $z = -2.077$, $p = .038$, $r = -.69$, which did not confirm our initial hypothesis (see Fig. 8). Running another analysis to uncover the preferred version of those who self-reported low knowledge of DEMO ($< = 1.5$), we found that they also grant a higher evaluation to Version A ($N = 3$; Version A: $Mdn = 4.64$, $SD = .68$; Version B: $Mdn = 2.55$, $SD = .51$; $z = -1.633$, $p = .102$, $r = -.94$).

Previous authors have identified that familiarity with a modeling language often positively influences its evaluation [10]. Our study found that the preferred option of Sample B (modeling language knowledgeable subjects) was Version A, rather than Version B that they were familiar with. Further studies must be conducted to explore this hypothesis.

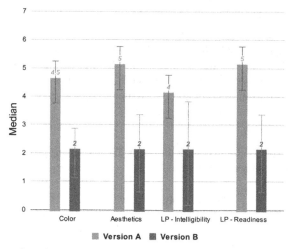

Fig. 7. Evaluation of version A and B, by the participants with self-reported knowledge of the modeled processes (sample A).

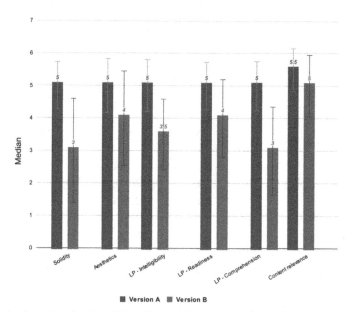

Fig. 8. Evaluation of version A and B, by the participants with self-reported knowledge of DEMO (sample B).

5.1 Empirical Quality

We ran a Wilcoxon test to assess hypothesis H_{iii}. We uncovered statistically significant differences in the evaluation of the scale EQ. According to our data, higher perceived EQ (Version A: $Mdn = 4.6$, $SD = .62$; Version B: $Mdn = 3.4$, $SD = 1.14$; $z = -3.063$, p

= .002), with a large [16] effect size ($r = -.65$) was achieved by Version A, confirming hypothesis H_{iii}.

When analyzing the EQ variables independently, we found that the variables Color, Solidity, Aesthetics, and Orientation also reached statistically significant results, showing that Version A was perceived as having higher EQ (see Table 2 and Fig. 5).

These results confirm that Version A revealed a higher level of perceived EQ; it is regarded as having a better arrangement and layout [11].

Table 2. Wilcoxon test's results compare the evaluation of diagrams' Version A and B, per item, in an overall analysis and per sample.

Items	Overall analysis		Sample A (modeled process knowledgeable)		Sample B (modeling language knowledgeable)	
	z ($N = 22$)	r	z ($N = 8$)	r	z ($N = 14$)	r
SQ (Color)	−2.950 (.003)	Large (−.63)	−2.414 (.016)	Large (−.85)	NS*	—
SQ (Solidity)	−2.425 (.015)	Large (−.52)	NS*	—	−2.438 (.015)	Large (−.65)
SQ (Aesthetics)	-3.397 (.001)	Large (−.72)	−2.266 (.023)	Large (−.8)	−2.842 (.004)	Large (−.76)
SQ (Shape)	NS*	—	NS*	—	NS*	—
SQ (Orientation)	−1.968 (.049)	Medium (−.42)	NS*	—	NS*	—
SPQ (Language perception-intelligibility)	−3.414 (.001)	Large (−.73)	−2.238 (.025)	Large (−.79)	−2.672 (.008)	Large (−.71)
SPQ (Language perception-readiness)	−3.346 (.001)	Large (−.71)	−2.116 (.034)	Large (−.75)	−2.799 (.005)	Large (−.75)
SPQ (Language perception-comprehension)	−2.936 (.003)	Large (−.63)	NS*	—	−2.401 (.016)	Large (−.64)
SPQ (Content relevance)	−2.722 (.006)	Large (−.58)	NS*	—	−2.070 (.038)	Large (−.55)
SPQ (Structured analysis)	NS*	—	NS*	—	NS*	—

* Non-significant

According to the literature, Color can represent a crucial visual differentiator [11]. Both representations use Color to distinguish between the ontological, infological, or datalogical facts (see Fig. 3). Feedback from the participants indicates that the Color and attractive Aesthetics of Version A improved the task's clear identification and understandability, which confirms previous claims that stress the relevance of these visual emphases to improve EQ and cognitive effectiveness [11].

The variable Shape did not reach statistically significant results. Further research is needed to evaluate the usage of symbols and their syntactic quality.

Previous studies claim that familiarity with a diagram often positively influences the evaluation of its Aesthetics [12]; however, our data only partially supports this claim. When comparing the evaluation given by Sample A and B, we found that Sample B (which has undergone DEMO training) evaluated the diagrams more positively than Sample A. Nevertheless, the preferred option for Sample B was still Version A of the Process Model (see Table 2, Fig. 5, and Fig. 8).

Our study evaluated the perceived EQ of the diagrams, but further studies should be conducted to technically evaluate all the metrics available within EQ in the SEQUAL model to uncover potential improvements and fully assess its EQ.

5.2 Social Pragmatic Quality

To evaluate SPQ, we included five items: Content Relevance, Language Perception - Intelligibility, Language Perception-Readiness, Language Perception-Comprehension and Structured Analysis. Results showed that our Hypothesis H_{iv} was true, as the participants evaluated Version A as having a higher SPQ (Version A: $Mdn = 4.8, SD = .62$; Version B: $Mdn = 3.5, SD = 1.06$; $z = -3.288, p = .001$), with a large [16] effect size ($r = -.7$) (see Table 2 and Fig. 5).

Analyzing the results of both samples separately, we found that the items Language Perception (Intelligibility, Readiness, and Comprehension) reached statistical significance and confirmed the participants' preference toward Version A in both samples (see Table 2, Fig. 7, and Fig. 8).

According to our data, Version A presented a higher level of perceived SPQ, that is, the participants disclosed that those diagrams were easier to understand when compared to Version B.

5.3 Other Improvements

When faced with the question "Imagine that in the course of your duties, you had doubts about which person/service you should forward the process to when the tasks under your responsibility are finished. For that I would prefer to consult… a….diagram version A - conference + Transaction Description Table; b…..diagram version B - DEMO; c….the legislation", subjects revealed that they clearly preferred to look up the information on Version A (Version A: $Mdn = 5, SD = .95$; Version B: $Mdn = 3, SD = 1.56$; $z = -2.906, p = .004, r = -.63$; and Version A: $Mdn = 5, SD = .95$; Legislation: $Mdn = 3, SD = 1.77$; $z = -2.857, p = .004, r = .62$). Data supports our hypothesis H_{vii}.

In one open-ended question, the participants were also asked for suggestions on improving the representations. Among the suggestions, the ones that gathered the most consensus were: to include, in the process diagram, the time restrictions of each task; and the ability to present, associated with the tasks, the organizational role responsible for executing the task, in some sort of overlay.

The participants from Sample A (experienced in the modeled processes) revealed that they would like to have included in the task shape (e.g., a collapsible box) the exception conditions of the task and the procedure in case of that exception (e.g., not happening within the expected timeframe; or other conditions like delivery of documents not being met). This information is already available in the transaction description table, but they considered it would also be helpful to have it represented in the diagrams as well.

The participants in our study emphasized that they would need to frequently update the diagrams because the new rules and procedures are frequently created and updated. Therefore, the diagrammatic representation of the model must be dynamic, subject to be frequently and easily changed. Participants in the study also reinforced the need to include informal descriptions in the diagrams.

Our experiment supports previous work that claimed that the Version A's Process Model representation is more accessible and easier to grasp ([3]), namely by professionals working with the represented processes and by other actors with self-reported knowledge of DEMO.

5.4 Foundations of a Theory of Representation Within DEMO

Our proposals and claims have led in the past to exciting discussions by the practitioners of the enterprise engineering discipline, which made clear that there is a need to assess and improve the way to present and communicate DEMO models [3]. From these discussions, we had the idea to propose developing a new Enterprise Engineering theory: the *X-theory*, taking the CHI letter from the Greek alphabet, standing for **C**ommunication of **H**uman-readable-representations and **I**nterpretation theory. Currently, DEMO's representations and symbols are not grounded in any theory, and the work presented previously constitutes an initial empirical work in the direction of a clear separation between the meta-model aspects of DEMO, and a more user-friendly representation of the models, as well as their boundaries, with higher perceived quality and functionality.

As discussed at the conference, a clarification of implementation independence or abstraction is necessary. Elements such as organizational functions used in the Transaction Description Table could be perceived as a breach of that abstraction but are already present in the current DEMO meta-model in the Actor Delegation Table and, as such, are not new additions. We do have the MU-theory [1] that explains very well and clarifies the notion of what are models and representations. However, we do not have any theory behind the DEMO methodology itself, clearly justifying why we have the current four aspect models and all associated representations as they exist now. Our impression is that the current set of aspect models and representations arose from practice and are certain conventions not thoroughly grounded in some theory. So the research we present now is questioning these conventions and trying to find more usable and functional representations, constituting first steps toward the *X-theory*. Among other things, we aim to understand what exactly the more adequate "aspects" and "representations" are to facilitate the interpretation and communication of DEMO model elements and their representations.

DEMO representations need to evolve to meet real-world needs, and DEMO researchers should strive to make the visual notation and language used in the representations more user-friendly, so it can be cognitively more effective, needing just a short introduction, instead of explaining complex theoretical postulates. The present work, which reports the high perceived Quality and Functionality of the new representations, even in subjects with self-reported knowledge of DEMO, is a step further to better understanding users' perceived representations and improving them.

Considering the results of our study, we can conclude that the perceived functionality, EQ, and SPQ are important factors to consider when creating visual notations and designing diagrammatic representations. Therefore, bearing in mind its importance, we argue to include as a foundation of the *X-theory*, the need to evaluate, for each proposed representation, the following principles:

- Perceived Functionality: the degree to which the stakeholders (especially the users) perceive the utility and functionality of the diagrams, considering them as more useful than other representations of the model.
- Visual Quality: the degree to which the diagram layout and aesthetics are readable and perceived as pleasant by the stakeholders (especially the users).
- Understandability: the degree to which the stakeholders (especially the users) comprehend the diagram.
- Dynamic Representation: the degree to which the diagram allows users to easily update the representation according to the evolution of the business and processes.

The state-of-the-art indicates us other directions that we should explore in future work [8, 12], namely: cognitive effectiveness (the speed, ease, and accuracy with which the user perceives the diagram), cognitive fit (the use of different visual dialects when required), semiotic clarity (each graphical symbol may only be associated to one semantic construct), perceptual discriminability (symbols should be smoothly distinguishable), semantic transparency (symbols look should be suggestive of its meaning), graphic economy (keep the number of different symbols cognitively manageable), dual coding (enrich diagrams with textual descriptions), physical quality (persistence, currency, and availability of the diagram), syntactic quality (the correct usage of the modeling language), semantic quality (relationship between the diagram and the modeling domain), perceived semantic quality (relationship between the knowledge of the stakeholders and their interpretation of the diagram), pragmatic quality (interpretation of the diagram by technical actors), social quality (relationship between the interpretation of the process modeled by different actors), deontic quality (contribution of the diagram to fulfill the overall goals of modeling), and comprehensiveness (degree in which the diagram represents the complete process that is meant to represent).

These factors should be used to evaluate and improve the visual notations of diagrams and other representations in DEMO. Users' evaluation should be included in any modeling project to assess how the diagrams are perceived and investigate improvements. Therefore, evaluation criteria and metrics need to be developed for each one of the principles of the *X-theory*.

Future work should continue discussing these postulates to define the basis of the *X-theory*-Communication of **H**uman-readable-representations and **I**nterpretation theory within DEMO.

6 Conclusions

In this paper, we present the results of the evaluation of the Version A, a new alternative way of representing the Process Model in DEMO (that includes elements from the standard Process, Cooperation, and Action Models) in comparison with the current standard way of representing the Process Model (Version B). Namely, we compare the newly proposed Process Diagram with the standard Process Structure Diagram. The objective of this comparison was not to evaluate the quality of different representations with semantic equivalence because they are not so. Version A was semantically enriched with elements we found necessary for our project. Furthermore, we removed elements that were considered irrelevant. The goal of the study presented in this paper was to evaluate the usability of the new representations for stakeholders in a large-scale modeling project as well as to ground our claim that the Process Aspect Model representations should be richer than they are at the moment to meet practical needs of the real world.

We also introduce some principles for the X-theory-Communication of Human-readable-representations and Interpretation theory within DEMO, namely: Perceived Functionality, Visual Quality, Perceived Pragmatic Quality, and Dynamic Representation, which derive from the realized study.

We found that the new representations proposed in [3] (Version A) are cognitively more effective than the current standard representations [1] (Version B), as the participants evaluated them with a higher level of perceived Quality and Functionality. Our study did not support previous claims, which mention that familiarity with a diagram positively influences the evaluation of the aesthetic factors. Our participants, knowledgeable in the modeling language, evaluated the aesthetic of Version A of the diagrams more positively.

Although the present study provides valuable insights into understanding the users' perceptions of the diagrams in DEMO, a few limitations should be recognized, and these may provide directions for future research.

We used a single data source, relying on self-reports from participants, so conclusions need to be taken with caution. Due to limited time and resources, it was not feasible to include more participants in the sample. Therefore, we had to use purposeful sampling to collect our data, which could have limited the generalization of our results. The sample in our study included only a group of Portuguese public officers and a group of Portuguese students with self-reported knowledge of DEMO.

Concerning the above limitations, we recommend future research to extend the present study into other industries and users from different backgrounds. Further studies with bigger samples are needed to explore differences in the perceived Quality and Functionality of the diagrams when controlling for the subjects' backgrounds. In these experiments, different speakers should do the initial briefings to account for a possible bias introduced by the presenter when presenting the diagrams.

In the questionnaire revision, it should be considered to include direct questions about what could be improved in diagrammatic representations. Furthermore, participants should be asked to explicitly point out the reasons for their preference over the diagrams. A practical exercise in evaluating how the participants perform using both versions of the diagrams should also be considered (measuring, for instance, speed, ease of use, and intuitiveness).

Further studies should be conducted to technically evaluate Version A in all the metrics established in the SEQUAL framework, uncover potential improvements and assess the cognitive effectiveness of the diagrams. This further research should also evaluate the Process Diagram in terms of effectiveness as viewpoints to the stakeholders and if they, in fact, address most of their concerns or if other elements of the whole view that also includes the Transaction Description Table should be added or replaced or even if there is the need for additional models (viewpoints) for different groups of stakeholders in line with [17, 18].

The present work contributes to the body of research on the evaluation of business process models, as it contributes to better understanding the users' perceptions over representations. First, it allows us to grow the body of knowledge with a user's perceptions study over the perceived Quality and Functionality of the DEMO representations. Second, we hope that this study initiates a series of evaluations of the users' perceptions of the DEMO diagrams, which may improve the representations, improve their perceived Quality and Functionality, and, consequently, grow the number of businesses using them. Third, the questionnaire we used to evaluate the perceived Quality and Functionality is available as an Appendix to this paper and may be used for further studies. Fourth, this study offers important implications for practice, as it gives valuable insights into the users' perceptions, which should be considered when representing the Process Model in DEMO. Further developments of a new version of representations of the PM should consider these suggestions.

Acknowledgments. Special thanks to the participants in the study that contributed with their fruitful insights and feedback. This work was supported by the Regional Development European Fund (INTERREG MAC), projects Dynamic eGov MAC2/5.11a/359 (MAC-2014-2020), and FiiHUB MAC2/2.3d/335 (MAC-2014-2020).

References

1. Dietz, J.L.G., Mulder, H.B.F.: The enterprise engineering theories. In: Dietz, J.L.G., Mulder, H.B.F. (eds.) Enterprise Ontology: A Human-Centric Approach to Understanding the Essence of Organisation, pp. 23–48. Springer International Publishing, Cham (2020). https://doi.org/10.1007/978-3-030-38854-6_4
2. Dietz, J.L.G.: Enterprise Ontology: Theory and Methodology. Springer (2006). https://doi.org/10.1007/3-540-33149-2
3. Pinto, D., Aveiro, D., Pacheco, D., Gouveia, B., Gouveia, D.: Validation of DEMO's conciseness quality and proposal of improvements to the process model. In: Aveiro, D., Guizzardi, G., Pergl, R., Proper, H.A. (eds.) EEWC 2020. LNBIP, vol. 411, pp. 133–152. Springer, Cham (2021). https://doi.org/10.1007/978-3-030-74196-9_8
4. Larkin, J.H., Simon, H.A.: Why a diagram is (Sometimes) worth ten thousand words. Cogn. Sci. **11**, 65–100 (1987). https://doi.org/10.1016/S0364-0213(87)80026-5
5. Bertin, J.: Sémiologie graphique. Les diagrammes, les réseaux, les cartes. Éditions de l'École des hautes études en sciences sociales (1973)
6. Mendling, J., Reijers, H.A., van der Aalst, W.M.P.: Seven process modeling guidelines (7PMG). Inf. Softw. Technol. **52**, 127–136 (2010). https://doi.org/10.1016/j.infsof.2009.08.004

7. Krogstie, J., Sindre, G., Jørgensen, H.: Process models representing knowledge for action: a revised quality framework. Eur. J. Inf. Syst. **15**, 91–102 (2006). https://doi.org/10.1057/pal grave.ejis.3000598

8. Moody, D.: The "Physics" of notations: toward a scientific basis for constructing visual notations in software engineering. IEEE Trans. Softw. Eng. **35**, 756–779 (2009). https://doi.org/10.1109/TSE.2009.67

9. Genon, N., Heymans, P., Amyot, D.: Analysing the cognitive effectiveness of the BPMN 2.0 visual notation. In: Malloy, B., Staab, S., van den Brand, M. (eds.) Software Language Engineering, pp. 377–396. Springer, Berlin (2011). https://doi.org/10.1007/978-3-642-19440-5_25

10. Sedera, W., Rosemann, M., Doebeli, G.: A process modelling success model: insights from a case study. In: Proceedings of the 11th European Conference on Information Systems, Naples Italy (2003)

11. Krogstie, J.: Quality of business process models. In: Sandkuhl, K., Seigerroth, U., Stirna, J. (eds.) PoEM 2012. LNBIP, vol. 134, pp. 76–90. Springer, Heidelberg (2012). https://doi.org/10.1007/978-3-642-34549-4_6

12. Krogstie, J.: SEQUAL specialized for business process models. In: Krogstie, J. (ed.) Quality in Business Process Modeling, pp. 103–138. Springer, Cham (2016). https://doi.org/10.1007/978-3-319-42512-2

13. ISO/IEC JTC 1/SC 7: ISO/IEC 25010:2011. https://www.iso.org/cms/render/live/en/sites/iso org/contents/data/standard/03/57/35733.html

14. Dietz, J.L.G., Mulder, H.B.F.: The DEMO methodology. In: Dietz, J.L.G., Mulder, H.B.F. (eds.) Enterprise Ontology: A Human-Centric Approach to Understanding the Essence of Organisation, pp. 261–299. Springer International Publishing, Cham (2020). https://doi.org/10.1007/978-3-030-38854-6_12

15. Pacheco, D., Aveiro, D., Gouveia, B., Pinto, D.: Evaluation of the perceived quality and functionality of fact model diagrams in DEMO. In: (forthcoming) (2021)

16. Field, A.P.: Discovering Statistics using IBM SPSS Statistics: and Sex and Drugs and Rock 'n' roll. Sage, Los Angeles (2013)

17. Sanjog Z.: TOGAF Knowledge Series #2: Views and Viewpoints. https://www.linkedin.com/pulse/togaf-knowledge-series-views-viewpoints-sanjog-zawar/

18. ISO/IEC JTC 1/SC 7: ISO/IEC/IEEE 42010:2011(en), Systems and software engineering — Architecture description (2011)

Use of EA Models in Organizational AI Solution Development

Kurt Sandkuhl[1,2](✉) [iD] and Jack Daniel Rittelmeyer[1] [iD]

[1] Institute of Computer Science, University of Rostock, Rostock, Germany
{kurt.sandkuhl,jack.rittelmeyer}@uni-rostock.de
[2] School of Engineering, Jönköping University, Jönköping, Sweden
kurt.sandkuhl@ju.se

Abstract. Digital transformation in combination with service ecosystems exploit and incorporate innovative technologies, such as artificial intelligence, Internet of things or data analytics. For most enterprises, new digital business models and participation in service eco-systems lead to severe changes of the enterprise architecture (EA) and the need for methodical support to systematically perform the resulting change process. The focus of this paper is on the implementation of AI applications in organizations. Based on the analysis of industrial case studies, our observation is that different kinds of AI applications require different prerequisites in an organizational IT landscape, some of which can be found in an EA model, and some enterprises intend to use AI but are not prepared for it. The work investigates, what information can be harvested from EA models to support requirements engineering and the evaluation of organizational readiness for AI planning and implementation. The main contributions of our work are (a) an enhanced and updated literature analysis on EA use for AI introduction, (b) an analysis of differences in requirements of different kinds of AI applications, and (c) an improved AI context analysis method prepared for addressing these differences. The improved method exploits insights gained in our work on what information regarding the requirements can be extracted from EA models.

Keywords: Enterprise architecture · AI context · Organizational AI solutions · Artificial intelligence · AI requirements engineering

1 Introduction

Digitalization of products, processes and services [1] unlocks a wide range of opportunities to transform business models and value chains as an instrument to increase competitiveness and to meet changing customer and market demands. Service ecosystems in combination with digital platforms [2] are considered important foundations for new digital business models that contribute to the development and implementation of corporate strategies. Digital platforms exploit and incorporate innovative technologies [3], such as Artificial Intelligence (AI), Internet of Things (IoT), Cloud Computing, and Data Analytics. From the perspective of most enterprises, new digital business models

© Springer Nature Switzerland AG 2022
D. Aveiro et al. (Eds.): EEWC 2021, LNBIP 441, pp. 149–166, 2022.
https://doi.org/10.1007/978-3-031-11520-2_10

and participation in service eco-systems lead to severe changes of the enterprise architecture (EA) and the need for methodical support to systematically perform the resulting change process. In this work, our focus in particular is on the implementation of AI applications in enterprises from both an engineering and an organizational perspective.

In previous work, we proposed and demonstrated an approach for extracting the primary requirements of organizational AI usage from EA models [4]. The result of the extraction is called "AI context" and includes organizational processes and roles as well as related IT systems. From using this approach, we learned that (a) different kinds of AI applications require different prerequisites in an organizational IT landscape, some of which potentially are captured and can be extracted from an up-to-date EA model, and (b) some enterprises intend to use AI, but are not sufficiently prepared for it, which ought to be discovered and addressed before starting AI implementation projects and failing due to complete due to missing essential prerequisites.

This paper intends to contribute to a better understanding of AI introduction into organizations and the potential of EA use for this purpose. Due to a lack of published research in the field (see Sect. 4), we decided to base our work on industrial case studies exposing different levels of AI readiness and different characteristics of AI applications. The main research question (RQ) for our work is: *In the organizational use of artificial intelligence solutions, how can enterprise architecture models be used to support the planning and implementation processes?*

The main contributions of our work are (a) an enhanced and updated version of a previous literature analysis on EA use for AI introduction, (b) an analysis of differences in requirements of different kinds of AI applications, and (c) an improved AI context analysis method prepared for these differences. The improved method exploits insights gained in our work on what information regarding the requirements can be extracted from EA models.

The rest of the paper is structured as follows. Section 2 introduces the research methods applied in the paper. Section 3 summarizes the background for our work from enterprise architecture management and discusses related work on AI readiness and requirements engineering for AI. Section 4 presents the results of the updated literature analysis on AI and EA. Section 5 introduces industrial case studies of organizational AI use. Section 6 analyzes the cases, presents observations and derives the conclusions for changing our initial method approach. Section 7 summarizes our findings and discusses future work.

2   Research Approach

Work presented in this paper is part of a research program aiming at methodical and technological support for the EA-based introduction of AI in enterprises. It follows the five stages of Design Science Research (DSR) [5], namely, problem explication, requirements definition, design and development of the design artifact, demonstration, as well as evaluation. This study concerns the first two DSR steps, problem explication and requirements definition for the design artifact. The paper starts from the following research questions which are based on the motivation presented in Sect. 1:

- *RQ1: What information can be extracted from enterprise architecture models to assess the readiness of enterprises for organizational AI use?*
- *RQ2: How to use EA models to extract information supporting different kinds of AI applications?*

The research method used for working on the research questions is a combination of literature study, descriptive case study and argumentative-deductive work. Based on the research questions, we started identifying research areas with relevant work for the questions and analyzed the literature in these areas. The purpose of the analysis was to find theories or experience reports on enterprise architecture use for AI implementation or determining AI readiness. Since the literature study showed a lack of publications in this area (see Sect. 4), we decided to analyze our own material from qualitative case studies in order to contribute to the field (see Sect. 5). Yin [6] differentiates various kinds of case studies: explanatory, exploratory and descriptive. The case studies presented in Sect. 4 have to be considered as descriptive, as they are used to describe the implementation of AI solutions in real-world environments and allow for investigating the use of EA models for this purpose.

Based on the analysis of the case study material and related work on AI readiness and AI requirements engineering, we derive an extension of our method for extracting the AI context from EA models. This method extension is still preliminary since we need more case material to support our deductive conclusions and also plan for lab experiments to further refine our method as part of future work.

3 Background and Related Work

Background for this paper is our initial method proposal for extracting the AI context from EA models (Sect. 3.1). Furthermore, we base our work on findings addressing factors for AI readiness (Sect. 3.2) and specific requirements when engineering AI applications (Sect. 3.3).

3.1 Method Support for AI context

In our previous work, we proposed a method supporting feasibility studies and requirements elicitation of AI applications [4]. The motivation for this method proposal was that many organizations look into the introduction or development of AI solutions but at the same time there is not much experience with the technical complexity of AI applications. Given the fact that organizational solutions have to be embedded in business processes, integrated in the information architecture of an organization and often also be connected to the existing application and technology landscape, our method support is positioned close to EA management and aims to exploit the content of EA models.

In general, we see AI projects as a kind of IS development or software development project and to our knowledge, there is no strong evidence implying that we would need radically different methodical instruments. Scoping of project content, requirement elicitation, specification and design of the solution, prototyping or software development will be required in AI projects – with specific approaches contributing to knowledge base development or preparing suitable data sets for machine learning.

EA models usually reflect an enterprise's business, information and application architecture, i.e., at least part of the required information for AI planning is captured in such models. Our method support assumes the existence of an EA model for the organization in question. If an EA model does not exist, the organizational context for the EA has to be developed. The proposed method consists of four steps, which include procedural steps, important concepts to observe and document, and a notation on how to do this:

- Step 1. Model organizational AI context: aims at extracting all information of organizational structures, processes and resources required for or affected by the planned AI solution from the EA model of the organization under consideration. The extracted information is captured in a conceptual model, i.e., represented by using a modelling language. This conceptual model ideally is a subset or view of the analyzed EA model of the organization.
- Step 2. Elicit AI requirements: aims at documenting the requirements from candidate AI technologies that have to be fulfilled if a certain candidate technology is to be used in an organization (we recommend that an AI expert is involved in this step).
- Step 3. Analyze AI context: systematically analyzes the AI context model (from step 1) using the AI requirements (from step 2) for each EA layer of the context model separately.
- Step 4. Decide on feasibility: gives support for deciding on feasibility based on the results from step 3.

The AI requirements elicited in step 2 have to be distinguished for every different AI technology. This is highly important because e.g., ontologies require expert experience and domain knowledge for the definition of rules. On the other side, machine learning approaches need suitable and sufficient training data. Examples for requirements are the data format and structure, the amount of data, the required data quality, if expert competencies are required, input and output data conversion as well as what quality criteria and performance constraints exist for an AI approach. More details about each step and an illustrative example are provided in [4].

The context model itself can be distinguished in different dependent and inter-related dimensions:

- Roles that provide the input or use the output of an AI application
- Processes that are going to be supported, automated or transformed by an AI solution
- Data structures that are used by an AI application and
- Applications that provide data for the AI solution

Concepts and a notation are not part of our method, because EA models already provide all necessary elements. Hence, we recommend to use established EA modeling languages like ArchiMate to create the context model and perform the requirements analysis [4].

3.2 AI Readiness

The concept of AI readiness according to Jöhnk et al. [7] was developed based on the theories of innovation and technology adoption as AI can be seen as each of them. In general, AI readiness describes if and to what extent a company is prepared ("ready") to adopt AI. Evaluating the AI readiness also helps to avoid projects from failing by depicting what kind of AI readiness level should be reached first before starting the adoption of a new AI solution. Furthermore, the AI readiness depends on the organizational context and the purpose of each AI solution individually. Jöhnk et al. [7] differentiate between AI readiness and AI adoption but emphasize that both should be used in conjunction with each other. The AI readiness of a company should not be evaluated just once before the AI adoption but rather iteratively after and for each AI adoption project, because the previous project changes the AI readiness of the company. The AI adoption can be divided into the steps of initiation, adoption decision and implementation. During the initiation, the first awareness for AI usage emerges and different AI possibilities are considered. Then the possibilities are evaluated and a decision for or against the AI project is made. Finally, the solution will be implemented and used, growing the acceptance of it, ideally. AI readiness, on the other hand, can be measured by specific factors. Jöhnk et al. [7] suggest five categories with 18 AI readiness factors and 58 illustrative indicators (see Table 1).

The 58 indicators are more precise than the 18 factors. Hence, they can be used for an easier and more accurate evaluation of the AI readiness. As an example, there are three indicators for the factor "Personnel" [7]:

- My organization has employees with AI know-how.
- My organization has AI specialists who have a deep understanding of AI technologies.
- My organization has business analysts who possess both domain and AI know-how.

In summary, the different AI readiness factors can be used to identify the overall readiness of a company for AI adoption. This also includes the context in which an AI application will be implemented and used and therefore aligns with the method described in Sect. 3.1. Because of that, we applied the readiness factors and indicators to three case studies to evaluate the readiness of the respective companies (Sect. 6.1).

Table 1. AI readiness factors per category by Jöhnk et al. [7]

Categories	AI readiness factors per category				
Strategic alignment	AI-business potentials	Customer AI readiness	Top management support	AI-process fit	Data-driven decision-making
Resources	Financial budget	Personnel	IT infrastructure		
Knowledge	AI awareness	Upskilling	AI ethics		
Culture	Innovativeness	Collaborative work	Change management		
Data	Data availability	Data quality	Data accessibility	Data flow	

3.3 AI Requirements Engineering

As expressed by the second research question in Sect. 2, one purpose of our research is to extract information from EA models for *different kinds of AI applications*. One approach to address this question would be to start from categorizations of AI applications and elaborate on the specific requirements of each application category. However, the existing categorizations proved not to be suitable as they focus on the technological principles, "inner" architecture, or intended functionality. The most cited textbook on AI [8], for example, distinguishes between problem-solving, reasoning and decision making, machine learning, deep learning, probabilistic programming, and multiagent systems; and elaborates in detail how algorithms and data processing should be implemented, but provides very little information on what to observe when designing such applications for an organizational context. The same is true for the periodic system of AI application[1] by BITKOM that has its focus on basic functions and the kind of input data required.

We propose to analyze real-world cases for organizational AI use instead and to take the perspective of requirements engineering (RE) for AI applications. More concrete, a taxonomy for RE of AI applications has been proposed by [9] that builds on [10] and elaborates on challenges during the RE activities elicitation, analysis, specification, validation, management and documentation. In each activity, the challenges are divided into data, model and system challenges. For our purpose, data and model-related challenges during elicitation, analysis, specification and validation are of specific interest, as we expect to find pertinent information in EA models. These challenges are:

- elicitation: availability of (large) datasets; lack of domain knowledge required for the model; undeclared consumers of AI application results
- analysis: imbalanced datasets; data silos; no trivial workflows to be supported
- specification: data labelling is costly, minimum viable model and end-to-end pipeline support
- validation: training data critical analysis; various data dependencies; entanglement of aspects in the model; high scalability issues for ML

Requirements to future systems (architecture or technology) and challenges to manage and document requirements of AI systems are not in the scope of our work and, thus, will not be part of the analysis.

4   Literature Analysis

As introduced in the overview of our research approach (Sect. 2), we first conducted a literature analysis to examine the use of EA for AI implementation which is presented here [11]. After a lot of feedback, we enhanced and updated the literature analysis and formulated a new RQ tailored for this research project. This is what we are going to present in this paper. The first version of the literature analysis analyzed the state of research on the influence of implementing AI applications on EAs. Its results showed that the introduction of AI affects the EA of a company, but it also revealed that not

---

[1] https://periodensystem-ki.de/Mit-Legosteinen-die-Kuenstliche-Intelligenz-bauen.

much research exists in this field so far. More precisely, no paper examines the specific influence on the EA (e.g. which EA layer or elements are influenced). Furthermore, no support is provided on how to deal with the arising changes and secure the functionality of the AI application and its integration in the company. Moreover, several papers mention the need for guidance with the selection of suitable AI technologies for different use cases, e.g., in the form of an AI technology catalogue [11].

We followed the method of structured literature review (SLR) by Kitchenham [12] which consists of six steps. The first step is the formulation of RQs. Based on our overall RQs (see Sects. 1 and 2), we formulated the following RQ for the literature analysis:

• *RQ-LA: Which theories or experience reports on enterprise architecture use for AI implementation exist?*

The second step was to conduct the search process itself to identify papers. Originally, we collected the following synonyms for the areas of AI and EA for an initial population (Table 2):

Table 2. Selected search terms for the SLR from [11]

Artificial intelligence	Enterprise architecture
Machine learning	Enterprise model
Deep learning	Business architecture
Support vector machines	Software architecture
Ontology	Information architecture
	IT-architecture

We then included the following additional terms for the AI topic in this new version of the literature analysis: "rule-based system", "expert system", "knowledge graph", "knowledge-based system". We then enhanced our original search strings with the new terms and applied it to the databases "Scopus", "Springer Link", "IEEE-Explore", "ACM Digital Library" and "AISeL" and adapted the strings to the respective query format. We chose these databases because they should cover the majority of research relevant for our field. Springer Link also provided the opportunity to search for German literature. This is the final search string which resulted in 240 found documents:

TITLE-ABS-KEY (("artificial intelligence" OR "machine learning" OR "deep learning" OR "support vector machines" OR "rule-based system" OR "expert system" OR "knowledge graph" OR "knowledge-based system") AND "enterprise architecture").

To be able to make well-grounded decisions of which papers are relevant, we applied the inclusion and exclusion criteria we introduced in our previous research (see Table 3) to the search results in the third step of the SLR (paper selection). We divided the inclusion criteria into the topics of AI and EA. They indicate the content a paper should contain to be considered as relevant, at least one criteria of each topic should be fulfilled. We further excluded papers that investigated the use of AI for the support of modelling tools and tasks which occurred often during the search process.

Table 3. Inclusion criteria for the SLR from [11]

AI	Organizational impact/Effects
AI1. Is AI investigated at all?	**EA1.** Is EAM investigated or are EAM concepts used (e.g., as a basis to investigate changes or as a method)?
AI2. Implementation Environment	**EA2.** Which parts of the organization can be affected by implementing an AI application? - **EA2.1.** Processes - **EA2.2.** Actors - **EA2.3.** Roles - **EA2.4.** Data - **EA2.5.** Applications
AI3. Implementation Factors, Guides, Recommendations	**EA3.** Is a specific method used to measure the effects?

The refined search discovered 6 new papers relevant to the research topic. For comparison, the original search conducted between March and May 2021 resulted in 9 relevant results. Nevertheless, the new findings cannot be traced back to the new search terms. Rather they are a result of the date the search was performed because nearly all papers were published recently between June and September 2021 and can also be found without the additional search terms.

In the fourth step, we extracted the data from the selected papers (data collection) and in the fifth step, we analyzed and interpreted our results. The summary of our approach in this section as well as the explanation of our findings represent the final sixth step of the SLR (documentation of results).

The majority of the identified papers were slightly enhanced versions of work found in the previous SLR. Because of that, they mainly did not provide further contributions relevant to this research. Nevertheless, one of the papers presented a relevant method for identifying business activities that could be replaced by AI systems [13]. However, despite introducing EA modelling at the beginning of the paper, the method itself consists of only tables, questions and steps that have to be answered. It helps to gather and systemize relevant information and helps to analyze if a business activity can be replaced by AI or not. But it does not use EA to accomplish that.

Overall, several papers were identified that are relevant to the research topic. However, the results do not help to answer RQ1 and RQ2. In conclusion, the small number of relevant results shows a lack of publications in this area. Because of that, we decided to use our case studies for further analyzations which will be described in the following sections.

5   Industrial Case Studies

We used three case studies for our investigation. Case study A was from the field of power garden products (Sect. 5.1), case B from payment transaction handling (Sect. 5.2) and case C from marketing (Sect. 5.3).

5.1 Case Study A: Manufacturer of Power Garden Products

The industrial enterprise considered in the case study is a world-leading producer of outdoor power products including chainsaws, trimmers, robotic lawnmowers, garden tractors, and watering systems. The company is in a transformation process where they see it as a necessity to transform their business model in order to stay competitive and to deliver improved value to their stakeholders. This transformation basically moves from outdoor power products without communication and interconnectivity features to networked ones, which also involves new features based on AI. This changes the product development and deployment processes, and also the customer care, sales and marketing departments. Figure 1 shows the areas of the EA-model that changed during the digital transformation process in the company.

As a result of the transformation, many products do not only have built-in electronics or embedded systems but also features based on networking and communication capabilities. The built-in IT is in many cases used for controlling the different mechatronic components of the product and for collecting data when the product is in use, either performance parameters or used product features, or the environment of the product. The networking features are used for communicating usage statistics, license information or location information (if anti-theft features are activated) to either the product owner or the back-office of the manufacturer. The data collected by these new features is supposed to be used for detecting maintenance needs of the devices, new sales opportunities, anomalies in functionalities indicating defects, or optimization potential for internal functions (e.g. for energy consumption) – to name only a few examples. The owner of the garden has access to services for operating, supervising and planning garden maintenance using mobile devices.

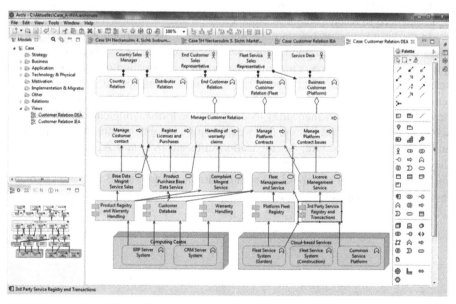

Fig. 1. Excerpt from EA-model of case A with focus on parts affected by digital transformation

Since many of the products offer similar functionality regarding networking and communication, the process of digital transformation included the design and implementation of reusable services and components for either the "digitized" product or the back-office infrastructure, which comprise an IT and service architecture for the IT built into the physical product. Furthermore, data management services including collections of time-series data and data warehouse-based services were implemented [14].

5.2 Case B: AI for Fraud Detection

Case study company B is a payment service provider offering various IT-based services for handling payment transactions for small and medium-sized banks. The company was among the first in Germany to process instant payment transactions (IPT). Instant payment solutions usually consist of the scheme layer (end-user solutions for the market), clearing layer (arrangements for clearing of transactions between payment service providers) and settlement layer (arrangements for settlement of transactions). Company B provides clearing layer and settlement layer functions in combination with value-added services, such as fraud detection, sanction screening and embargo checking. The case emerged when the company decided to explore possibilities of AI use in IPT handling and is also the basis for the initial method development [4].

After a requirements analysis, the case study company performed a feasibility study that examined different AI-based solutions for detecting fraudulent transactions [15] and how to integrate them into the existing EA. In the business architecture, the future roles expected to use the AI solution for IP fraud detection were identified. These roles are the ones who need to understand the decisions of the AI solution. The business process steps to be automated by the future AI components also had to be determined and the related affected tasks of other processes were located, i.e. what process steps deliver input and need to receive output information.

In the information architecture, the focus was on the information required for the fraud detection (and what applications or services provide or consume this information) and what information is missing. The required information for fraud detection is spread between different data sources (payment monitoring system, core banking system, customer transaction history). With this distribution onto different data sources, a new integrated data set is mandatory to allow for a performant implementation of the AI solution. Integrating data "on the fly" would require too much time. In the application and technology architecture, the applications affected by a new AI solution, because they provide or receive data, were identified.

Figure 2 shows an excerpt of the architecture model for case B with a focus on the investigation of suspicious transactions.

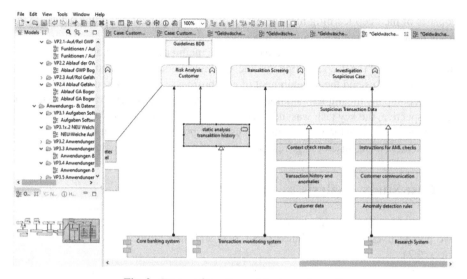

Fig. 2. Excerpt from the architecture of case B

5.3 Case C: AI for Object Recognition and Marketing Support

Case study company C is a content-marketing enterprise specialized in the creation and distribution of online videos, and in using these videos for marketing purposes. This company aims at new business models exploiting the possibility to create interaction with the users and new innovative media formats. In particular, free online videos have a high reach in the advertising-relevant target group. Such videos contain several scenes and show mostly fashion-related content applicable for content-related advertising. For example, if a video shows a close-up of a male face wearing sunglasses, advertisements should be placed for these glasses. Knowing what kind of object is shown in the video, therefore, is crucial for the service. Traditionally, the objects in videos were identified by manual "tagging" of the videos. This approach is labor-intensive and difficult to scale up due to the need to hire and train the workforce. Automatic image detection technologies can enable more efficient and cost-effective operations.

The case study company started to develop an innovative technological approach by combining a technique from the symbolic and approximate sub-disciplines of AI research [16]. The aim is to apply knowledge captured in an ontology to improve the process of object recognition in videos, which is based on an artificial neural network (ANN) and a deep-learning approach. The ontology is supposed to capture the relevant knowledge for the application field of discovering fashion items in videos. This knowledge includes, for example, a taxonomy of fashion items, environments suitable for specific fashion categories (mountain, skiing, outdoor), social contexts relevant for fashion categories (weddings, parties), and more. Furthermore, the ontology is also used to capture combinations of fashion items relevant for defined marketing purposes, for example, the fashion for a particular target group. For each concept in the ontology, there is a corresponding classification model in the deep learning part of the system. This part consists of the deep learning management software component providing access to the ANN database containing available models.

From an organizational perspective, both the maintenance of the ontology, the continued training of the deep learning module, the integration of the automatic tagging into existing processes and the development of new business services based on this platform had to accompany the implementation of the AI solution described above. From a technical perspective, the key task was the integration with the existing marketing and content distribution engine, which also includes customer profiles, campaign management and advertisements. Because of page restrictions, the EA model is not included in this paper.

6   Case Study Analysis

To answer our research questions presented in Sect. 2, we analyze our case data from two perspectives: the AI readiness (Sect. 6.1) and the requirements engineering view (Sect. 6.2).

6.1   EA-based AI Readiness Analysis

Analysis of the case material from Sect. 5 for answering RQ1 (Sect. 2) was done using the readiness factors depicted in Table 1 in Sect. 3.2. For each readiness factor, we went through the available EA models. The result of this step is summarized in Table 4. The letters in brackets indicate the case(s) the information was retrieved from.

Table 4. AI readiness factors retrieved from EA models of the cases

Categories	AI readiness factors in the cases
Strategic Alignment	*AI-business potentials, customer AI readiness, top management support*: no information available in any case *AI-process fit; data-driven decision-making*: established processes and their connection/linkage to data sources [A, B]
Resources	*Financial budget, personnel*: no information available in any case *IT infrastructure*: current technology and application infrastructure [all]
Knowledge	*AI awareness, upskilling, AI ethics*: no information available [all]
Culture	*Innovativeness, change management*: no information available Collaborative work: supporting applications and technology [A]
Data	*Data availability, data accessibility, data flow* current information architecture [all] *Data quality*: no information available [all]

For the readiness regarding strategic alignment, only established processes can be extracted from the models in cases A and B. These processes are the basis for evaluating how much data-driven decision making already exists. In the category of resources, the existing IT infrastructure is well-documented in all cases. The other factors are not visible. For the knowledge category, no relevant information could be retrieved in any of the cases. Not surprisingly, there is no relevant information regarding the change culture and innovativeness retrievable from the models. However, the existence of tools for collaborative work can be discovered in the model of case A. For the data category, much information regarding readiness can be found in the information architecture of all cases with respect to what data are available, how to access data is visible in services and interfaces and what flow exists is shown by the connection to other applications and the business architecture.

In summary, the EA models of our case studies contained only some information for a few readiness factors that were pertinent for judging the AI readiness of the organizations. All this information had to be interpreted or complemented by a domain expert in AI and someone knowledgeable in the organization's internal structures and processes. The small amount of extracted information in combination with the need for interpretation by experts raises doubts if EA models really should be used for this purpose. We conjecture that the domain experts probably would have reached similar conclusions without the EA model.

6.2 EA-based Requirements Analysis

Section 3.3 identified important aspects of AI applications that AI requirements engineering currently considers as a challenge. Extraction of information regarding these aspects from EA models would support AI requirements engineering. Furthermore, contrasting the extracted information between different kinds of AI applications can help to tailor the method for AI context modeling for different kinds of AI by identifying specific activities required for the different kinds of AI.

As preparation to extract relevant information from EA models, the challenges discussed in Sect. 3.3 are examined from the viewpoint of what information potentially could be found in EA models and how to identify it. For this purpose, we propose to focus on the modeling language used for the EA (for example ArchiMate), i.e. to identify concepts or classes in the modeling language that are likely to capture relevant information. The result of this examination is shown in Table 5.

With exception of the challenges classified as "not available", there are concepts in the ArchiMate modelling language available that could be used to capture relevant information in an EA model for the challenges. Instances of these concepts should be closely investigated when examining the EA models of the three use cases as indicated in Table 5. The result of this examination is summarized in Table 6 that provides examples from the cases. Again, the letters in brackets indicate the cases.

Table 5. Challenges of AI applications and potential sources in EA-models

Challenge	Potential information in EA models/how to identify?
Availability of (large) datasets	Data architecture: data objects related to process or actor/role to be supported by AI
Domain knowledge required for the model	(not available)
Consumers of AI application results	Business architecture: actor or role related to AI application or connected service
Imbalanced datasets; data silos	Data architecture: attributes of relevant data objects; Application architecture: service or interface
No trivial workflows to be supported	Business architecture: process flow to be supported
Data labelling	(not available)
End-to-end pipeline support	Business and application architecture: at least one component or interface or service for all processes or business services connected in a workflow
Training data critical analysis	Data architecture: attributes of relevant data objects;
Data dependencies	Data architecture: dependencies between relevant data objects
Entanglement of aspects in the model	Application architecture: dependencies between relevant interfaces or services

Table 6. Retrieved information from case study EA-models for the AI-challenges

Challenge	Information from EA models
Availability of (large) datasets	[A]: "Fleet Management" data as a basis for sales support in"Manage Platform Contracts" [B]: "static analysis transaction history" data as a basis for "Risk Analysis Customer"
Consumers of AI application results	[B]: "Compliance Officer". [C]: "Channel Manager" role is a user of object detection
Imbalanced datasets; data silos	[A]: all log data and transaction data for fleet services in "Platform Fleet Registry"
No trivial workflows to be supported	[B]: many refinement levels of "Investigation Suspicious Case" [C]: "modify semantic net" in "semantic advisor"
End-to-end pipeline support	[B]: sub-processes and their connections to the information architecture of the "fraud detection" process
Training data critical analysis	[C]: video data in "brand wire repository"
Data dependencies	[B]: "Research System" and its dependencies to other data sources
Entanglement of aspects in the model	[A]: no clear separation of business and information architecture on refinement levels

One result with respect to RQ2 from the cases is that the general process for AI context analysis is suitable for different kinds of AI applications, such as deep learning-based applications (case C), decision support based on integration and cleansing various data sources (case A), real-time decision making based on real-time and historic data (case B) or time-series analysis and pattern detection (case A). As suspected, the differences between the different kinds of AI applications lie in the detailed activities to be performed (i.e., the steps in the method components) and the information to look for. These differences are elaborated in Sect. 6.3 when discussing the extension of our AI context method.

6.3   Extension of the AI Context Method

Section 6.2 showed what relevant information for AI requirements engineering can be retrieved from EA models. This result is one input to extending our AI context method. The second relevant aspect are the differences between different kinds of AI applications. In order to visualize these differences, we focus in particular on the data aspects, which are also part of the readiness investigation. Table 7 shows those AI differences in the different cases.

Table 7. Differences between different kinds of AI applications

Case	(Types of) data relevant for AI	Purpose the data is used for
A	Time-series data from IoT devices (power garden products)	Discovery of anomalies showing technical problems
	Text documents with maintenance reports	Knowledge extraction for improvements of maintenance/construction
	Fleet management log-data and transaction data	Detection of patterns indicating sales opportunities
B	Payment transaction data	Fraud detection in transactions
	Payment history per customer and overall bank	Fraud detection in transactions using context for a higher level of precision
C	Video data for training classifiers and detectors	Object recognition
	Vocabularies and knowledge structures for ontology	Detection of object context in the object recognition process

The analysis of the cases showed that the required data sources, i.e., the relevant applicants or storage systems, usually were represented in the EA models but sometimes difficult to discover due to missing attribute values, refinement levels or unclear naming and description of the model elements. This motivates an additional step 3a in our method "enrich the EA model" as a complement to step 3 "analyze AI context" to be performed optionally if step 3 discovers incompleteness of the model attributes or descriptions (see Fig. 3). The step is in particular important for the following data sources:

- Images, videos and audio recordings: we observed that the repository or storage system was shown in the model but discoverable only by company-insiders due to the naming (case C: "brand wire repository" contained the required videos for detector training),
- AI applications depending on the evaluation of historic data: we found that sources of historic data were visible and easily identifiable, but the extent of stored historic data (is the amount sufficient for machine learning purposes?) and its quality was not described in the attributes of the model elements (case A maintenance reports archived for the last 5 years; case B: customer transactions and payment histories),
- Data sources to be integrated for joint evaluation: AI applications including real-time decision making that is based on the integration of data from many different sources which cannot be done performantly "on the fly" need detailed information about acceptable processing times, possibilities to extract data from operational systems or the use of proxies.

Additional descriptions of the model element or attributes would be useful in all the above cases.

The most significant change need, discovered for our method approach is an additional method step 5 for "Designing the future EA" (see Fig. 3). The feasibility study (method step 4) made clear that a serious investigation on feasibility has to include the initial design of new or changed data, application and business architectures prepared for the AI application, and the migration planning from the current to the future situation. Only if migration is not only possible but also economically acceptable and resource-wise doable, the implementation should be started. However, designing the future EA is tightly related to the actual AI application development. This is why elaboration of this additional step requires substantial additional work to be done in a future research step.

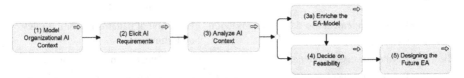

Fig. 3. Extended AI context-method

7 Concluding Remarks and Future Work

From our perspective, for the investigation of AI readiness, EA models can only provide complementary information. Our analysis in Sect. 6.1 basically showed that the models only included little information for some readiness factors that were relevant and that this information had to be interpreted or elaborated by a domain expert in AI and someone knowledgeable in the organization's internal structures and processes. Thus, in an AI readiness investigation, the EA models should be used if available but are no critical resource.

On the other side, the extraction of information from AI models for requirements engineering and feasibility study purposes is fully possible and recommendable, as – from our viewpoint – valuable information can be obtained. The earlier developed method support proved itself useful in the three cases. Useful method extensions have also been proposed and their elaboration in detail has to be part of future work.

Additionally, during our research the questions arose if AI applications could be treated as "just another piece of IT" and if it should be included more explicitly at the business layer as it needs more explicit alignment of roles/responsibilities between human intelligence and AI? Because of the results of the model application and the EAM models, we argue that AI is more complex. Especially because of the different AI technologies that exist, there are many more specific requirements compared to e.g. an isolated small software program for a factory without many APIs.

Future work will additionally have to be of conceptual and empirical nature: the proposed method extensions from Sect. 6.3 have to be properly elaborated and documented, for example by providing a method handbook and instructions for modelers. Furthermore, more industrial cases have to be performed using the method extension and the findings from our work. The main limitation of our research currently is the small number of cases.

Moreover, the literature search could be improved again with a look into intersecting research areas like intelligence amplification (IA) and human-machine symbiosis as well as process modelling. Whereas the first two have overlapping topics with the area of AI, both AI and IA applications often focus on the substitution or improvement of business processes that are a part of an EA and are highly relevant in the area of process modelling as well.

References

1. Matt, C., Hess, T., Benlian, A.: Digital transformation strategies. Bus. Inf. Syst. Eng. **57**(5), 339–343 (2015). https://doi.org/10.1007/s12599-015-0401-5
2. van Alstyne, M.W., Parker, G.G., Choudary, S.P.: Pipelines, platforms, and the new rules of strategy. Harv. Bus. Rev. **94**, 54–62 (2016)
3. Berman, S.J., Bell, R.: Digital transformation: creating new business models where digital meets physical (2011)
4. Sandkuhl, K.: Putting AI into context-method support for the introduction of artificial intelligence into organizations. In: 2019 IEEE 21st Conference on Business Informatics (CBI), vol. 1, pp. 157–164 (2019)
5. Bichler, M.: Design science in information systems research. Wirtschaftsinformatik **48**(2), 133–135 (2006). https://doi.org/10.1007/s11576-006-0028-8
6. Yin, R.K.: Applications of Case Study Research. Sage, Los Angeles (2011)
7. Jöhnk, J., Weißert, M., Wyrtki, K.: Ready or not, AI comes—an interview study of organizational ai readiness factors. Bus. Inf. Syst. Eng. **63**, 5–20 (2021)
8. Russell, S., Norvig, P.: Artificial intelligence: a modern approach (2002)
9. Belani, H., Vukovic, M., Car, Ž.: Requirements engineering challenges in building AI-based complex systems. In: 2019 IEEE 27th International Requirements Engineering Conference Workshops (REW), pp. 252–255 (2019)
10. Lwakatare, L.E., Raj, A., Bosch, J., Olsson, H.H., Crnkovic, I.: A taxonomy of software engineering challenges for machine learning systems: an empirical investigation. In: International Conference on Agile Software Development, pp. 227–243 (2019)

11. Rittelmeyer, J.D., Sandkuhl, K.: Effects of artificial intelligence on enterprise architectures - a structured literature review. In: 2021 IEEE 25th International Enterprise Distributed Object Computing Workshop (EDOCW), IEEE (2021). https://doi.org/10.1109/edocw52865.2021.00042

12. Kitchenham, B., Brereton, O.P., Budgen, D., Turner, M., Bailey, J., Linkman, S.: Systematic literature reviews in software engineering-a systematic literature review. Inf. Softw. Technol. **51**, 7–15 (2009)

13. Takeuchi, H., Ichitsuka, A., Iino, T., Ishikawa, S., Saito, K.: Assessment method for identifying business activities to be replaced by AI technologies. Procedia Comput. Sci. **192**, 1601–1610 (2021). https://doi.org/10.1016/j.procs.2021.08.164

14. Kaidalova, J., Sandkuhl, K., Seigerroth, U.: Product-IT inclusive enterprise architecture management: an approach based on ecosystems, customer journey and data-driven business opportunities. CSIMQ **26**, 1–25 (2021). https://doi.org/10.7250/csimq.2021-26.01

15. Diadiushkin, A., Sandkuhl, K., Maiatin, A.: Fraud detection in payments transactions: overview of existing approaches and usage for instant payments. CSIMQ **20**, 72–88 (2019). https://doi.org/10.7250/csimq.2019-20.04

16. Towards more robust fashion recognition by combining of deep-learning-based detection with semantic reasoning (2021)

Author Index

Amaral, Glenda   21, 42
Andringa, Sytze P. E.   58
Aveiro, David   114, 129

Bork, Dominik   3

De Vries, Marné   74

Gouveia, Bernardo   114, 129
Guizzardi, Giancarlo   21, 42

Krouwel, Marien R.   95
Kulkarni, Vinay   10

Op 't Land, Martin   95

Pacheco, Dulce   114, 129
Pinto, Duarte   114, 129

Rittelmeyer, Jack Daniel   149

Sales, Tiago Prince   21, 42
Sandkuhl, Kurt   149

Yorke-Smith, Neil   58

Printed in the United States
by Baker & Taylor Publisher Services